Beginning Ballerina Programming

From Novice to Professional

Anjana Fernando
Lakmal Warusawithana

Apress®

Beginning Ballerina Programming: From Novice to Professional

Anjana Fernando
Mountain View, CA, USA

Lakmal Warusawithana
Mountain View, USA

ISBN-13 (pbk): 978-1-4842-5138-6
ISBN-13 (electronic): 978-1-4842-5139-3
https://doi.org/10.1007/978-1-4842-5139-3

Managing Director, Apress Media LLC: Welmoed Spahr
Acquisitions Editor: Steve Anglin
Development Editor: Matthew Moodie
Coordinating Editor: Mark Powers

Cover designed by eStudioCalamar

Cover photo by Gaelle Marcel (www.unsplash.com)

Distributed to the book trade worldwide by Springer Science+Business Media, 1 New York Plaza, New York, NY 10004, U.S.A.. Phone 1-800-SPRINGER, fax (201) 348-4505, e-mail orders-ny@springer-sbm.com, or visit www.springeronline.com. Apress Media, LLC is a California LLC and the sole member (owner) is Springer Science + Business Media Finance Inc (SSBM Finance Inc). SSBM Finance Inc is a **Delaware** corporation.

For information on translations, please e-mail editorial@apress.com; for reprint, paperback, or audio rights, please email bookpermissions@springernature.com.

Apress titles may be purchased in bulk for academic, corporate, or promotional use. eBook versions and licenses are also available for most titles. For more information, reference our Print and eBook Bulk Sales web page at www.apress.com/bulk-sales.

Any source code or other supplementary material referenced by the author in this book is available to readers on GitHub via the book's product page, located at www.apress.com/9781484251386. For more detailed information, please visit www.apress.com/source-code.

Printed on acid-free paper

To my mother and father.
—Anjana

I dedicate this to my mother, father, wife, and two sons.
—Lakmal

Table of Contents

About the Authors

Anjana Fernando is a director of developer relations for the CTO office at WSO2. He has built up his expertise in data analytics and enterprise integration by leading several products at WSO2. His latest role is as part of the Ballerina project, where he has been involved in the design and implementation of the language and its runtime, currently working on ecosystem engineering and evangelism activities. Anjana also presents frequently at events, such as ApacheCon, API World, WSO2Con, KubeCon, BallerinaCon, DeveloperWeek, and many tech meetups. Anjana earned a first-class honors degree in software engineering from the Informatics Institute of Technology, Sri Lanka, which is affiliated with the University of Westminster, UK. He also has a master's degree in computer science from the University of Colombo School of Computing.

Lakmal Warusawithana is the senior director of developer relations for the CTO office at WSO2. Lakmal has a long history of working in open source, cloud, and DevOps technologies and was previously the vice president of the Apache Stratos PaaS project. Lakmal is an architect for the containerization and deployment orchestration of Ballerina, an open source programming language. Lakmal has presented at numerous events, including ApacheCon, CloudOpen, QCon, JaxLondon, Cloud Expo, Cloudstack Collaboration Conference, WSO2Con, KubeCon, ContainerCamp, DeveloperWeek, API Summit, and many tech meetups. Lakmal holds a Bachelor of Science (Hons) Special in Computer Science from the University of Colombo, Sri Lanka.

About the Technical Reviewer

Sameera Jayasoma is the lead architect and developer of the Ballerina language compiler and runtime. Also, he is the director of platform architecture at WSO2. He is a member of WSO2's architecture team, which drives the overall development and enhancement of WSO2 platform capabilities. He is also one of the lead architects behind WSO2 Carbon, WSO2 Update Manager, and the Ballerina language project. He has presented at many conferences, including ApacheCon, OSCON, QCon, and WSO2Con, and he has conducted technical workshops on Java, microservices, and OSGi. Sameera holds a first-class honors degree in computer science and engineering from the University of Moratuwa, Sri Lanka.

Acknowledgments

We would like to thank all the people who helped us in writing this book, particularly our technical reviewers, Sameera Jayasoma, Prabath Siriwardana, Sudheera Fernando, Shafreen Anfar, Anupama Pathirge, and Ruchith Fernando. We are also grateful for our families for their support throughout the project. Special thanks goes to Dr. Sanjiva Weerawarana, the creator of the Ballerina programming language, who has also mentored and guided us throughout our careers.

—Anjana Fernando and Lakmal Warusawithana

Introduction

Ballerina is a new cutting-edge programming language designed to write modern, connected applications.

Beginning Ballerina Programming provides an opportunity to learn the Ballerina language during your first encounter with programming computers. The book starts off by introducing basic computer organization, along with essential programming constructs, and gradually progresses to more advanced use cases, such as network programming and data security.

The first chapter covers the foundational operations of a computer, binary systems, and how data can be encoded in binary data to represent any information. From there, the book explains basic programming structures, such as variables, types, and the usage of functions, before covering the code organization and error handling aspects of Ballerina.

Once you have a solid understanding of the basics, we move on to more complex topics, beginning with concurrency, then input/output systems, and finally network programming. We then explore a few popular topics in data security and database programming.

The book aims to give readers an overall knowledge of programming and practical usage. So even though you are a novice starting to program for the first time, the knowledge you will gain from this book will take you well on your way to a professional programming career.

CHAPTER 1

Getting Started

In this chapter, we will learn the importance of computers, and how it affects our day to day life. We will start off by taking a look at the basic components that makes up a computer, and how they work together, along with a brief overview on digital data representation. And finally, we will be writing our first computer program.

Computers and Coding

It is no secret that computers have become an integral part of our lives. You can do your online banking from anywhere in the world; this is made possible by computers. Modern medical procedures, from MRI tests to laser eye surgery, are performed using advanced computer hardware and software. Self-driving cars offer a glimpse of the future of transportation. The limitations of humans do not hinder machines that can perform certain tasks better than we can. Take the latest Tesla vehicles—more than hardware, they advance their features using software upgrades. Just by updating the car's software, users will be able to get better power management, thus getting better mileage; in addition, users can update the automatic driving technology for a safer ride (see Figure 1-1).

A. Fernando and L. Warusawithana, *Beginning Ballerina Programming*,
https://doi.org/10.1007/978-1-4842-5139-3_1

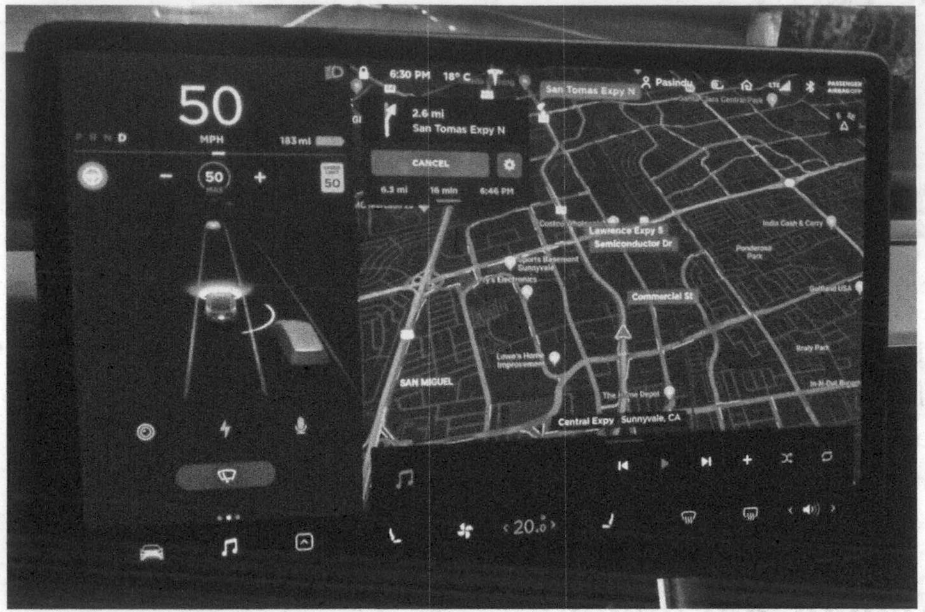

Figure 1-1. *Computer software–assisted driving*

Most modern businesses are now reliant on computer systems. All successful companies have their own software departments. It is no longer enough to use off-the-shelf software products to get something done; you need your own team to build customized applications and to maintain them in-house. Therefore, the demand for computer programmers is higher than ever. And it remains one of the highest-paid jobs in the world.

One of the Miami Heat's "Big Three," NBA All-Star Chris Bosh started as a coder in college. He frequently talks about how it helped in his life and that everyone should learn to code at some point. Learning to code is one of the most interesting experiences you can have in your life. Regardless of whether you are learning programming as a hobby or in the interest of making it a full-time profession, it will help improve your logical thinking, teach you how problems can be approached methodically, and help you learn how to optimize solutions.

Programming Languages

This book will teach you the basics of how computers work and how to program them. Ballerina is one of the languages that you can use to program a computer. Programming languages are used in a manner similar to how we use spoken languages. There are many dialects around the world whose sole purpose is to enable people to communicate with each other. A single thought can be expressed in numerous ways through different languages.

For example, the English phrase "What is your name?" can be said in many different languages. In Sinhala, it's "ඔයාගේ නම කුමක් ද?" In French, it's "Quel est votre nom?" In the end, it still means the same for everyone.

The same is true with programming languages, except that their purpose is to tell a computer what to do. There are many programming languages, such as C, C++, Java, and Go, but the computer will understand the same final *machine-level instructions*.

You might be wondering, "Why are there so many programming languages?" Even if programming languages ultimately mean the same thing for a computer in the end, each one has its own unique way of expressing certain needs. Some languages may be better for writing computer games, some may be better for network communications, and so on. There is no perfect programming language. It all depends on the type of computer programming you will be doing.

There are varying degrees of specialization for programming languages. For example, languages such as R and MATLAB are used specifically for statistical and mathematical computations. PHP and JavaScript are mainly used in the web development domain. Languages like C/C++ are mostly used for systems programming, which is related to operating systems code and embedded systems.

The Ballerina programming language is defined as a general-purpose programming language, but it also has built-in features to help write network-distributed applications. In a language such as C, these tasks are comparatively harder to do, because we need to think about low-level details, such as explicit memory management. This is something you need when you are doing systems programming, but not necessarily in general applications programming. For instance, the C language would be good for writing an operating system, but it would be hard to use Ballerina in that scenario. This is because of a compromise between the overall user control of resources and the user friendliness of the language in general programming. One of these aspects is automatic memory management in Ballerina, whereas in C, you must do your own memory management. We will be learning more about these as we advance through the chapters.

Computer Organization

Before we start programming, it's important to understand how a typical computer system works. This is not an in-depth guide on how a computer works but rather just a high-level overview of how things work together.

Figure 1-2 shows the three main components of a computer.

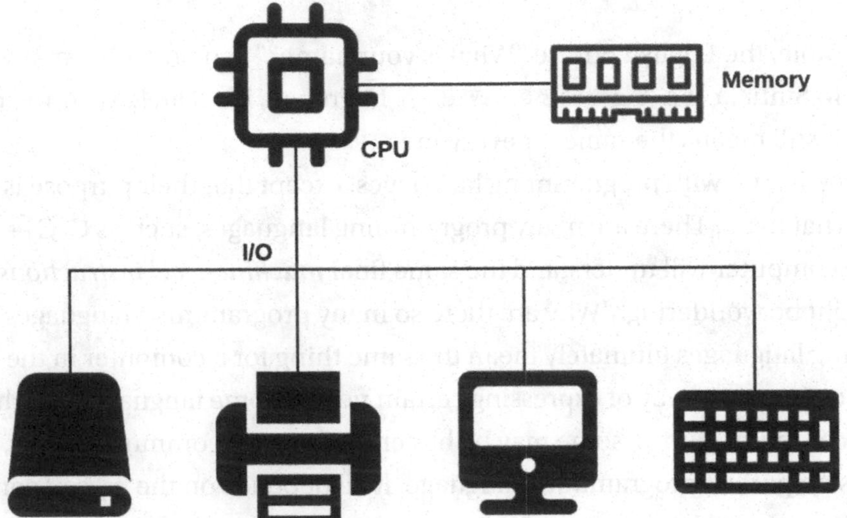

Figure 1-2. *High-level computer organization*

CPU

The central processing unit (CPU) is the brain of the computer. It takes in external instructions and performs the required actions defined by the instructions. These can be mathematical operations, reading and writing to memory, or input/output (I/O) operations. I/O operations include, for example, accessing devices, such as a display devices or printers. This is very much like a human brain, which coordinates all the body's functions to make things happen. One notable difference is that our brains already have some initial programming at the time of birth and then learn to do new things as we mature. Computer CPUs are not that advanced yet; it's still necessary for programmers to give them instructions on what to do. But with the advent of artificial intelligence (AI) techniques with computer code and improved hardware, the push for computers to learn and *think* on their own is on.

Instruction Sets

Each CPU has its own instruction set. Basically, instructions are the commands that it understands. This is similar to a dictionary of possible words in a written language. The most popular instruction set is the x86/x64 instruction set originated by Intel and Advanced Micro Devices (AMD). The instructions are nothing more than a sequence of numbers, representing some specific action to be executed by the CPU. Listing 1-1 contains a set of CPU instructions to perform a simple calculation.

Listing 1-1. x86 Assembly Code for Addition

```
mov eax, 10
mov ebx, 20
add eax, ebx
mov [esi+8], eax
```

Those are the CPU instructions to calculate 10 + 20 and store a result in a specific place. We also call this the *assembly code,* which means it is the lowest-level code actually running in a CPU. These instructions are translated into binary code, to a target set of numbers, using an assembler. It maps each of the instructions and the other values mentioned in the assembly code to a numerical format identified by the CPU. This binary code is also called the *machine code* for a CPU.

The actual numerical representation of the preceding code in the x86 architecture is displayed here in hex (base 16) numbers:

```
B8 0A 00 00 00 BB 14 00 00 00 01 D8 89 46 08
```

It is these numbers that are fed into the CPU to execute the required processing.

People used to program in this low-level assembly language in the early days of computers. But as memory capacities and CPU capabilities increased, programmers were able to write much more complicated programs. In this situation, coding with this lower-level form is time-consuming and hard to manage. This drove the development of higher-level programming languages to define and then translate or compile those programs to CPU instructions. Listing 1-2 shows an example of a higher-level language code to perform the same operation as the assembly code in Listing 1-1.

Listing 1-2. High-Level Code for Addition

```
a = 10;
b = 20;
x = a + b;
```

This code looks simpler and is more natural for a human programmer. There are many more higher-level constructs that developers use in programming languages, such as conditional execution, loops, and functions. A *compiler* does us a big favor by converting our higher-level—more human friendly—language code to the low-level machine code understood by the CPU.

Primary Memory

The primary memory of a computer is where the storage that is required for the CPU resides (Figure 1-3). This is used for CPU instruction calculations and other operations that need a temporary storage area to carry out their work. This can be input data for processing, intermediate data that is required for calculations, and a storage area for containing the program instructions themselves. This area of memory is also known as *random access memory* (RAM). Here, unlike in spinning magnetic disks or optical disks, any data point can be instantly accessed, without waiting for something mechanically to reposition itself to read the data. This type of memory is much faster than secondary memory, e.g., hard disks.

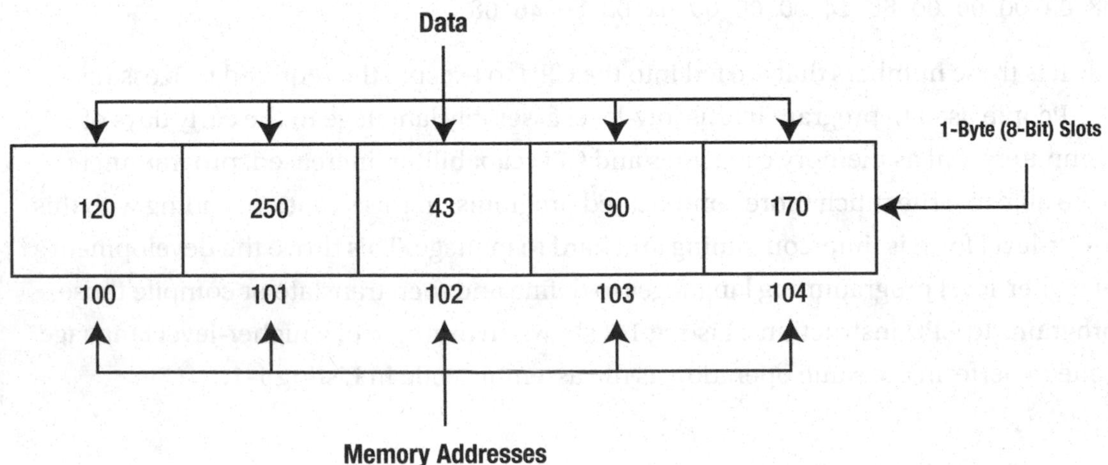

Figure 1-3. *Main memory layout*

Primary memory can be visualized as a set of slots in the computer to store values. It consists of a finite number of slots that we can refer to by a number representing the slot position. We call this slot position a *memory address.* For example, if we have a main memory capacity of 200 slots, these 200 slots can be used to store a specific value and be read back later by the CPU. The only thing you need to know is the specific index of the slot to access the data you are interested in. That is, CPU code may instruct the computer to fetch the data in the 101st slot, perform some modifications to that data, and write it back to the 102nd slot.

Now that you know about primary memory, how much data does one of those slots actually hold? This is generally the lowest addressable unit of data in computers, known as a *byte*. A byte of data is made up of 8 *bits.* And a bit is a single base 2 number. In our day-to-day lives, we use the decimal number system, which is base 10. This simply means each digit can hold 10 states, from 0 to 9. So if you have space to write two digits, you will be able to store 10^2 values, from 0 to 99. Computers store the data as binary; that is, it uses base 2 numbers, so if you have 8 bits, that means you can have 2^8, or 256, states.

You've learned how the CPU can access a specific memory location and how it can get access to one byte of data and that you can store a numeric value of 0–255 there. But what if you want to store a bigger value than that? In this case, you simply use more than one slot to store that value. In computer programming, we generally represent an integer value with 64 bits, or eight 8-bit slots. This will give us the ability to represent 2^{64} states. That is, if we consider it as a signed number (numbers with minus values), we will be able to store a number value starting from -9,223,372,036,854,775,808 to 9,223,372,036,854,775,807 ($-2^{64}/2$ - $2^{64}/2-1$). That is more than enough for our typical uses, or if needed, we can combine more bytes and create larger structures as well.

Memory bytes can be used to store various kinds of data. The trick lies in the way you *encode* your data to be stored as bytes. For example, what if we want image data to be saved in memory? A digital image is composed using pixel values, where each pixel contains red/green/blue (RGB) components, which represents the respective color component intensity of the pixel. The most common way to encode the pixel value is to represent each color component using one byte of data, so you get 2^8=256 color shades of that component. In this manner, you will be storing each pixel value with 24 bits, which gives you the ability to represent 2^{24}, or about 16 million, colors.

Figure 1-4 shows a zoomed-in image with each pixel showing, as well as the single-pixel color components. Here the highlighted pixel's RGB value is a hexadecimal (base 16) value of 746508. This means R=74, G=65, and B=08 in hexadecimal values of each color component.

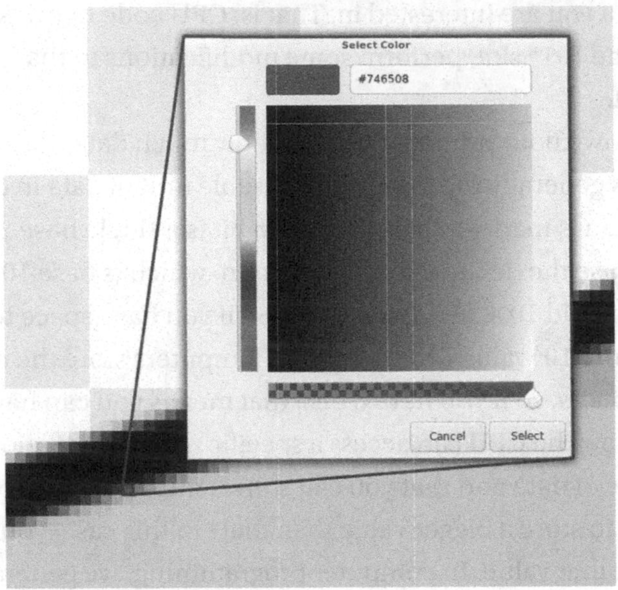

Figure 1-4. *Image pixel representation*

Similar techniques are applied for audio. Pulse code modulation (PCM) is often used to represent digital audio by analyzing an analog audio signal. This is done by taking samples of the intensity of the analog audio signal (the amplitude) in certain time intervals (the sample rate).

Figure 1-5 shows the use of PCM operation, where each sample S(t) is recorded at given T time intervals from the analog audio signal.

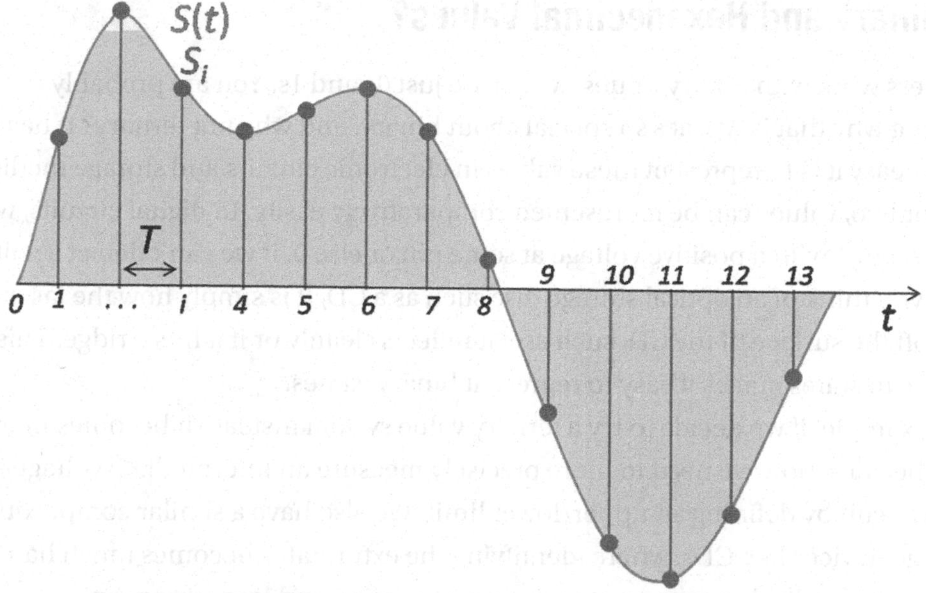

***Figure 1-5.** Digital audio representation*

If we take more samples, with each sample having a higher accuracy, we will get a better reproduction of the original analog signal, which results in clearer audio. For example, CD-quality audio has a sample size (resolution) of 16 bits and a sample rate of 44.1 kHz. That is, the S(i) value has a 16-bit value, which means it can have 2^{16} (65536) values for representing the sample amplitude, and it takes 44,100 of these samples per second.

A CD generally holds about 847 MB of data (even though they are commonly marked as 700 MB CDs). This is due to the additional error correction data used for general data storage. But in audio CDs, the full 847 MB of storage can be used. Since we now know about sampling size and sample rates for audio CDs, we can check the maximum amount of digital audio that can fit in a CD.

- *Storage required for one second of audio*: 44100 * 2 (16 bits, 2 bytes) * 2 (two channels, stereo) = 176,400 bytes
- *Number of seconds of audio in a CD*: 847 × 1000 × 1000 ÷ 176400 = 4801
- *Number of minutes in an audio CD*: 4801 ÷ 60 ≈ 80 minutes

This calculation shows how a CD can hold 80 minutes of audio using a digital audio encoding mechanism.

Why Binary and Hexadecimal Values?

Computers work with binary values, which are just 0s and 1s. You are probably wondering why that is. What's so special about binary, and why not ternary? It has to do with how easy it is to represent these values in electronic circuits and storage mediums. Binary, or two, values can be represented comparatively easily. In digital circuits, we can represent 1 with a positive voltage at some pin or else 0, if we can't detect a voltage there. If you think of an optical storage disc such as a CD, it is simply how the laser beam reflects off the surface of the CD, such as if it reflects cleanly or if it hits a ridge. This clear difference in states makes it easy to represent binary values.

For example, if we decide to try a ternary value system instead, it becomes much trickier, because now we need to more precisely measure an intermediate voltage in a digital circuit by defining an upper/lower limit. We also have a similar complexity for storage devices like CDs, where identifying the extra states becomes much harder. Therefore, generally, binary systems are easier to define and less error prone.

But what is the deal with hexadecimal (hex) values? We see these values often when we talk about binary values. This is because when we have larger binary values, it is easier to show them as hex (base 16) values. In hex values, the first 10 states are represented using 0–9 numbers, and the other six states are represented using the characters A–F. Also, it is easier to convert from binary to hex. This is because a single hex digit can be mapped to 4 bits, or rather 1 byte (8 bits) can be mapped to two hex digits. So, especially when we talk in byte granularity, we can always represent them fully as hex values.

For example, the 1110 0110 binary value in hex is E6. This is also written as 0xE6, where hex values are prefixed with 0x to signal that they are base 16 (hex) numbers.

Input/Output

The input/output subsystem is what is used by the CPU to communicate with other devices in the computer and the outside world. These devices include hard disks, display monitors, printers, keyboards, network devices, etc. From computer programs, we can provide CPU instructions to communicate with these devices by transferring from and to primary memory.

In our first Ballerina program, we will be bringing all the parts of a computer together to show a message on our display monitor.

The First Ballerina Program

Now that we know the basics of how a computer works, let's see how to write our first computer program using Ballerina.

Installing Ballerina

Ballerina consists of a compiler and a runtime. The compiler is used to convert our program code to a representation that the runtime will use to execute CPU instructions. Ballerina can be downloaded from `https://ballerina.io/downloads/` for all major operating systems. Follow the instructions available in the respective installers to install Ballerina.

After the installation, verify the installation by typing `ballerina --version` from a terminal window on the respective operating system. This will print the installed Ballerina version if it was successfully installed.

Ballerina IDE Plug-in

The source code of Ballerina programs can be written in any simple text editor available with your operating system. Ballerina also provides support for the Visual Studio Code (VS Code) integrated development environment.

VS Code offers additional functionality compared to a simple text editor. It can improve your development experience by providing features such as syntax highlighting of the source code, as well as other types of assistance such as code autocomplete, templates, and library lookups. These code assist features are useful when you are proficient with the basics, and it will make advanced users more productive with their development.

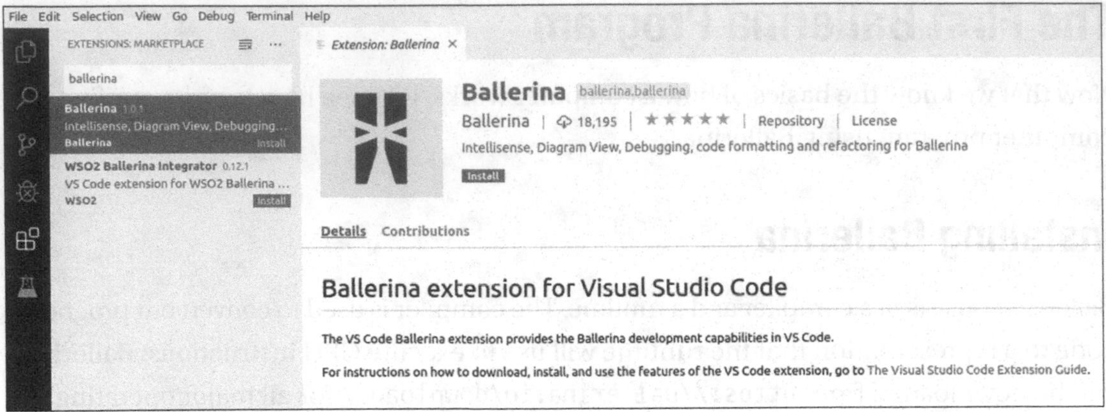

Figure 1-6. *VS Code Ballerina plug-in installation*

The VS Code Ballerina plug-in can be installed simply by searching for *Ballerina* using the plug-in search mechanism in VS Code. You will be able to select and install the Ballerina plug-in.

Now in VS Code, you can create any new file with the `.bal` extension, and the plug-in features will be available to the source code when editing these files. In the next section, let's create our first Ballerina program.

Hello, World!

Open your favorite text editor (e.g., `Nano, Notepad, VS Code`), and enter the code shown in Listing 1-3.

Listing 1-3. hello.bal

```
import ballerina/io;

public function main() {
    io:println("Hello, World!");
}
```

Save the file as `hello.bal`.

Open a terminal and navigate to the location where you saved `hello.bal`. Here, run the following command:

```
$ ballerina run hello.bal
Hello, World!
```

You have now successfully run your first Ballerina program!

Let's try to understand what is meant by this code.

The `import` declaration statement at line 1 says to make the *module* `io` from the *organization* `ballerina` available to our code. This module will be accessible to us with the alias `io`.

We call the statement in line 4 a *function call* or an *invocation*. It basically says to execute a specific functionality defined in the `println` function in the `io` module. As you may have guessed, this function is used to print a message out to our console.

This example program uses many concepts to illustrate how to use the Ballerina programming language. We will learn more about these in detail in the coming chapters. For now, we will simply write the instructions inside the `main` function, which is in the space between lines 4 and 5. A *function* is simply a reusable unit of programming code that can be executed when needed. The `main` function is a bit special, because it is the entry point to the Ballerina program. That is, this is the section that gets executed automatically when the program is started.

Comments

You can put code comments in your programming code to note something related to the code you have written. This can be an explanation of the logic you have followed or basically anything that would help someone who is reading the code. Comments are ignored by the compiler, and they will not affect the outcome of the program logic.

You enter comments in a Ballerina program by using the // prefix. Any content after // in the same line will be ignored by the compiler.

Here's an example:

```
io:println("Hello, World!"); // prints a message
```

Summary

In this chapter, we covered the basics of computer organization, the binary data representation, and encoding techniques; in addition, we wrote our first Ballerina program to output a message to the console.

In the next chapter, we will extend our knowledge of programming to create more useful programs. This will include using variables, performing conditional execution, and creating functions.

CHAPTER 2

Programming Basics

In this chapter, you will learn the basics of programming, such as how to use simple data types and variables, how to implement flow control, and how to organize and reuse logic by writing your own functions.

Types and Variables

Variables are simply locations in memory with a given name. This gives you a chance to store something in memory to be later used or modified in your program. Every variable has a type associated with it that defines the values that can be stored in the variable.

Let's do a demonstration by writing a small program, shown in Listing 2-1, to calculate the area of a circle. The formula for this is $A = \pi * r^2$ ($\pi \approx 3.1415$).

Listing 2-1. circle_area.bal

```
import ballerina/io;

public function main() {
    int radius = 5;
    float area = 3.1415 * radius * radius;
    io:println(area);
}
```

```
$ ballerina run circle_area.bal
78.53750000000001
```


A. Fernando and L. Warusawithana, *Beginning Ballerina Programming*,
https://doi.org/10.1007/978-1-4842-5139-3_2

Here, we have declared two variables: `radius` and `area`. Line 4 contains the declaration of the variable `radius`. This line starts with the type of the variable, followed by the variable name, then the equal sign, and finally the literal value 5. Literal values are explicit fixed values in the code, which are meant to be used as is. So, line 4 can be read as follows: "declare a variable named `radius`, which is of type `int`, and assign it an initial value of 5."

We call each of the lines at lines 4, 5, and 6 a code *statement*. A statement must always end with a semicolon (`;`). A variable declaration statement takes either of the following forms:

```
<type> <variable_name>;
<type> <variable_name> = <initialization_expression>;
```

A variable can be declared with or without an initial value.

```
int age;
```

The previous line declares the variable age of type `int`, but it is not assigned a value yet. Before a variable can be used for reading its value, it must be first initialized.

A variable with the type `int` is used to store integer values, and no other type of values can be stored. For example, we will not be able to store numbers with decimal points. If we need to support values with decimal points, we will have to declare variables with a different type that will allow those values.

This is what is done in line 5, where we declare the type of the variable `area` as `float`. This means it is a floating-point value that can store numbers with fractional values. The value of `area` is calculated using an *expression*. An expression is a clause that will evaluate to some value. This can be a specific calculation, such as `3.1415 * radius * radius` or even a single literal value. For variable assignment statements, the general format is as follows:

```
variable = <expression>;
```

You can picture this operation as follows: the right-hand side (RHS) is evaluated first, and the result flows to the left-hand side (LHS) to the variable. Assigning a value as such can be done immediately when the variable is declared or later with assignment statements.

Let's update our code to add an extra assignment to the `radius` variable and repeat the calculation (see Listing 2-2).

Listing 2-2. circle_area2.bal

```
import ballerina/io;

public function main() {
    int radius = 5;
    float area = 3.1415 * radius * radius;
    io:println(area);
    radius = 10;
    area = 3.1415 * radius * radius;
    io:println(area);
}
```

```
$ ballerina run circle_area2.bal
78.53750000000001
314.15000000000003
```

Naming Variables

The variable names that are used in Ballerina are called *identifiers*. These can be any Unicode string but with some specific restrictions. The identifier should start with a letter or an underscore (_). The rest of the characters also cannot contain symbols such as programming operators, e.g., +, -, and &. Also, identifiers cannot contain keywords in Ballerina, which are the terms used to build up the syntax in the language. These are, for example, `public`, `function`, and `import`. For a full list of reserved keywords, please refer to the Ballerina language specification: `https://ballerina.io/spec/`.

If a Ballerina keyword is critical for a variable name, a mechanism known as the *quoted identifier syntax* can be used. This is done by prefixing the name with a single quote ('). This usage is mainly useful in field names of Ballerina record types, which will be introduced in Chapter 3.

An example usage of variable names is shown here:

```
int _count = 5;
string 'function = "add";
float personHeight = 2.5;
```

The identifiers are also case sensitive, where the names `personHeight` and `PersonHeight` are two distinct names and will not conflict. A general notation used in naming is *hump notation*. This is where the first letter of the identifier is lowercase, and the first letter of the following words are capitalized, e.g., `streetAddress`, `firstName`. The name for the notation is because the identifiers resemble the hump of a camel. This notation is also known as *camel case*.

It's important to use meaningful names for variables, for example, `areaCircle` and `areaBox` instead of `a1` and `a2`. The code you write now has to be read later, either by you or by other users. At this point, the logic that is intended should be apparent by reading the code; therefore, using meaningful identifiers is important.

Simple Types

A simple type is a type that is defined as the primitive set of types available in the language, which is not based on another type. The following table defines each simple type:

Name	Supported Values
`boolean`	`true, false`
`byte`	8-bit unsigned integers: `10, 150`
`int`	64-bit signed integers: `10, -1259, 289`
`float`	64-bit IEEE 754-2008 binary floating-point numbers: `1.0, -35.1, 1.453e10`
`decimal`	128-bit IEEE 754-2008 decimal floating-point numbers: `3.435e10, 3.10, -10.0003`
`string`	Unicode strings: `"hello"`, "ආයුබෝවන්"
() - nil	()

Boolean Type

Boolean values are used in situations where you have only true or false values, and fittingly the only possible literal values for Boolean are `true` and `false`. An example usage of the Boolean type is shown here:

```
boolean finished = false;
```

The previous code is used in declaring the variable `finished` with the type `boolean`, and it is given the initial literal value `false`.

Subsequent assignment operations can be done to modify the value of the variable.

```
finished = true;
```

Integer Types

Integer types in Ballerina are represented by the `int` and `byte` types. The difference is simply the amount of memory used to store each value, which mandates the range of values possible in each type. `int` is a 64-bit signed integer type, and `byte` is an 8-bit unsigned integer type. A signed integer type is something where its values can be used to store both positive and negative values. The opposite is unsigned types, which have only positive values. The byte type has a value range from 0 to 2^8-1 (0 to 255). And the `int` type has a value range from -2^{63} to +2^{63}-1 (-9223372036854775808 to 9223372036854775807).

A mechanism known as *two's complement* is used to represent signed integers as binary values. The exact approach used for this is out of the scope of this chapter. But if you are curious, check Appendix A for a detailed explanation of how this is done.

Let's take a look at how the integer types can be declared.

```
byte myByte = 53;
int myInteger = 11530;
int myOtherInteger = -640;
```

The literal integer values 53, 11530, and -640 are used to give initial values for the variables. These are base 10 values we use in our day-to-day life. It is also possible to provide literal integer values in base 16, also known as *hexadecimal*. The following shows some follow-up assignment operations used to update the variable values using hex values:

```
myByte = 0xFF;     // 255 in base 10
myInteger = 0x10; // 16 in base 10
```

Hexadecimal integer literals are prefixed with 0x to distinguish them from base 10 numbers. The 16 possible values for each digit are represented using 0–9 and A–F, which represents the values 10–16.

Floating-Point Types

In Ballerina, numbers with fractional components are represented using floating-point types: `float` and `decimal`. Floating-point numbers are internally represented using the scientific notation based on a binary encoding. This representation contains two main parts; one is the actual digits that make the number, and the other represents the position in the digits where the radix point is situated. The radix point is said to be *floating* because of this representation.

The `float` type, represented using the 64-bit IEEE 754-2008 floating-point standard, converts the decimal fractional values to binary fractional values. In this conversation, it is not possible to always exactly represent the decimal fractional value as it is, as binary fractions. Because of this behavior, there can be rounding errors when we represent decimal values using the `float` type. Appendix A explains how floating-point values are represented in binary data.

Because of the accuracy issues in representing decimal values as binary floating-point values, it is not recommended to use floats in domains such as currency processing, where even slight accuracy errors can build up to bigger issues with time. In those situations, we will use special data types to represent currency. The `decimal` type in Ballerina is suitable for this domain. The `decimal` type is used when we want to represent numbers with decimal fractions without rounding errors. It uses a special binary encoding mechanism to represent the decimal fractions correctly.

How floating-point typed variables are declared and the usage of their literal values are shown here:

```
float roadWidth = 1245.5;
float distanceToSun = 9.296e7;
decimal sharePrice = 153.59;
```

The notation with *e* (or E) is used to denote the number of times the preceding value should be multiplied by 10. This is basically using scientific notation to represent the value. In this manner, the value of the variable `distanceToSun` equals $9.296 * 10^7 = 92960000.0$.

A floating-point literal value can also state explicitly what its type is. This is done by adding the suffix `f` or `d` to the value, e.g., `3.14f`, `1.005d`, for denoting float and decimal values, respectively. Generally, this is not required since the type of the value is detected by the context it is in. For example, the previous `distanceToSun` variable has the type `float`. Thus, it expects and considers the expression used to assign its value. In this case, the literal value `9.296e7` is a float value. Let's see a scenario when the floating-point type suffixes become useful.

Type Inference with var

In Ballerina, we can use the var keyword in place of the type descriptor, where the type of the variable is inferred from the value that is provided for its initialization.

```
var name = "Nimal";
var age = 18;
var height = 182.88;
var distanceToSun = 9.296e7f;
var sharePrice = 153.59d;
```

In the previous code snippet, we have not given the exact type in the variable declaration but rather used var to infer the type of the variable using the given value. In this manner, the variable name is inferred as a string type from the compiler, and age is inferred as an int. Also, the variable height is given a floating-point literal value, where by default this get inferred as a float type. The variable sharePrice here is inferred as a decimal type since we explicitly mentioned the literal value given is of decimal type.

In this manner, we can use the floating-point type suffixes to eliminate any possible ambiguity for the compiler in resolving the types of literal values.

Why both decimal and float?

The question may arise, why are there two different floating-point types, and why can't we always use decimal? This is because the float type takes less memory than decimal (64 bits versus 128 bits), and also its operations are typically faster compared to decimal because of the special dedicated floating-point calculation circuitry available in CPUs.

Generally, the float type is usable for the majority of our use cases. So, we should use decimal only when it's actually required for the specific advantages it provides over the float type.

Numeric Conversions

Sometimes you may need to convert between numeric data types in a program. For example, if you have a floating-point value, you may need to convert it to an integer value. Or it could be that you have a value of type int, but you actually need it in a byte-typed variable. These operations are done using the cast operator (<>) in Ballerina.

The following example converts from a `float` value to an `int`:

```
float a = 53.56;
int b = <int> a;
```

After the previous conversion operation, the value of b will be 54. The reason is that the conversion automatically rounds the value to the closest integer.

The following example converts an `int` value to a `byte` value, where the byte is a smaller capacity type compared to the `int`. So, in the conversion, there is a chance that the conversion may fail because the integer value is too big to fit into the target variable.

```
int a = 70;
byte b = <byte> a;
```

The previous code will execute properly, since the integer value 70 is a supported value for a `byte` value. Let's see a typical problem case.

```
int a = 1500;
byte b = <byte> a;
```

The previous code will fail during the conversion operation at runtime by resulting in a panic. This is because the integer value 1500 is unable to fit into an 8-bit unsigned integer (`byte`) typed variable. Ballerina error handling and panics will be covered in depth in Chapter 5.

string Type

A `string` is used to store text in your program. In a `string` variable, you can store any sequence of Unicode characters. The following example contains the declarations of `string`-typed variables with `string` literals used to initialize them:

```
string city = "Colombo";
string myFriend = "සුනිල්";
string myOtherFriend = "சிவா";
```

Escape Sequences

In strings, there are special characters known as escape sequences, which start with the escape character \. For example, if we need to add double quotes (`""`) to a string, we cannot add it directly, since it will become a syntax error because of the string bounded by double quotes in its definition, and the compiler will get confused because of the mix of double quotes. This is where we need to use the escape character to create a sequence with \, which can be used to add the double quotes to the final string. The following table contains the escape character sequences and their usages:

Escape Character Sequence	Description
\n	New line character
\r	Carriage return character
\t	Tab character
\\	Backslash
\"	Double quotes

Listing 2-3 shows an example of how to use escape sequences.

Listing 2-3. escape_sequences.bal

```
import ballerina/io;

public function main() {
    string message = "I remember my uncle saying \"great power " +
                     "comes great responsibility\".";
    io:println(message);
    message = "Shopping List:\n\tBread\n\tEggs\n\tButter";
    io:println(message);
}
```

```
$ ballerina run escape_sequences.bal
I remember my uncle saying "great power comes great responsibility".
Shopping List:
        Bread
        Eggs
        Butter
```

Function	Description
`indexOf(string substr, int indexFrom)`	Searches the current string for the given substring from the given index location
`substring(int startIndex, int endIndex)`	Returns a substring from the current string starting with `startIndex` (inclusive) to `endIndex` (exclusive)
`startsWith(string substr)`	Returns a Boolean value indicating if the current string starts with the given string
`endsWith(string substr)`	Returns a Boolean value indicating if the current string ends with the given string
`trim()`	Removes any whitespace characters from the beginning and the end of the string
`length()`	Returns the length of the string
`toLowerAscii()`	Returns a string with the current string's English letters turned to lowercase
`toUpperAscii()`	Returns a string with the current string's English letters turned to uppercase

In the previous code snippet at lines 4 and 5, we can see how escape sequences have been used to add double quotes to the string. And at line 7, escape sequences have been used to add line breaks and tabs.

nil Type

The `nil` type/value is special. This represents a nothing or a void value in Ballerina. The `nil` type and value are both represented in the code using `()`. This usage is especially useful when we are using optional values and return types in functions. This will be covered in more detail when introducing union types in Chapter 3.

Mathematical Calculations

We already saw some mathematical calculations in action when we multiplied variables in the sample program in Listing 2-1. Let's go through the main supported mathematical operators that are available in Ballerina.

Operands are values given in relation to the operator. These can be either variables, literal values, or any other expression. The number of operands is decided based on if it is a unary, binary, or ternary operator. This means the operator works with one, two, or three operands, respectively.

Arithmetic Operators

The following binary operators are used to do arithmetic operations on given two values.

Operator	Description	Example
+	Add	`a + b`
-	Subtract	`a - b`
*	Multiply	`a * b`
/	Divide	`a / b`
%	Remainder of the value after a is divided by b. For example, 5 % 3 is equal to 2	`a % b`

The arithmetic operators are mostly self-explanatory. Listing 2-4 shows an example of the arithmetic operators in action.

Listing 2-4. arithmetic_sample.bal

```
import ballerina/io;

public function main() {
      int a = 1 + 4;
      int b = a + 10;
      float c = b * 2.5;
      io:println(a, ":", b, ":", c);
      int d = a % 3;
```

```
09     int e = a / 3;
10     io:println(d, ":", e);
11     float f = a / 3.0;
12     io:println(f);
13     int g = a + b * 2;
14     int h = (a + b) * 2;
15     io:println(g, ":", h);
16 }
```

```
$ ballerina run arithmetic_sample.bal
5:15:37.5
2:1
1.6666666666666667
35:40
```

In line 9, the division operator works in a way that, since two integer values are involved, the result is also an integer value. This result is always a rounded-down integer value. For example, if you execute the expression 11/6, the result will be 1. Also, as shown in line 11, even if one of the numbers is a `float` value, then the result would also be a `float` value.

When executing an expression with multiple arithmetic operators, as shown in lines 13 and 14, operator precedence comes into play, that is, figuring out which operator to be executed first in an expression. In line 13, the expression `a + b * 2` is executed by first evaluating `b * 2` and then adding the result to `a`. This is because the multiplication operator has higher precedence than the addition operator. So, in scenarios where you need to evaluate the addition first and do the multiplication with the result, we can wrap the `a + b` section with parentheses, where parentheses always get higher precedence compared to other operators. This behavior is shown in line 14.

The arithmetic operator precedence order in Ballerina is as follows (ordered from highest to lowest):

- `()`
- `*`
- `/`
- `%`
- `+`
- `-`

Assignment Operators

These are used to assign a value to a variable and can be used to combine an arithmetic operation at the same time of the assignment. The operators that are used to combine the arithmetic operators with the assignment are called *compound operators*.

Operator	Description	Example
=	Assigns the value of the expression at RHS to LHS	a = b
+=	Simplified for a = a + b	a += b
-=	Simplified for a = a - b	a -= b
*=	Simplified for a = a * b	a *= b
/=	Simplified for a = a / b	a /= b

Making Decisions

Decision-making in programming is often a combination of conditional and logical operators and the use of flow control constructs. The following sections introduce these concepts in detail and cover how and when to use them.

Comparison Operators

These operators are used to create Boolean expressions to do comparisons between two given expressions.

Operator	Description	Example
==	Deep equals	a == b
<	Less than	a < b
<=	Less than or equal	a <= b
>	Greater than	a > b
>=	Greater than or equal	a >= b
!=	Not deep equals	a != b

(*continued*)

Operator	Description	Example
===	Exact equals	a === b
!==	Not exact equals	a !== b

The === operator checks for exact equality, where in the case of simple types, it checks if the values are identical. Otherwise, in the case of reference types, it checks if the memory location information stored in the reference typed variable is identical.

The == operator checks for deep equality, whereas for simple types, with the exception of floating-point values, it behaves the same as the === operator.

For simple types, other than the `float` type, == and === provide a similar result. The difference in usage of these two operators will be specially made clear when we check reference types in Ballerina, which are introduced in Chapter 3.

In the case of the `float` type, positive and negative zero are both equal when used with ==, but they are not with ===. For the decimal type, it takes in the precision when considering the deep and exact equals. For instance, with decimal values, `5.0 == 5.00` is true, but `5.0 === 5.00` is false.

Listing 2-5 contains sample code that shows the comparison operators in action.

Listing 2-5. comparison_operators.bal

```
import ballerina/io;

public function main() {
    int a = 10;
    int b = 20;
    int c = 10;
    boolean d = a == c;
    boolean e = a == b;
    boolean f = a < 10;
    boolean g = a <= 10;
    io:println(d, ":", e, ":", f, ":", g);
}
```

```
$ ballerina run comparison_operators.bal
true:false:false:true
```

Logical Operators

The logical operators are used to combine two Boolean expressions to result in a single expression or else complement a given Boolean expression.

Operator	Description	Example
&&	Executes a logical AND operation on the given two operands	`boolean x = a && b;`
||	Executes a logical OR operation on the given two operands	`boolean x = a || b;`
!	Executes a logical NOT operation on the given operand	`boolean x = !a;`

AND Operator

The AND (&&) operator is used to combine two conditions to create a single expression, which evaluates to `true` if both given conditions are true. Let's take a simple example. To serve in the military, a man needs to be at least 152 cm tall and at least 17 years old. Let's write a Boolean expression to decide this.

```
height >= 152 && age >= 17;
```

The previous Boolean expression uses the variables `height` and age and creates a compound expression (an expression created by combining other expressions) using the AND operator. The result of this expression can be assigned to a variable, as shown here:

```
boolean canJoinMilitary = height >= 152 && age >= 17;
```

The Boolean expression can also be used directly in flow control constructs, such as the `if/else` statement, which you will see in the upcoming "Flow Control" section.

The AND operator also tries to do the minimum amount of processing to get the final result. This is done by short-circuiting the evaluation. If the first condition is false, it skips evaluating the second condition. This is done because, if the first condition is false, the whole compound expression will result in a `false` value anyway, regardless of what the second condition evaluates to. Because of this, for example, if `height=100`, the age `>= 17` expression is not executed at all.

OR Operator

The OR (||) operator is used to create a compound expression that will result in `true` if at least one of the conditions is evaluated to true. As an example, let's take the criteria used to check how children are allowed to fly on a plane. A child must be at least 12 years old, or else an adult must accompany the child. Let's write a Boolean expression to show this scenario and store the result in a Boolean variable.

```
boolean canFly = age >= 12 || adultAvailable;
```

Here, `adultAvailable` is a Boolean variable representing if an adult is accompanying the child. Similar to the AND operator, the OR operator also does short-circuit evaluation in executing its logic. If the first condition here evaluates to `true`, there is no reason to evaluate the second condition, but rather it will return true immediately.

NOT Operator

The NOT (!) operator can be used to swap the Boolean value of an expression. This can be useful when we want to simplify a complex compound Boolean expression. Let's check the following scenario:

```
boolean gotoBeach = !(temp > 70 || weather == "rain")
```

Here, we are checking if we can go to the beach. The criterion is to check all the scenarios that are not suitable for a beach visit. If there is high temperature or rain, we cannot go to the beach, so we simply get the result by negating the full result of the possibility of not being able to go to the beach.

But interestingly, we can avoid the usage of the NOT operator in the previous scenario by rewriting the compound Boolean expression in a different manner.

```
boolean gotoBeach = temp <= 70 && weather != "rain";
```

The previous provides the same result, but sometimes, to keep our thought process clearer and to make the logic more readable, we may decide to use a specific organization of our logical expressions.

Combining Logical Operators

The logical operators can be combined in a single compound expression to create more complex logic. Let's take our initial military enlistment requirements and make the example common for both men and women.

```
boolean canJoinMilitary = ((gender == "male" && height >= 152) ||
(gender == "female" && height >= 147)) && age >= 17;
```

In the previous logic, we have said for men, a height of 152 cm is required, and for women, a height of 147 is required, and both men and women must be at least 17 years old.

As with arithmetic operators, logical operators also have an operator precedence. The ordering is as follows, from highest to lowest precedence: NOT, AND, OR. To control the order explicitly, we can use parentheses to group subexpressions as done in the previous example. For example, let's remove the outermost parentheses from the first part of the expression, as shown here:

```
(gender == "male" && height >= 152) || (gender == "female" && height >= 147)
&& age >= 17;
```

This gives us three main subexpressions, as shown earlier. But because of operator precedence rules, the AND (&&) will execute first, which means it will execute `(gender == "female" && height >= 147) && age >= 17` and then `(gender == "male" && height >= 152)`. But this will give incorrect logic because the age check will be done only for women. So, what we need is for `(gender == "male" && height >= 152) || (gender == "female" && height >= 147)` to execute first and finally `age >= 17`. The only way to do this is to override the operator precedence for logical operators by adding more parentheses to drive the order of operations for the logic.

Flow Control

So far we have written code in a way that all the statements are executed continuously from the start to the end. But in real life, and in turn in our computer programs, things don't always work like that. We generally look at certain factors, and depending on those factors, we change our actions. For example, if today is a cold day, you will wear a jacket, or else, you will not wear it. We need to make similar decisions in our computer programs.

Let's take a look at how Ballerina's flow control constructs help in implementing logic in our programs.

if Statement

The `if` statement is used to check for a condition, and if that condition is true, it will execute a given set of statements. The general format of an `if` statement is as follows:

```
if <boolean_expression> {
    <statement1>
    <statement2>
    ...
}
```

In the code block between the open and close parentheses, we can provide a list of statements to execute if the given Boolean expression is evaluated to `true`. If it is false, the statements inside the `if` code block will not be executed, but rather it will skip through those statements and continue to execute the statements after the `if` statement block.

Let's look at an example of an `if` statement, where we are checking if a person's age is over the legal drinking age, shown here:

```
int age;
...
if age >= 21 {
   io:println("Legal to drink");
}
```

The previous code snippet shows how the Boolean expression `age >= 21` is used as the condition for the `if` statement, and if it evaluates to `true`, the `print` statement will be executed.

What if we now want to do something if the person is not over the legal age to drink? That is, if the person is over the drinking age, we print that, or else, we need to print a different message. We can of course have another `if` statement after the first `if` statement with the inverse condition.

```
if age >= 21 {
    io:println("Legal to drink");
}
if age < 21 {
    io:println("Not legal to drink");
}
```

The previous code gets the job done. But there is actually an easier way to do it, by adding an `else` clause to the original `if` statement.

```
if age >= 21 {
    io:println("Legal to drink");
} else {
    io:println("Not legal to drink");
}
```

The statements inside the `else` code block are executed if the `if` code block is not executed. It can simply be read as follows: "*If* the given condition is met, execute the statements in the `if` block, *else*, execute the statements in the `else` block."

Nested if/else Statements

The `if/else` statements can be nested; that is, other `if/else` statement can be stated inside an outer `if/else` statement to create more advanced logic. Let's extend our earlier scenario to see if the person is at least allowed to drive if he or she is not allowed to drink.

```
if age >= 21 {
    io:println("Legal to drink");
} else {
    if age >= 16 {
        io:println("Can just drive");
    } else {
        io:println("Not even allowed to drive");
    }
}
```

We can see that there is another nested `if/else` happening in the outer `if` statement's `else` clause. For similar patterns for nested `if/else` statements, there is a shorthand version that can be used. This is shown in the following code snippet:

```
if age >= 21 {
    io:println("Legal to drink");
} else if age >= 16 {
    io:println("Can just drive");
} else {
    io:println("Not even allowed to drive");
}
```

So, similar to the previous code, whenever we want to check for a new condition when the earlier condition is false, we can use the `else if <boolean_expression>` syntax.

In certain simple nested `if` statement situations, it may be convenient to combine the conditions to a single Boolean expression and have a single `if` statement. Let's check the following scenario. It checks two conditions now: if the country is USA and also if the age is greater than or equal to 21.

```
if country == "USA" {
    if age >= 21 {
        io:println("Legal to drink");
    }
}
```

The previous logic can also be written in the following manner:

```
if country == "USA" && age >= 21 {
    io:println("Legal to drink");
}
```

There we have simply used a conditional operator to combine two conditions and make a single Boolean expression, thus allowing us to eliminate the nested `if` statement.

Ternary Conditional Operator

To demonstrate the usage of the ternary conditional operator, let's first implement a simple coin toss scenario using conditional logic.

```
string result;
if math:random() > 0.5 {
    result = "Heads";
} else {
    result = "Tails";
}
```

Here, a random number is generated, and its value is checked using an `if/else` statement to assign the resulting value to a variable. This logic can be turned into a single line of code using the ternary conditional operator in the following manner:

```
string result = math:random() > 0.5 ? "Heads" : "Tails";
```

The ternary conditional operator consists of the following format:

```
<bool_expr> ? <expression_to_execute_when_bool_expr_is_true> : <expression_
to_execute_when_bool_expr_is_false>
```

The previous expression works in a way that the Boolean expression mentioned on the left side of the ? character is used to decide which one of the two expressions is to be evaluated on the right side of ?. These two expressions are separated by a : character. If the Boolean expression evaluates to `true`, then the first expression is executed, and its value becomes the result of the whole expression, or else, the second expression is executed and used as the result. Since this whole construct represented with the ternary conditional operator represents an expression, its result can be assigned to a variable with a variable assignment statement, as shown in the previous code.

Loops

Loops are used whenever we want to execute a specific code block repeatedly. The other obvious approach would be to actually write the same code multiple times in the program. But this will not be a pleasant experience to have, and it won't be practical to always do that.

while Loop

The primary approach in looping in Ballerina is the use of the `while` loop.

The `while` loop construct has the following format:

```
while <loop_condition> {
   statements...
}
```

In a `while` loop, the code block between the parentheses is executed repeatedly, while the loop condition represented by the Boolean expression is evaluated to `true`.

Listing 2-6 illustrates a simple example of printing 100 numbers from 0 to 99.

Listing 2-6. print_numbers.bal

```
01 import ballerina/io;
02
03 public function main() {
04     int i = 0;
05     while i < 100 {
06         io:println(i);
07         i += 1;
08     }
09     io:println("End.");
10 }
```

```
$ ballerina run print_numbers.bal
0
1
2
3
...
98
99
End.
```

In the previous code, at line 5, the `while` condition is evaluated first, and since the initial value of `i` is 0, the expression `i < 100` is evaluated to `true`. Because of this, the loop condition is fulfilled, and the execution moves into the `while` loop body code block. Now the statements inside the loop body are executed sequentially, which are at lines 6 and 7, which result in the value of variable `i` being incremented as well. After line 7, with the end of the `while` loop body, the execution again loops back to line 5. Here, now the value of `i` is 1, and still the loop condition `i < 100` evaluates to `true`; thus, the loop body is executed again.

A single execution of statements inside the loop body is known as a *loop iteration*. The previous scenario executed 100 loop iterations in this manner, and at the final iteration, i becomes equal to 100, and the loop condition at line 5 is not evaluated to true anymore. Now with the loop condition not fulfilled, the program execution jumps from line 0 to line 9 directly, skipping the loop body.

break

The break statement can be used to immediately jump out of a loop. This is used when you do not use the loop condition or, else, do not want to wait till the end of the loop iteration until the loop condition is evaluated but rather want to exit the loop right away.

continue

The continue statement is used to skip the rest of the statements in the current loop iteration and continue onto the next loop iteration immediately.

Listing 2-7 demonstrates a sample program that uses the break and continue statements.

Listing 2-7. loop_sqrt.bal

```
import ballerina/io;
import ballerina/math;
import ballerina/lang.'float as floats;

public function main() returns error? {
  while true {
    string input = io:readln("Enter a positive number (q to exit): ");
    if input == "q" {
        break;
    }
    float n = check floats:fromString(input);
    if n < 0 {
        io:println("Not a positive number, try again.");
        continue;
    }
    io:println(math:sqrt(n));
  }
}
```

```
$ ballerina run loop_sqrt.bal
Enter a positive number (q to exit): 90
9.486832980505138
Enter a positive number (q to exit): 431
20.760539492026695
Enter a positive number (q to exit): -55
Not a positive number, try again.
Enter a positive number (q to exit): q
```

The previous scenario implements a user interface for prompting the user for a positive number and prints the square root of the given number. This is done continuously until the user quits by entering `q`. Here, we are using a `while` loop with the condition set to the literal Boolean value `true`. This means that the loop condition is always fulfilled, and the loop construct will never end on its own. This is called an *infinite loop* since it will loop forever.

The only way the loop is exited is using the `break` statement at line 9, which checks for user input for the quit instruction. Also, if the user enters an incorrect value, i.e., a negative value, the rest of the loop body statements are skipped using a `continue` statement at line 14. This results in the execution going back to the top of the loop, which will prompt the user to enter a new value again.

Something to note is that the usage of `break` and `continue` is not the only way to implement those behaviors. A careful design of the loop's logic can be done with conditional statements to result in the same scenario.

foreach Loop

The `foreach` loop in Ballerina is most often used in iterating elements in structured values, such as arrays and maps. These data types will be introduced in Chapter 3. The `foreach` loop also can be used with range expressions. A range expression can be used in generating a numerical value range that can be iterated through a `foreach` loop. Let's rewrite our number printing example in Listing 2-8 to use a `foreach` loop with a range expression.

Listing 2-8. print_numbers_foreach.bal

```
import ballerina/io;

```

```
public function main() {
    foreach int i in 0...99 {
        io:println(i);
    }
    io:println("End.");
}
```

```
$ ballerina run print_numbers_foreach.bal
0
1
2
3
...
98
99
End.
```

The range expression `0...99` represents all the integer values between 0 and 99 inclusive. The syntax `0..<99` can be used to signal the second value is exclusive, so in this case, the `foreach` loop will iterate from 0 to 98.

Variable Scopes

The scope of a variable is the area of program source code where the variable can be referenced from, or simply the visibility of a variable. So far, we have defined all our variables inside the `main` function. A variable declared inside a function is known as a *local variable*. This type of a variable is accessible only to the code in the function itself and has the lifetime of the function call. More specifically, a local variable is in scope, i.e., visible, in the same code block after the line it was declared on, and in any nested code blocks till the end of the containing code block.

The variable scopes, and their behavior with nested code blocks, are demonstrated in Listing 2-9.

Listing 2-9. var_scopes.bal

```
1  import ballerina/io;
2
3  public function main() {
4      int i = 0;
5      // io:println(count);
6      int count = 10;
7      while i < count {
8          io:println(i);
9          int j = i + 1;
10         io:println(j);
11         if (j > 5) {
12             int x = j * 2;
13             io:println(x);
14         }
15         i += 1;
16     }
17     // io:println(j);
18 }
```

if statement code block

while loop code block

"main" function code block

In lines 4 and 6, the variables `i` and `count`, respectively, have been declared in the `main` function body's code block. Because of our scoping rules, these variables are addressable from the line they were declared on, to the end of the code block they were defined in, which is the `main` function body, which ends at line 18. Also, these variables are accessible in the nested code blocks, such as the `while` loop body code block and even in the further nested `if` statement body.

At line 5, if we uncomment the line there, it tries to access the variable `count`, which is yet to be declared in the following line. Even though it is referenced in the same code block, according to the rule that the variable must be declared in an earlier line relative to the place it tries to access it, it gives the following compile-time error:

```
error: .::var_scopes.bal:5:16: undefined symbol 'count'
```

A similar situation arises when line 17 is uncommented, where the variable `j` is declared in the `while` loop body, and thus, its scope ends with the end of the `while` loop body, and it is no longer accessible afterward. A scoping mechanism that follows this type of rule is known as having lexical (or static) scoping.

There are variables that are defined at the module level; thus, they have module-level scope. This means they can be accessed from anywhere in the module, and if they are declared `public`, they can even be accessed from other modules as well. You can find more about module-level scope in Chapter 3.

Making Sense of Bits and Bytes

In this section, we will take a look at the operations that can be performed to understand and extract information from binary encoded data.

Bitwise Operators

These operators are used to do operations on each bit level of given numeric values. Let's take a look at some statements with bitwise operators.

```
int a = 5;       // 00000101₂
int b = 9;       // 00001001₂
int x = a & b; // x = 1
x = a | b;       // x = 13
```

When using a bitwise operator, we execute the corresponding logical operator against each bit value in the same bit position in the binary numbers. Figure 2-1 shows how these calculations are done using the low-order bits (8 bits) of the previous numbers.

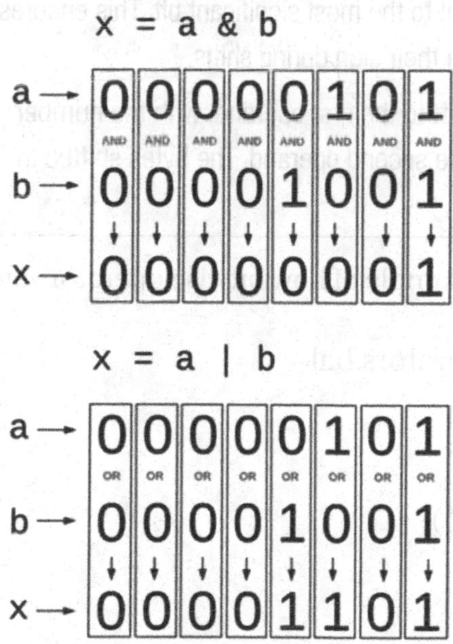

***Figure 2-1.** Visualization of Bitwise AND/OR Operations*

<table>
<tr><th>Operator</th><th>Description</th><th>Example</th></tr>
<tr><td>&</td><td>Executes a bitwise AND operation on the given two operands for each bit position.</td><td><code>boolean x = a & b;</code></td></tr>
<tr><td>|</td><td>Executes a bitwise OR operation on the given two operands for each bit position.</td><td><code>boolean x = a | b;</code></td></tr>
<tr><td>^</td><td>Executes a bitwise Exclusive OR (XOR) operation on the given two operands for each bit position. This is similar to the OR operation, where the only difference is bit values 1 and 1 results in 0.</td><td><code>boolean x = a ^ b;</code></td></tr>
<tr><td>~</td><td>Executes a bitwise NOT operation on the given operand for each bit position.</td><td><code>boolean x = ~a;</code></td></tr>
<tr><td><<</td><td>Executes a left shift to the first operand, with the number of shifts given by the second operand. The bytes shifted in from the right are 0.</td><td><code>a = b << 2;</code></td></tr>
<tr><td>>></td><td>Executes a right shift to the first operand, with the number of shifts given by the second operand. The bytes shifted in from the left is equal to the most significant bit. This ensures signed values retain their sign during shifts.</td><td><code>a = b >> 2;</code></td></tr>
<tr><td>>>></td><td>Executes a right shift to the first operand, with the number of shifts given by the second operand. The bytes shifted in from the left are 0.</td><td><code>a = b >>> 2;</code></td></tr>
</table>

Listing 2-10 shows an example of how bitwise operators are used in Ballerina.

Listing 2-10. bitwise-operators.bal

```
import ballerina/io;

public function main() {
    int a = 5;
    int b = 9;
    int c = a & b;
    int d = a | b;
    io:println(c, ":", d);
```

```
    int e = 16 >> 1;
    int f = -10;
    int g = f >> 1;
    int h = f >>> 1;
    int i = f << 2;
    io:println(e, ":", g, ":", h, ":", i);
}
```

```
$ ballerina run bitwise-operators.bal
1:13
8:-5:9223372036854775803:-40
```

As you may have noticed, for the bit-shift operators, for each right shift, the number gets divided by two, since all the bit positions move one position to the right. And in the same manner, left shifts will multiply the value by two. The unsigned right shift ignores the sign bit and thus will not retain the same sign of the number and will not have the same number being multiplied by two property.

Bitmasks, Flags, and Encoding

Bitwise operations are critical in implementing masking operations. *Masking* is the act of extracting, removing, or updating certain parts of a binary value.

For example, in an integer value, if we want to extract only the lower 8 bits of the value, we can do the following:

```
int value = 1550; // [00000110 00001110]2
int mask = 255;   // [00000000 11111111]2
int lower8bit = value & mask; // [00000000 00001110]2
```

We can also switch on a specific bit on a number using an OR operation and a bitmask.

```
mask = 128; // [00000000 10000000]2
value  = value | mask; // [00000110 10001110]2
```

A value can be toggled in a specific bit location using the XOR operation and a bitmask.

```
mask = 2; // [00000000 00000010]2
value  = value ^ mask; // [00000110 00001100]2
```

The previous pattern is useful in encoding a set of related states or flags in a single value. An example usage would be to store game controller button press states in a single value. So when the controller is sending a signal to the game, we know exactly which buttons are pressed at a given time. We do this by representing each button state in a specific bit position in an integer.

- *Bit 0*: Up
- *Bit 1*: Down
- *Bit 2*: Left
- *Bit 3*: Right
- *Bit 4*: Shoot
- *Bit 5*: Jump

So, what is a possible event coming into our game? The user may be jumping right, while shooting. Listing 2-11 shows how we can represent this in an event and how we can understand this state in a program.

Listing 2-11. game-event-masks.bal

```
import ballerina/io;

public function main() {
    int UP = 1;      // [0 0 0 0 0 0 0 1]
    int DOWN = 2;    // [0 0 0 0 0 0 1 0]
    int LEFT = 4;    // [0 0 0 0 0 1 0 0]
    int RIGHT = 8;   // [0 0 0 0 1 0 0 0]
    int JUMP = 16;   // [0 0 0 1 0 0 0 0]
    int SHOOT = 32; // [0 0 1 0 0 0 0 0]

    int event = RIGHT | JUMP | SHOOT; // creating the event
    if ((event & UP) == UP) {
        io:println("UP");
    }
    if ((event & DOWN) == DOWN) {
        io:println("DOWN");
```

```
    }
    if ((event & LEFT) == LEFT) {
        io:println("LEFT");
    }
    if ((event & RIGHT) == RIGHT) {
        io:println("RIGHT");
    }
    if ((event & JUMP) == JUMP) {
        io:println("JUMP");
    }
    if ((event & SHOOT) == SHOOT) {
        io:println("SHOOT");
    }
}
```

```
$ ballerina run game-event-masks.bal
RIGHT
JUMP
SHOOT
```

Notice how the bitmask can again be used to retrieve whether a specific flag is set in the event using the bitwise AND operator.

Another useful technique used with bitmasks and bitwise operations is bit encoding. An example of this is the encoding of red, green, blue (RGB) values of a color image pixel. Each color component is represented using 1 byte (8 bits). So, we read in one pixel value as 24 contiguous bits, which can be stored in an integer typed value. One of the operations we may want to do when we have these 24 bits is to extract the separate R, G, B component values. This can be done using a combination of bitmask operations and bit shifts, as demonstrated in Listing 2-12.

Listing 2-12. rgb-extractor.bal

```
import ballerina/io;

public function main() {
    int RED = 0x0000FF;
    int GREEN = 0x00FF00;
```

```
    int BLUE = 0xFF0000;

    int rgbValue = 0xAEFF01;
    int red_component = rgbValue & RED;
    int green_component = (rgbValue & GREEN) >> 8;
    int blue_component = (rgbValue & BLUE) >> 16;

    io:println("R: ", red_component);
    io:println("G: ", green_component);
    io:println("B: ", blue_component);
}
```

```
$ ballerina run rgb-extractor.bal
R: 1
G: 255
B: 174
```

The bitmask variables RED, GREEN, and BLUE are used to isolate the color components using bitwise AND operations. Afterward, the right bit shifts are used to move the bit values that are in the middle of the binary number to the far right to represent them as 8-bit values.

Functions

A function is basically a definition of a code block that can be reused in any point in a program. It also promotes better structure of your overall code by splitting complex logic into smaller units of code. So, if you find yourself repeating the same type of logic in many places, it is a strong indication that this logic can be turned into a function and invoked (or called) from the places where its functionality is required.

To demonstrate this, let's take the scenario of calculating permutations mathematically. For example, if you are given four unique digits, how many different two-digit numbers will you be able to create? Let's say the digits are 1, 4, 5, 7; a few possible answers would be 14, 15, 75, 74, and 45. What is the total number of numbers we can generate? The answer is 12.

The formula to get this number is as follows:

$$ {}_{n}P_{r} = n! \,/\, (n - r)! $$

The previous formula gives us the total number of permutations, given the total number of choices - n, and the number of items considered at a given time - r. So, in our previous scenario, it is four things taken at two things at a time. So, the expression we need is ${}_{4}P_{2} = 4! \,/\, (4 - 2)! = 4! \,/\, 2!$.

The ! sign denotes the factorial of a number. If you say `n!`, this means `n * (n - 1) * (n - 2) ... * 1`. So, our earlier example becomes the following:

$$ \begin{aligned} {}_{4}P_{2} &= 4 * 3 * 2 * 1 \,/\, (2 * 1) \\ &= 4 * 3 \\ &= 12 \end{aligned} $$

Listing 2-13 illustrates a program to compute the number of permutations using the previous formula.

Listing 2-13. perm1.bal

```
import ballerina/io;

public function main() {
    int n = 4;
    int r = 2;
    int x = n - r;
    int nf = 1;
    int xf = 1;
    int i = n;
    while i > 0 {
        nf = nf * i;
        i = i - 1;
    }
    i = x;
    while i > 0 {
        xf = xf * i;
        i = i - 1;
    }
```

```
    int result = nf / xf;
    io:println(result);
}
```

```
$ ballerina run perm1.bal
12
```

The previous program calculates ${}_4P_2$, which gives the result 12.

Now, we would like to solve instances of the problem in a single program, namely, ${}_4P_2$ and ${}_5P_3$. The simple solution would be to do the same logic twice in the code. This approach is shown in Listing 2-14.

Listing 2-14. perm2.bal

```
import ballerina/io;

public function main() {
    int n = 4;
    int r = 2;
    int x = n - r;
    int nf = 1;
    int xf = 1;
    int i = n;
    while i > 0 {
        nf = nf * i;
        i = i - 1;
    }
    i = x;
    while i > 0 {
        xf = xf * i;
        i = i - 1;
    }
    int result = nf / xf;
    io:println(result);

    n = 5;
    r = 3;
```

```
    x = n - r;
    nf = 1;
    xf = 1;
    i = n;
    while i > 0 {
        nf = nf * i;
        i = i - 1;
    }
    i = x;
    while i > 0 {
        xf = xf * i;
        i = i - 1;
    }
    result = nf / xf;
    io:println(result);
}
```

```
$ ballerina run perm2.bal
12
60
```

The preceding program did get the job done, but we can feel that duplicating the logic in the code does not seem to be the right approach. We have simply updated the variable values for the problem, and the code to the formula is repeated. This does not look like a scalable solution to the problem we have. Let's refactor our solution to define our permutation count calculation as a separate function.

A function allows us to create a reusable code block, which can be *called* or *invoked* from any part of your program. Also, a function can have parameters, which allows the code block inside the function to work with different values each time a function call is made.

Listing 2-15. perm3.bal

```
import ballerina/io;

public function main() {
    int result1 = perm(4, 2);
    int result2 = perm(5, 3);
```

```
06     io:println(result1);
07     io:println(result2);
08 }
09
10 function perm(int n, int r) returns int {
11     int x = n - r;
12     int nf = 1;
13     int xf = 1;
14     int i = n;
15     while i > 0 {
16         nf = nf * i;
17         i = i - 1;
18     }
19     i = x;
20     while i > 0 {
21         xf = xf * i;
22         i = i - 1;
23     }
24     int result = nf / xf;
25     return result;
26 }
```

```
$ ballerina run perm3.bal
12
60
```

Listing 2-15 contains the identical functionality as Listing 2-14, but the code is much shorter and readable. The logic that calculates the number of permutations is moved to the function `perm`, which takes two parameters: `n` and `r`. So now, we can invoke this function multiple times in our code with different parameter values. The function invocations are shown in line 4 and line 5. A function call simply jumps into the target function call and executes the function with the given parameter values, and if there is any return value, this is returned to the place the function was originally called. In our code, we can see the function results are stored in the variables `result1` and `result2`.

Figure 2-2 shows a visualization of the code execution with the function calls.

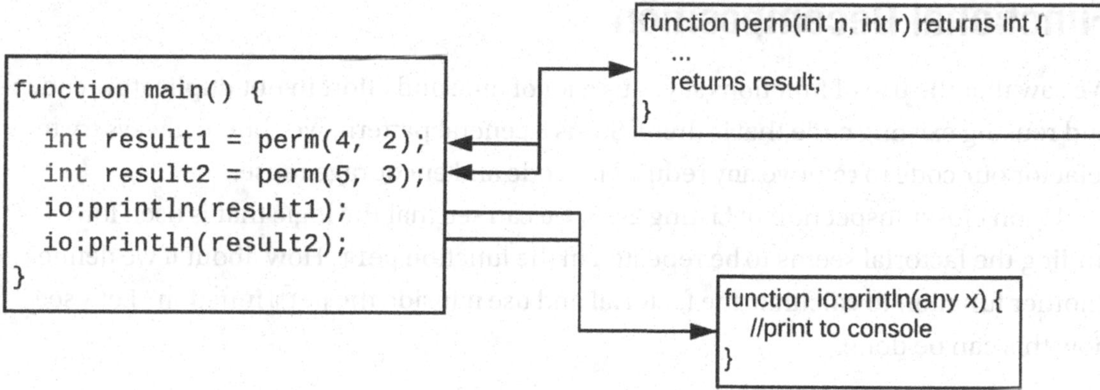

***Figure 2-2.** Program execution with function calls*

The general format of a function definition is as follows:

```
[access_modifier] function <name>(<type> param1, <type> param2...) [returns
<type>] {
   statements...
}
```

The access modifier can be either `public` or an empty value, which implies having a private access modifier. A function can be defined as returning a value—for example, some calculation that was done, or else, it may not return anything, which is equal to returning a `nil` value. If the function does not return anything, the `returns <type>` section is not required.

In our `perm` function, the parameters for it are the `n` and `r` values, which are of `int` types, and it returns an `int` type as the result.

The general format for a function call statement is as follows:

```
[<type> <var> =] <function_name> (argument1, argument2, ...)
```

A function invocation may or may not have arguments when it is called, depending on its definition. Also, if a return type is defined for the function, the function invocation is treated as an expression, and in a function call statement, its value must be assigned to a variable.

In the event that we want to ignore the return value of a function without assigning it to a variable, we can use the special variable _ to assign the return value. An example function call that ignores its return value is shown here:

```
_ = funcCall(a, b);
```

Functional Decomposition

We saw that the use of functions saves us a lot of time and effort in not duplicating code and reusing existing code that is there. So, as a general pattern, we should always try to refactor our code to remove any redundant code and encourage reuse.

Upon closer inspection of Listing 2-16, we can see that the logic that is used for finding the factorial seems to be repeated in the function `perm`. How about if we define another function to calculate the factorial and use it inside the `perm` function? Let's see how this can be done.

Listing 2-16. perm4.bal

```
import ballerina/io;

public function main() {
    int result1 = perm(4, 2);
    int result2 = perm(5, 3);
    io:println(result1);
    io:println(result2);
}

function perm(int n, int r) returns int {
    int x = n - r;
    int nf = fact(n);
    int xf = fact(x);
    int result = nf / xf;
    return result;
}

function fact(int n) returns int {
    int nf = 1;
    int i = n;
    while i > 0 {
        nf = nf * i;
        i = i - 1;
    }
```

```
    return nf;
}
```

```
$ ballerina run perm4.bal
12
60
```

Listing 2-16 introduces a new function `fact`, which is called twice from the function `perm` to do the factorial operations. We can immediately see that our overall code is more organized now, and it's clearer to read. We have removed the code redundancy, and with that, we remove the tendency to make mistakes while duplicating code, thus making it much easier to validate the correctness of the code. So even though the line count of Listing 2-15 and Listing 2-16 is basically the same, the breaking up of code in Listing 2-16 gives us many more advantages of code maintainability and readability.

Summary

In this chapter, we explored the fundamental features we need to understand when writing meaningful computer programs. We covered data types, variable declarations, conditional execution, and finally creating your own functions. We now have a good foundation in basic programming to tackle more advanced topics in the upcoming chapters.

CHAPTER 3

Lists, Mappings, and Objects

So far, we have been using simple types to implement our scenarios. In this chapter, we will be looking into the structural and behavioral types that are available in Ballerina. These types will help us in modeling and solving complex problems more efficiently.

There are also a few other special types that can be created, which are critical in Ballerina's type system. Union types are one of them. Let's start off by getting to know what they are and how we can use them.

Union Types

A union type is created by combining two or more existing types together. The union type descriptor takes the following form: `T1|T2`. A *type descriptor* is the construct that is used in defining a specific type. The type `T1|T2` represents the set of values, which is made up by combining all the values of type `T1` and all the values of type `T2`. This basically means that any values belonging to `T1` and `T2` are compatible with the type `T1|T2`.

Let's take the following example:

```
int|string id;
```

The `id` is declared as a union type of `int|string`. This means that the variable `id` can be assigned with any `int` value or any `string` value. So, it's possible to have either an `int` or a `string` value in the runtime for the variable `id`. In this way, we can do the following assignment operations to the variable `id`:

```
id = "ABC";
id = 10;
```


A. Fernando and L. Warusawithana, *Beginning Ballerina Programming*,
https://doi.org/10.1007/978-1-4842-5139-3_3

In certain situations, you may need to know whether the value of `id` is of a specific type. For example, in the runtime, you need to check whether `id`'s value is a `string`. This can be done using the type test expression. This is a Boolean expression that takes the following form: `<variable> is <type>`.

```
boolean idIsString = id is string;
```

Here, the expression returns `true` if the `id` is indeed a `string` at the point of evaluation. A common usage of this is with conditional statements to execute specific logic if the value is of a specific type.

```
string prefixedId;
if id is string {
    string sid = <string> id;
    prefixedId = "ID" + sid;
} else {
    int nid = <int> id;
    prefixedId = "ID" + nid.toString();
}
```

The previous code shows how to use a type test expression to check whether the value is of a certain type and how to do a cast to assign it to a variable of the type we want. But the Ballerina compiler is aware of the type test operation in the conditional statement, and it knows that after the condition check, inside the `if` statement block, the `id` variable will surely be of `string` type. Because of this, inside the `if` statement code block's scope, the `id` is considered as a `string` value. In the same manner, inside the `else` code block, the variable `id` can only be the rest of the union type other than `string`, which means it can only be an `int`. So, with this behavior, we can rewrite the previous code snippet in the following way:

```
string prefixedId;
if id is string {
    prefixedId = "ID" + id;
} else {
    prefixedId = "ID" + id.toString();
}
```

Let's take a look at an extended example of a union type constructed using three basic types.

```
int|string|boolean status = getStatus();
if status is int {
    // status is an int in this scope
    int a = status;
} else {
    // status is string|boolean in this scope
    if status is string {
        // status is string in this scope
        string b = status;
    } else {
        // status is boolean in this scope
        boolean c = status;
    }
}
```

In the previous scenario, the `getStatus()` function returns a value of type `int|string|boolean`. The `if` statement checks whether it is an `int` in the condition, so in its block it becomes an `int` value, and in the `else` statement, since we have eliminated the type to be an `int`, we are left with `string|boolean`. Here, we can do further type tests to narrow down to further simple types and use them as required.

Optional Types

An optional type is denoted using `T?`, which is equivalent to the union type `T|()`. This basically expresses the type as either `T` or `nil`. The usage of optional types is frequently seen when we want to represent a value of a type or the state that a value is not there at all.

Let's take a look at a sample scenario of using optional types. We have implemented a system, where it can retrieve the scores of an exam for a student for a specific subject. This is implemented using the following function:

```
function getExamScore(string studentId, string subject) returns int? {
...
}
```

The return type of the preceding function is marked as `int?`. We could have just used `int`, but what if the student hasn't taken this specific subject? We can return `0` as a default value, but this can mean the student has taken the exam and scored `0`, or else he hasn't taken it at all. So, to resolve this ambiguity, in the event that the student hasn't taken this specific subject, we can return a `nil`, `()`, value to state that there is no score for this specific subject and student. A possible usage of the previous function is shown here:

```
int? score = getExamScore("W530033", "Organic Chemistry");
if score is int {
    io:println("Score: ", score);
} else {
    io:println("The student has not taken the subject");
}
```

But, if we actually wanted to record a final score for the subject? Regardless of whether the student sat for the subject, we can use a conditional expression to return a default value if the score is `()`.

```
int finalScore = score is () ? 0 : score;
```

Here, we are checking whether the `score` value is `()`. If so, we return `0`, or else, we return the actual `score` value. Here, the conditional expression works in a similar way as in an `if/else` conditional statement when evaluating a type test expression, where the optional typed `score` variable becomes an `int` when the condition `score is ()` is false. A shorthand version of the previous statement can be written using the Elvis - `?:` operator.

```
int finalScore = score?:0;
```

The expression `score?:0` reads as follows: if the optional typed variable `score` is `()`, return `0`, or else, return the value of `score`. In this way, the variable `finalScore` will always have a valid score to be reported as the final score.

Any Type

The any type is a special type in Ballerina, which is a union of all the possible types, excluding the `error` type. So, basically any possible value, other than an `error` value, can be assigned to a variable of type any.

```
any myvar = 50;
myvar = "mystring";
myvar = 1.56;
myvar = true;
```

The previous code snippet shows that a variable of type any is declared and how it is assigned various simple type values, such as `integer`, `string`, and `boolean` values.

Arrays

So far, we have stored a single value in its own dedicated variable. For example, let's say you wanted to store your exam result scores in some variables. You can do something similar to the following:

```
int mathsScore = 92;
int physicsScore = 85;
int chemistryScore = 80;
```

Now you get the requirement of calculating the class average for each subject. That means you need to store subject scores for all the students in the class. The class has 40 students, so this looks like doing a lot of typing to store the scores in variables to start with. This would look like the following:

```
int mathsScore1 = 77;
int mathsScore2 = 81;
int mathsScore3 = 92;
...
int mathsScore40 = 86;
int physicsScore1 = 70;
int physicsScore2 = 77;
...
```

But there is a better way of doing this, which is by using *arrays*. An array is a value that contains a list of values of the declared type. So, using a single variable, we can store multiple values in it. Let's see how we can use this to store all the math scores of students.

```
int[] mathsScores = [];
mathsScores[0] = 77;
mathsScores[1] = 81;
mathsScores[2] = 92;
...
```

Here, an integer array type is declared using `int[]`. In the same manner, we can create an array of any type. For example, an array of strings would be defined as `string[]`. On the right-hand side of the assignment, the `[]` is used as the array constructor, where an empty array is provided by default, but can also provide a specific set of values, for example: `[77, 81, 92]`.

We can visualize an array as having numbered slots, and we can store and retrieve values from these slots, as shown in Figure 3-1.

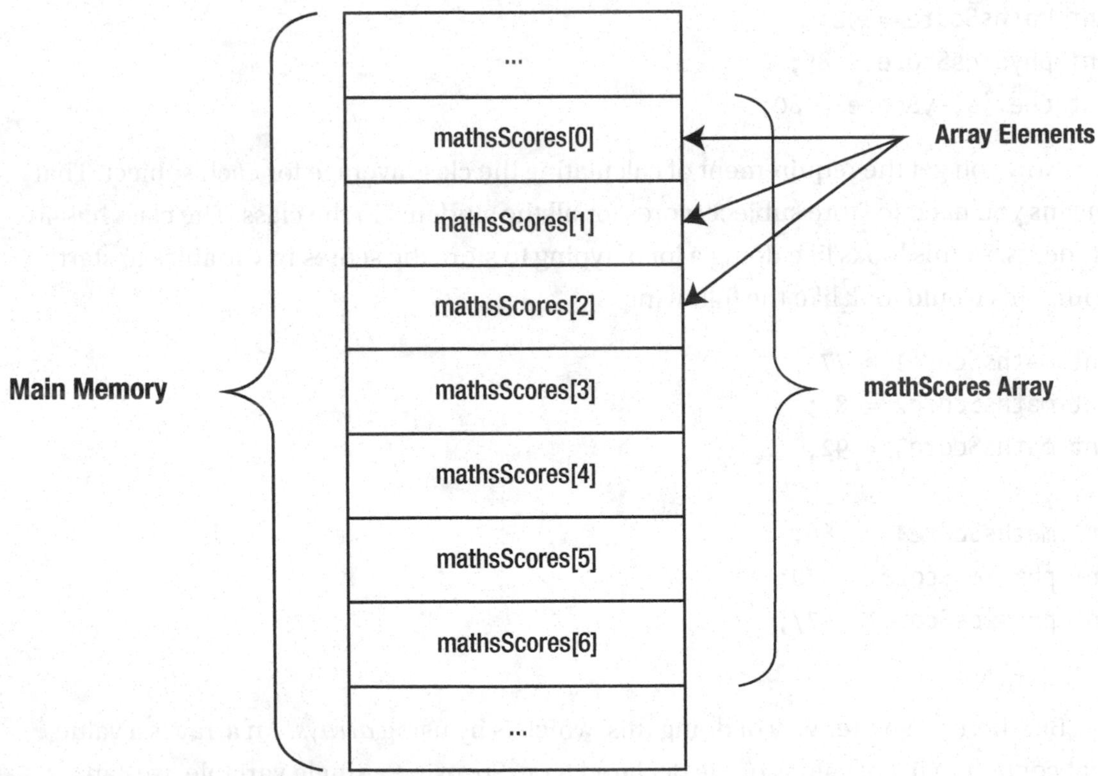

Figure 3-1. *Array layout in main memory*

We call one of these slots an *array element*. An array element is accessed by giving the element index value, which starts from 0, not 1. We call this strategy 0-based indexing, which relates to using index 0 as the first element in an array, 1 is the second, 2 is the third, and so on.

An array element can be referenced for setting its value and also as an expression for reading the value using the `<variable>[index]` format.

```
io:println(mathsScores[2]); // prints the third value in the array
```

The array index itself can be given dynamically by means of an integer expression. For example, we can have an integer variable to refer to the index of an array. This is especially useful when we are populating a big array with the use of a loop. Let's take a look at an example of this:

```
int[] mathsScores = [];
int i = 0;
while i < 40 {
    mathsScores[i] = check ints:fromString(io:readln("Enter score: "));
    i += 1;
}
```

In the previous code, we do 40 loop iterations, and then the loop counter is used as the index into the array to store the integer value read from the user. The `check` keyword is used as a special mechanism in error handling. The exact usage of this will be explained in Chapter 5.

Array Creation Modes

There are two approaches to creating arrays based on the behavior of array lengths. Let's see the functionality of each option.

Dynamic-Length Arrays

If we do not provide an explicit array length in the array type descriptor, the array length becomes dynamic. This is the approach we used in our earlier examples. In this format, the array type descriptor does not mention any integer value between the square brackets, and the array size dynamically increases as we assign values to the array elements. In the RHS value when declaring the array variable, we can provide an empty array value with [] or provide the initial values of the array. This approach is demonstrated in the following code snippets:

```
// dynamic length array with three initial values
int[] mathsScores = [77, 81, 92];

// dynamic length array with an initial empty array
int[] mathsScores = [];
mathsScores[0] = 77; // array size increases to 1
mathsScores[1] = 81; // array size increases to 2
mathsScores[9] = 70; // array size increases to 10
```

In the last statement in the previous code snippet, we directly set the 10th element in the array. In this case, what happens to values between index 1 and 9? These array elements are automatically filled with what are known as *filler* values for each type. For the integer type, this is the value 0. Table 3-1 shows how the filler value maps to the given type.

Table 3-1. *Type Descriptor Filler Values*

Type	Filler Value
`Boolean`	`false`
`Int`	`0`
`Byte`	`0`
`Float`	`+0.0f`
`Decimal`	`+0.0d`
`string`	`""`
`Array/tuple`	`[]`, if there is a valid constructor for the type
`Map/record`	`{}`, if there is a valid constructor for the type
`Object`	`new T()`, if this is valid

Array Operations

There are a number of built-in array functions that can be used to retrieve useful information about the array and also do certain manipulations. Let's take a look at some of the prominent operations that are available.

push/pop

The push and pop functions represent the operations done on a stack data structure. A stack has the property of having a *last in, first out* (LIFO) behavior. This means the last element inserted will be the first element retrieved.

For a real-life stack operation example, think of a stack of plates you create after you wash them. You pick up the plates in the inverse order from the way you put them in the stack; that is, you first pick up the last plate you washed.

The array push function works by adding elements to the end of an array. The pop function removes one element from the end of the function and returns the element that was removed.

```
mathScores.push(90, 85, 65); // adds 90, 85, 65 to the end of the array
int removedElement = mathScores.pop(); // removes 65 from the array
```

The push function is defined having a variable length parameter, which is called a 'rest' parameter, with this, any number of values can be passed in the function invocation.

shift/unshift

These operations have similar actions as push/pop functions, but they work from the other end of the array. The shift function is used to remove the first element from the array and return the value. The unshift operation adds the given values to the beginning of the array.

```
int[] mathScores = [90, 88, 75];
int firstScore = mathScores.shift(); // array is now [88, 75]
mathScores.unshift(95, 80, 85);      // array is now [95, 80, 85, 88, 75]
```

Another common data structure used is the queue. A queue has the property of being *first in, first out* (FIFO). We see this commonly in real life. For example, if we queue up at a supermarket to pay, the people get served in the order they came in. This behavior can be implemented in an array using a combination of the push and shift functions.

```
int[] mathScores = [90, 88, 75];
mathScores.push(85); // now [90, 88, 75, 85]
mathScores.push(93); // now [90, 88, 75, 85, 93]
int score1 = mathScores.shift(); // now [88, 75, 85, 93]
int score2 = mathScores.shift(); // now [75, 85, 93]
int score3 = mathScores.shift(); // now [85, 93]
```

The previous operations show how the push function is used to queue two new scores into the array and how we dequeued multiple scores from the array using the `shift` function.

slice

The `slice` function is used to generate a subarray of the current array. The first parameter is the start index of the array to start creating the subarray, including the element at this index. The second parameter is the last index position used to create the slice in the array. This value is non-inclusive, which means, the value at the second parameter index in the array is not returned in the slice. But rather, the slice will contain values up to the index right before the second parameter. The following example demonstrates this behavior.

```
int[] mathScores = [90, 88, 75, 85, 92];
int[] scoreSlice = mathScores.slice(1, 4); // scoreSlice = [88, 75, 85]
```

In the previous code, the `scoreSlice` variable contains the values of `matchScores`, in the range from index 1, which contains the value 88, and up until index 4 (non-inclusive), so it will actually contain until the value at index 3, which is 85.

Fixed-Length Arrays

In a fixed-length array, the array values must be given when the array is first initialized. An example usage is shown here:

```
int[3] mathsScores = [77, 81, 92];
```

In the array type descriptor itself, the fixed array size is given, and with the array initialization, its initial values also must be provided. The following statement also represents the same behavior, by providing * as the array length, where now the fixed array length is automatically inferred from the initial value set.

```
int[*] mathsScores = [77, 81, 92];
```

Something to note is that `int[*]` and `int[]` are not the same. Where the first option is always a fixed length, with the length inferred, and the latter option is always a dynamic-length array declaration.

Iterating Arrays

Array items can be iterated by using a while loop, which will use our own loop counter to access each element in the array. This approach is shown here:

```
int i = 0;
while i < mathsScores.length() {
    io:println("Score: ", mathsScores[i]);
    i += 1;
}
```

We can also achieve the same functionality by using the foreach loop, which has the previously used pattern implemented in its core functionality.

```
foreach var score in mathsScores {
    io:println("Score: ", score);
}
```

The foreach loop operates on an iterable type, where it iterates through the elements and returns a single element from the iterable type to a given variable. Most of the basic structured types are iterable, including arrays.

Multidimensional Arrays

Multidimensional arrays in Ballerina are emulated. This is because Ballerina does not support true multidimensional arrays, where it should have all the elements inside the multidimensional array in a contiguous memory block. In Ballerina, it can rather do an array of arrays. This means an array element type itself is another array.

As an example, let's take an image that shows two-dimensional information by way of pixel color values at a specific row and a column. If we consider the color intensity is encoded in an int value, the image values of a picture can be stored using the following type:

```
int[][] imageData = [];
```

The previous imageData variable is declared as a two-dimensional integer array. In this way, each array element in imageData would be of type int[], which can be seen as a specific pixel image row in our example.

Setting array values in a multidimensional array is done in the same manner as any other value. The following code snippet shows how an imageData's entries can be updated using assignment statements:

```
imageData[0] = [150, 110, 20];
```

Also, in the same manner, we can set or retrieve a specific value in the multidimensional array by providing the exact location of the entry.

```
int[][] imageData = loadImage();
int px1 = imageData[10][42]; // read pixel value at (10,42)
imageData[25][50] = 150;     // set pixel value at (25,50)
```

Using a similar pattern, we can extend our arrays to have as many dimensions as we need.

Keeping Inside the Bounds

In accessing and setting array element values, sometimes we may refer mistakenly to element locations that are outside the allowed bounds in an array. In a fixed-size array, we cannot go above the size of the array (or below 0), in both accessing and setting values. This will be disallowed at compile time itself if we use constant values for the index. For example, the following code will not compile:

```
int[*] mathsScores = [77, 81, 92];
io:println(mathsScores[3]);
```

This tries to access the fourth element in an array, which has a fixed size of 3. The compiler gives an error similar to the following:

```
error: .::test.bal:5:28: list index out of range: index: '3'
```

The compiler was able to catch this error only because we used a constant value for the array index. If a variable is used instead, this will not be caught at compile time, but rather a runtime error will be raised.

```
int[*] mathsScores = [77, 81, 92];
int n = 3;
io:println(mathsScores[n]);
```

The previous code executes, and in the runtime, it raises the following error:

```
error: {ballerina/lang.array}IndexOutOfRange message=array index out of
range: index: 3, size: 3
```

In the same manner, for dynamic-length arrays, we can face with similar issues, if we try to access array elements that are not in the current bounds.

```
int[] mathsScores = [];
mathsScores[5] = 90;
io:println(mathsScores[6])
```

The previous code will also raise the following error in the runtime:

```
error: {ballerina/lang.array}IndexOutOfRange message=array index out of
range: index: 6, size: 6
```

Even though dynamic-length arrays are automatically extended with array insertion operations, it is not the same for accessing values. If the accessed entry is not in the current bounds of the array, it will also raise an index out-of bounds error.

Tuples

A tuple is similar to a fixed-length array; its elements are addressed using an integer index value, but it has the property that each element can have its own type, compared to an array, where all the array elements need to be of the same type. The general format to declare a tuple is as follows:

```
[<type1>, <type2>,...] <var_name> = [<val1>, <val2>, ...];
```

Let's extend our earlier school subject scores example to use a tuple to record a person's name and all their math, physics, and chemistry subject scores.

```
[string, int, int, int] result1 = ["sunil", 90, 88, 85];
[string, int, int, int] result2 = ["nimal", 85, 75, 80];
[string, int, int, int] result3 = ["jack", 80, 70, 78];
```

In the previous manner, we managed to group a student's related subject scores to a single data structure. The individual attributes of the tuple can be accessed using a similar syntax to array element lookup using an index.

```
string name = result1[0];
int mathsScore = result1[1];
int physicsScore = result1[2];
int chemistryScore = result1[3];
```

The previous can also be written in a shorthand manner, using a mechanism known as *tuple destructuring*.

```
var [name, mathsScore, physicsScore, chemistryScore] = result1;
```

Here, the variables names `mathsScore`, `physicsScore`, and `chemistryScore` are declared and assigned values using the same relative location in the variable list from the tuple attribute locations. That is, the variable `name` is assigned `result1[0]`, the variable `mathsScore` is assigned `result1[1]`, and so on. The usage of `var` indicates that the variable types are also inferred from the type of the attributes at the tuple's respective positions.

In the same manner, already existing variables can be used with the tuple destructuring.

```
[name, _, _, chemistryScore] = result1;
```

Here, it is possible to use the special variable name _ in order to ignore the values while destructuring.

Defining New Types

It is possible in Ballerina to create a new type based on an existing type descriptor. This operation takes the following form:

```
type <type_name> <type_descriptor>;
```

This is similar to giving an alias to a type descriptor. For example, our earlier tuple type, `[string, int, int, int]`, can be defined as a new type in the following manner:

```
type ExamResult [string, int, int, int];
```

Here, we have defined the type `ExamResult` to represent the tuple type descriptor we have used here. Now, we can simply refer to the newly declared type and create our values.

```
ExamResult result1 = ["sunil", 90, 88, 85];
ExamResult result2 = ["nimal", 85, 75, 80];
ExamResult result3 = ["jack", 80, 70, 78];
```

In this way, rather than repeating a long type descriptor, we have used an identifier that is easier to use.

Keeping up with our earlier example of storing all students' scores, we can now simply create an array of the `ExamResult` type to store the results of each student.

```
ExamResult[] results = [];
results[0] = ["sunil", 90, 88, 85];
results[1] = ["nimal", 85, 75, 80];
results[2] = ["jack", 80, 70, 78];
```

Now we have an array of a structure that is used to store all the subject scores, alongside the student's name. What if we wanted to store and look up these result entries so that we could provide the student name and access the required information? If we are using an array, we would need to iterate through all the records and see if there is such an entry. However, there is a better way to do this; in the next section, we will learn about the map type and how it can be used to solve our problem.

Maps

The map type is used when you need to store entries as key-value pairs. A given string key value is connected to a given specific value. Using maps, the stored entry value can be looked up using the associated key value.

A `map` value can be created using the following form:

```
map<T> data = { <key1>: <value1>, ...};
```

The type `T` is the type of the values that will be stored in each entry value, where the entry key is always a string.

Let's update our example to store the subject scores against a student's name. The requirement is that a user should be able to easily look up a student's score by providing the student's name. For now, let's start off by creating a map that will just contain the math scores for a student.

```
map<int> mathScores = { "sunil": 90, "nimal": 85 };
```

Here, the map value `mathScores` is created with two entries given at initialization; the key `"sunil"` is associated with the value 90, and the key `"nimal"` is associated with the value 85.

In a map, only a single value is associated with a given key. An entry value is set with a given key using the following syntax:

```
mathScores["jack"] = 75;
```

If the key `"jack"` is already there, it will replace the existing associated entry value with 75, or else, it will add a new map entry with the given key-value pair.

A value from a map is looked up similarly to how the map entry is referenced for adding or updating an entry in the map. The following code snippet shows how a map lookup is done:

```
int? jacksMathScore = mathScores["jack"];
if jacksMathScore is int {
    io:println("Jack's Math Score: ", jacksMathScore);
} else {
    io:println("Jack didn't do the math exam");
}
```

Here, `int?` represents the union type `int|()`. This basically signals that the return value can be either `nil` or an `int`. As a general case, for any map created with the value type as `T`, the lookup value type will be `T?`. In this manner, we need to do a type test on the result of a map lookup to check if the entry is available in the map or not.

We have so far worked with a simple type as the map entry value type, but we can of course provide a structural type for it as well. Let's create a new tuple type in order to represent all the subject scores a student has.

```
type ExamResult [int, int, int];
```

Now that we have a new type to represent all the subject scores at once, we can use this as the entry value in a map.

```
map<ExamResult> examResults = {};
examResults["sunil"] = [90, 85, 80];
examResults["nimal"] = [85, 82, 65];
```

Now at this point, with the map `examResults`, we can conveniently look up all the subject scores of a specific student by providing the name.

```
ExamResult? sunilsResult = examResults["sunil"];
if sunilsResult is ExamResult {
    int sunilPhysicsScore = sunilsResult[1];
}
```

Map Operations

Similar to the built-in functions available in arrays, maps have a list of functions that are used to provide information on the array and to manipulate entries. Table 3-2 summarizes the most often used operations that are there.

***Table 3-2.** Built-in Map Functions*

Operation	Description
`hasKey(string)`	Checks whether the entry with the given key is available
`keys()`	Returns the list of keys in the map as a `string[]`
`entries()`	Returns a map with the value containing a `[key, value]` tuple as the value in the new map
`remove(string key)`	Removes the entry with the given key
`length()`	Returns the number of entries in the map

Iterating a Map

The map itself is an iterable type, which can be used with the `foreach` loop to iterate its values. This is done in the following manner:

```
foreach var scoresValue in examResults {
    io:println("Scores Value: ", scoresValue);
}
```

The map keys can be iterated by using the `keys()` function to retrieve the keys array and iterating through them.

```
foreach var name in examResults.keys() {
    io:println("Name: ", name);
}
```

If we need the key-value pairs together one by one, we can iterate the value returned from `entries()`, which will provide us with a `[key, value]` tuple in each iteration.

```
foreach var [name, scores] in examResults.entries() {
    io:println("Name: ", name, ", Scores: ", scores);
}
```

Performance Considerations of Maps and Arrays

As we have seen, maps and arrays have their own usages. We should also have a general idea of how the data storage and access happen in these two data structures.

The array storage is done using a continuous block of memory, and it offers a quick store and access operation. When we say *quick*, we mean these operations are constant-time operations, where every store operation and every access operation will take the same amount of processing, and thus the same time, regardless of the size of the array.

A different aspect would be searching for a specific value in an array. For example, let's say we have an array of integers, and we are searching to see whether a specific value is there in the array. We would write code similar to the following:

```
int[] values = [1, 3, 30, 35, 325, 503];
int searchVal = check ints:fromString(io:readln("Enter value: "));
foreach var val in values {
    if val == searchVal {
        io:println("value found");
        break;
    }
}
```

The `values` array has six elements, and if the user enters `1`, the value would be found in the first loop iteration itself; or, if the user enters `503`, it will take six iterations to find the element. Basically, if we say the size of the array is `n`, the average number of loop iterations would be `n/2`. Here, we can consider the execution time of the algorithm to be proportional to the number of iterations done here. So, since the number of iterations we need to do is `n/2`, the execution time of this is proportional to `n`, that is, $t \propto n$.

In evaluating the efficiency of algorithms, we often use the big O notation. A detailed explanation of this notation is outside the scope of this book. But the general idea is it is often used in expressing the time or space complexity of an algorithm by showing how it is proportional to the input size `n`. Time complexity is when we consider the execution time of the algorithm, and space complexity is when we consider the amount of memory used in the algorithm. In our examples, we will primarily be talking about the time complexity.

So, since in our earlier example our search algorithm is directly proportional to the input size, we say it has O(n) execution time complexity. Again, this simply means $t \propto n$. We also call this specific situation as an algorithm having linear-time complexity, since the time linearly increases with the input size. This notation basically gives us a hint on how the algorithm performs with the variation of the input size. For example, if we have an algorithm with $O(n^2)$, this means the execution time grows exponentially with the input size. For example, if the execution time for an input size of 1 is 1 millisecond, for an input size of 2, this will become 4 milliseconds, and for an input size of 3, it would become 9 milliseconds and so on.

We mentioned earlier that array access operations are constant-time operations. That is, if we know the location of an array element, we will access the element directly. And the array size does not have any effect on this operation. So, our execution time `t` is proportional to 1, or $t \propto 1$. So, in big O notation, this is an O(1) operation, or a constant-time operation.

Computational Complexity for Map Operations

The map data structure is implemented using special techniques, which makes it possible to generally have O(1) time complexity in insertion and retrieval operations. This basically means the size of the map does not affect the lookup or the insertion performance of maps. This is different from the linear search used in arrays, where the execution time grows with the input size. This is mainly applicable if we are using largely growing data structures and we want to be aware of the performance implications.

There are some cases, in smaller input sizes, where an array can be actually faster than a map lookup operation. The reason is that the map operation has comparably complex logic to implement its lookup operation, and this constant-time operation may be costlier than the smaller size array linear lookup. But when the input size becomes larger, the execution time grows in the array lookup case, passing the constant-time lookup execution time of the map. So, unless we have a similar scenario such as doing a large number of search operations on a smaller dataset, generally an algorithm with a better execution time complexity delivers better results.

Records

A record is similar to a tuple type with names for its fields. Rather than using an index to access the fields, we will be providing a field name to access a record's fields. Let's again extend our exam results scenario to represent this information in a record type.

```
type ExamResult record {
    string name;
    int mathsScore;
    int physicsScore;
    int chemistryScore;
};
```

The record type descriptor used for defining the previous type `ExamResult` is as follows:

```
record {
    string name;
    int mathsScore;
    int physicsScore;
    int chemistryScore;
}
```

This is similar to the `ExamResult` tuple type we defined earlier, but now we have field names in defining each field. A value of this record can be created in the following manner:

```
ExamResult result1 = { name: "sunil", mathsScore: 90,
                       physicsScore: 85, chemistryScore: 80 };
```

The `record` value is initialized in the same manner as we initialize a `map` value, by providing the field names and its values. We must provide all the field values, since none of the fields is marked as an optional field, nor is it marked as having a default value. Let's take a look at how we can make a field optional and how to provide a default value.

```
type ExamResult record {
    string name = "Jane Doe";
    int mathsScore;
    int physicsScore;
    int chemistryScore?;
};

ExamResult result2 = { mathsScore: 90, physicsScore: 85,
                       chemistryScore: 80 };
ExamResult result3 = { name: "nimal", mathsScore: 90,
                       physicsScore: 85 };
int? nimalsChemistryScore = result3?.chemistryScore;
if nimalsChemistryScore is int {
    io:println("Nimals's Chemistry Score: ", nimalsChemistryScore);
} else {
    io:println("Nimal did not take the chemistry subject");
}
```

In the updated record definition, now we have a default value for the field name as "Jane Doe". So, any time this value is not explicitly provided, the default value will be set for the field. As for the field chemistryScore, we have now made it optional by adding the suffix ? to the field name, so when creating record values, this field value is not required. When accessing this record field, we need to use the special ?. operator to access the optional field, which returns the corresponding optional type for the type mentioned in the record field.

Open and Closed Records

In an open record, in the runtime, we can add new fields that are not explicitly defined in the record. In closed records, this is not possible. Records are by default open. Using our earlier definition of the ExamResult record definition, let's see how we can define new fields in the record values.

```
result1["age"] = 25;
anydata sunilsAge = result1["age"];
if sunilsAge is int {
    io:println("Sunil's age: ", sunilsAge);
}
```

Here, we basically treat the record value similar to a map<anydata> value. The type anydata is a special type representing the following union type:

```
()|boolean|int|float|decimal|string|(anydata|error)[]|map<anydata|error>|
xml|table
```

Now, using the map value set and get syntax, we can set and get field values that are not part of the explicit record definition.

If we want to disallow this behavior, we can close the record using the following manner:

```
type ExamResult record {|
    string name = "Jane Doe";
    int mathsScore;
    int physicsScore;
    int chemistryScore?;
|};
```

The | signs covering the field list in the record symbolize that the record is closed, and with this, the map field access syntax cannot be used on record values.

Record Rest Fields

A record rest field can be added to the earlier closed record to make it an open record type. This allows optional fields of a specific type. Let's update our ExamResult record type to add a rest field.

```
type ExamResult record {|
    string name;
    int mathsScore;
    int physicsScore;
    int chemistryScore?;
    int...;
|};
```

Now even though this is an open record type, we have restricted the optional fields to be integer fields only. For example, we probably can define new integer fields for subjects that may come into existence later.

```
ExamResult result1 = { name: "sunil", mathsScore: 90,
                       physicsScore: 85, chemistryScore: 80 };
                           result1["biology"] = 82;
```

Here, we have set the new field biology with an int value. The field access can be done in the same manner as we did for optional fields, but now, we know the type will be int? since with the rest field definition, we are only allowed to have int values as extra.

```
int? sunilsBioScore = result1["biology"];
if sunilsBioScore is int {
    io:println("Sunil's biology score: ", sunilsBioScore);
} else {
    io:println("Sunil has not taken the biology subject");
}
```

Subtyping in Records

Subtyping is a general concept in Ballerina related to compatibility between types. If we have the two types T1 and T2 and if all of T2's values are compatible with the type T1, we call T2 a *subtype* of T1. Also, in this situation, it is said that a value of T2 is of type T1. Let's further clarify this with an example.

We will be creating two new record types, Person and Student.

```
type Person record {
    string name;
    int age;
};

type Student record {
    string name;
    int age;
    string studentId;
};
```

Here, the Student record type has all the fields defined in the Person record type as well. So, if we create values of Student, they will be compatible with the Person type as well because the Person type is defined as having two mandatory fields, name and age, which are also available in Student. Because of this, Student is said to be a subtype of Person.

Let's see some examples of how values of each of the types can be used.

```
Person p1;
Student s1 = { name: "john", age: 30, studentId: "W200530"};
p1 = s1;
```

Here, we have declared variable p1 of type Person, and we also have a variable s1 of type Student. Now, since Student is a subtype of Person, the value s1 is compatible with the type Person, thus making it assignable to variable p1.

But can we now assign p1 to s1? Not directly. Rather, it requires an explicit type cast operation to do so.

```
s1 = <Student> p1;
```

The previous code successfully executes, because p1 actually has all the fields of a Student, since we initially defined it as a Student value. Let's see what happens if we update the code for p1 to only be a Person.

```
Person p1 = { name: "john", age: 30 };
Student s1;
s1 = <Student> p1;
```

Now at this point, the program exits with the runtime error, while executing the type cast operation.

```
error: {ballerina}TypeCastError message=incompatible types: 'Person' cannot
be cast to 'Student'
```

This is because the runtime value of p1 is not actually compatible with s1.

Even the explicit cast is not allowed for types that do not have a chance of being compatible with each other in the runtime. Basically, you can do a cast on a variable only if the casting type is a subtype of the variable's declared type. Only at this point is there a chance of success, or else, it will never work; thus, the compiler will not allow us to write such code. This is how it is evaluated in our cast operation as well, where p1's casting type, Student, is a subtype of p1's declared type, Person.

Objects

An object is basically a record with behavior. This behavior is created by defining functions inside the object itself. These functions associated with the object are known as *methods*.

Let's start off by converting our earlier `ExamResult` `record` type to an `object` type, as shown in Listing 3-1.

Listing 3-1. exam_results.bal

```
import ballerina/io;

type ExamResult object {

    public string name;
    public int mathsScore;
    public int physicsScore;
    public int chemistryScore;

    public function __init(string name, int mathsScore,
                           int physicsScore, int chemistryScore) {
        self.name = name;
        self.mathsScore = mathsScore;
        self.physicsScore = physicsScore;
        self.chemistryScore = chemistryScore;
    }

    public function average() returns int {
        return (self.mathsScore + self.physicsScore +
                self.chemistryScore) / 3;
    }

};

public function main() returns error? {
    ExamResult result1 = new("sunil", 90, 85, 80);
```

```
    int avg = result1.average();
    io:println("Sunil's exam score average: ", avg);
}
```

```
$ ballerina run exam_results.bal
Sunil's exam score average: 85
```

Here, we have defined the object type `ExamResult`. The object type, similar to a record, has a list of fields. Each field in an object has a visibility, which is controlled using access modifiers. These access modifiers are as follows:

- **Public**: The `public` access modifier signals that the field can be read by anyone, even from outside the current module.
- **Private**: The `private` access modifier makes the field accessible only within the object only.
- **Module-level**: No access modifier is mentioned, and it is considered as the module-level visibility, which allows code only within the same module to have access to the object fields.

Object Methods

There are two methods defined in the object: `__init` and the `average` methods. The `__init` method is a special method, which is known as the *object initializer*. This method is called when an object value is created with the `new` expression. The `__init` method's return type should be of type `error|()`. Since our method returns `()`, i.e., no return type, the return type is compatible. In an error situation inside the object initializer, we can return an `error`, which would fail the object creation.

A list of arguments can be provided with the `new` expression and passed into the object initializer. In the `new` expression, optionally the object type can be mentioned, but it is not required.

```
ExamResult result1 = new ExamResult("sunil", 90, 85, 80);
```

Basically, if the object type is not explicitly given in the new expression, it infers the type by checking the context. The explicit type must be given if this inference is not possible, for example, if the LHS variable contains a union type.

The usage of methods in an object is to provide the behavior for the object. It has full access to the possible data encapsulated inside the object as fields. Inside methods, we need to use the special variable `self`, which represents the current object itself when referring to any fields in the object. This usage is shown inside `__init` and the average methods.

The average method in the previous example is defined to simply return the average of the three subjects that are stored inside the object. This average is calculated by accessing the object that the method is associated with. This is especially useful when the field values are not exposed to the outside world, and these methods build up the interface of the object's functionality that can be used by consumers.

Subtyping in Objects

Considering subtyping in objects, when we have two object types `T1` and `T2`, in order for the `T2` type to be a subtype of T1, T2 needs to have all fields or methods in T1 with the field types being a subtype of the corresponding type in T1.

The method compatibility is checked by verifying that each method in T1, its parameters, and the return types should be a subtype (can be the same type) of the corresponding types in T2.

This is roughly similar to the rules we had for records, but with methods also coming into consideration.

Abstract Objects

Abstract objects simply define the interface of an object; thus, it will have field declarations and the signatures of the methods, and it will not contain default values of fields. Only subtypes of this object type will provide concrete implementations.

Let's explore the usage of this concept using the sample scenario shown in Listing 3-2.

Listing 3-2. animal_print.bal

```
import ballerina/io;

type Animal abstract object {

    public string name;
    public string class;

```

```
    public function sound() returns string;

};

type Dog object {

    public string name = "Dog";
    public string class = "Mammal";

    public function sound() returns string {
        return "bark";
    }

};

type Owl object {

    public string name = "Owl";
    public string class = "Bird";

    public function sound() returns string {
        return "hoot";
    }

};

function printAnimal(Animal animal) {
    io:println("Animal name: ", animal.name, ", class: ",
                animal.class, ", sound: ", animal.sound());
}

public function main() {
    printAnimal(new Dog());
    printAnimal(new Owl());
}
```

```
$ ballerina run animal_print.bal
Animal name: Dog, class: Mammal, sound: bark
Animal name: Owl, class: Bird, sound: hoot
```

In the previous sample, we have defined the abstract object type `Animal`. Also, we have a function `printAnimal` that takes in a value of type `Animal`. The `printAnimal` function does not care about the exact concrete implementation of the `Animal` object type, but rather, it expects a compatible type to be passed in, so it can access the fields and the methods that are defined in the abstract object type.

The object types `Dog` and `Owl` are of type `Animal`, since they have defined their fields and methods to be compatible with the `Animal` type. In our code, we only interact with the abstract type `Animal`, and we do not need explicit knowledge of the internal implementation details of the concrete types, nor should we be interested. Using this pattern, we have effectively decoupled the concrete implementations from the usage of the abstract type in our code. This is the general usage of *data abstraction*.

Objects or Records?

Because of similarities in these types, we may sometimes stop and wonder which type to use between the two. A `record` type's generally usage is to create a data structure to hold related data fields together. But if we really need to encapsulate some data and define behavior to act on that data in the object, we are presented with the `object` usage.

Reference Types and Value Types

Simple types that we have used, such as `int` and `float`, are directly stored in a variable or a member field. These are known as *value types*. All the structured and behavioral types that are mentioned in this chapter are called *reference types*. That is, what is actually stored in the variable or a member field is a reference to the actual value. The reference value basically represents a memory location where the actual target value is stored.

So when we are passing in a reference value to a function, or assigning it to a variable, we are basically copying the reference value, not the target value itself. In this way, if we change the target value from one of the references, this will be seen using other variables that have the same reference value.

Listing 3-3 shows an example scenario demonstrating this behavior.

Listing 3-3. value_reference_copying.bal

```
import ballerina/io;

public function main() {
    map<int> ages = { };
    ages["sunil"] = 25;
    int count = 10;
    io:println("Ages before update: ", ages);
    io:println("Count before update: ", count);
    updateAges(ages);
    updateCount(count);
    io:println("Ages after update: ", ages);
    io:println("Count after update: ", count);
}

public function updateAges(map<int> ages) {
    ages["sunil"] = 30;
    io:println("Ages in updateAges: ", ages);
}

public function updateCount(int count) {
    int myCount = count;
    myCount = 20;
    io:println("Count in updateCount: ", myCount);
}
```

```
$ ballerina run value_reference_copying.bal
Ages before update: sunil=25
Count before update: 10
Ages in updateAges: sunil=30
Count in updateCount: 20
Ages after update: sunil=30
Count after update: 10
```

In the previous example, we are creating a map value and an int value and passing them to two separate functions, and the passed-in values are modified inside the functions. After these update functions are called, we are printing the values again in the main function to see whether there is any effect on the values it has in the main function.

From the program output, we can see that the int value is not changed in the main function, but the map value represented by the ages variable has been updated. The reason for this behavior is because the int type is a value type when passing to the function, and also when assigning the value to another variable in the updateCount function, it is creating a copy of the actual value. Because of this, the updated int value is visible only in the updateCount function, but not in the main method's variable.

But in the case of the variable ages, the passed-in value to the function is a reference to the actual map value; thus, the variable inside the function updateAges also points to the same reference and thus to the same value. Any update done using the same reference value will result in updating the same target value as well.

Deep and Exact Equality

As we covered in Chapter 2, deep equality (==) and exact equality (===) work differently for value and reference types. For simple types (except floats), both operators work in the same way, where they compare the value stored in the variable.

In the case of reference types, the exact equality operator (===) checks to see whether it's the same reference value, or the memory location, stored in two variables. In the case of deep equality (==), it ignores the reference value and instead checks the target value represented by the reference value. If the target value also contains fields that are reference values, this operation is done recursively until all nonreference types are reached.

Listing 3-4 demonstrates the aforementioned behavior.

Listing 3-4. ref_deep_exact_equals.bal

```
import ballerina/io;

public function main() {
    map<string> m1 = { "name" : "jack"};
    map<string> m2 = { "name" : "jack"};
    io:println(m1 === m2);
    io:println(m1 == m2);
}
```

```
$ ballerina run ref_deep_exact_equals.bal
false
true
```

Here, the map variables `m1` and `m2` hold references to two separate map values. Since they are two different map values, the reference values stored in `m1` and `m2` will be different. But the map content pointed at by these two different references are similar, where they have similar entries. Therefore, the deep equality evaluates to `true`, but the exact equality evaluates to `false` because the variables are holding different reference values.

Constants and Singleton Types

Constants are declared at the module level in Ballerina as compile-time constant values, which means the initial value of them cannot be changed after initialization.

The following format is used when defining a constant:

```
const [type] <var_name> = <const_expr>;
```

An example constant definition is shown here:

```
const PI = 3.1415;
```

Here, the type of the constant is inferred from the value that is set, so the type is optional in the constant declaration. But the same thing can be written in the following manner as well:

```
const float PI = 3.1415;
```

Constants are also often used in defining an enumeration of values, by defining a new type with the list of constant values. The following shows an example of this pattern:

```
const ON = "ON";
const OFF = "OFF";
type SWITCH_STATUS ON|OFF;
...
SWITCH_STATUS livingRoomSwitch = ON;
```

A singleton type is basically a type definition that can contain only a single simple value. An example singleton type is shown here:

```
type IO_ERROR "IO_ERROR";
```

Also, a notable built-in singleton type is `nil`, where its type and the only single value are represented with `()`.

Singleton types are often used when defining error types; we will see this usage in Chapter 5.

Summary

In this chapter, we looked beyond simple types and ventured into the world of structural types. We covered list types in arrays and tuples, mapping types with maps and records, and also behavioral types with objects. We also saw the importance of special type descriptors such as unions and their usages.

CHAPTER 4

Code Organization

In this chapter, we will be looking at how proper code organization should be done when programming with Ballerina. This includes exploring the general development workflow of a computer programmer, including coding best practices, design patterns, automated testing, and functional reuse and sharing.

Ballerina Projects and Modules

Ballerina is not just a programming language and a compiler, but rather a full platform for application development. It has its own project and module concepts that can be used as the primary approach for organizing your program code.

Single Source File Programs

So far, we have been writing a single source file for Ballerina programs. You can directly build and run Ballerina programs consisting of single source files without any problem. Especially for smaller programs, this is a convenient approach to development.

Run or Build?

The Ballerina tool `ballerina` can be used to directly run a program by providing the source file, or you can build the source code first. We have used the `ballerina run <source>` command to run the programs so far. This command actually does the two-step process of building the program first and then running it. The building process compiles the source code, packages up dependencies, and creates the final executable program to be run. So, each time we issue a `ballerina run <source>` command, the build operations are repeated and the generated executable is run.

Listing 4-1 shows how we can do a build with the `ballerina` tool.

A. Fernando and L. Warusawithana, *Beginning Ballerina Programming*,
https://doi.org/10.1007/978-1-4842-5139-3_4

Listing 4-1. print_time.bal

```
import ballerina/time;
import ballerina/io;

public function main() {
    io:println(time:toString(time:currentTime()));
}
```

```
$ ballerina build print_time.bal
Compiling source
        print_time.bal

Generating executables
        print_time.jar
```

As shown in Listing 4-1, the Ballerina build command is executed with ballerina build <source>. This generates the new file named print_time.jar.

The .jar file is of the type Java archive. This represents the binary executable that will run in the Java Virtual Machine (JVM), which is the target runtime environment used for running Ballerina programs.

Now, we have the source code compiled, and the final executable is built, so we can use the ballerina run <executable> command to run the program.

```
$ ballerina run print_time.jar
2019-11-15T16:29:43.927-08:00
```

Note that we are providing the executable .jar file to the ballerina run command, not the source file. In this way, there is no source code compilation that needs to be done; rather, the executable file is directly run. You may also notice that the execution is now much faster, since the build process of the code has already happened.

So, even though in our examples in the book, we directly compile and run the code in a single ballerina run <source> command, when we are running our final programs in a real-world production setup, we should always build the application first and then run the built executable separately. This makes sure we will not be re-compiling the source code each time we run the program, thus wasting time. In addition; at the time of execution, we reduce the possibility of external tampering with the program's logic because of the availability of the source code.

Ballerina Projects

As your programs get more complicated, you may want to organize your code a bit more methodically. You can start by splitting high-level functionality into individual modules. A single module will contain independent functionality that can be brought together to build a larger Ballerina project.

A Ballerina project is created using the `ballerina new <project_name>` command.

Let's build a sample Ballerina project to demonstrate the Ballerina project features and show how to manage the modules that make up its functionality.

```
$ ballerina new calculator
Created new Ballerina project at calculator

Next:
    Move into the project directory and use `ballerina add <module-name>` to
    add a new Ballerina module.
```

You can see that with the previous command execution, we have created a new project called `calculator`. The execution of this command creates a directory structure similar to the following:

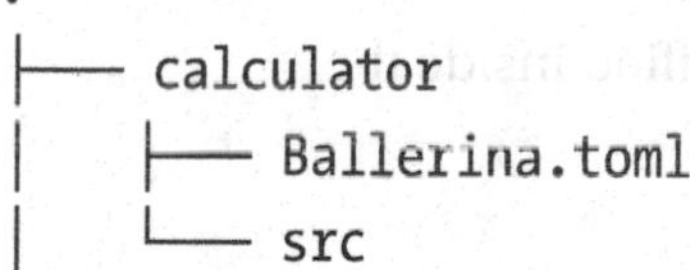

```
.
├── calculator
│   ├── Ballerina.toml
│   └── src
```

The Ballerina project is represented by the directory `calculator`, and inside this directory, there is a `Ballerina.toml` file and a `src` directory created. The `Ballerina.toml` file represents project metadata, and the initial content will be similar to the following:

```
[project]
org-name="laf"
version="0.1.0"

[dependencies]
```

The TOML (Tom's Obvious, Minimal Language) format has a simple structure, where all entries are based on key-value pairs. Also, these key-value pairs can be grouped using tables. For example, in our previously generated `Ballerina.toml` file, `project` and `dependencies` are tables. Under the `project` table, we have defined `org-name` and `version`, which are keys, while `laf` and `0.1.0` are their respective values. The `org-name` and version properties mentioned here are used in relation to the definition of individual modules in the project, and the `dependencies` section provides additional information on the dependencies used in this project.

The `src` directory contains the source code and resources for each module in the project. Next, we will learn about how Ballerina modules can be used as dependencies in a project and how we can define our own modules as well.

Ballerina Modules

A Ballerina module represents a grouping of functionality and data in the code. That is, a module is a specific set of services, functions, variables, and types that can be grouped into a single module. A module is identified by two parts.

- **Organization**: A logical name given when grouping modules together
- **Module name**: The name of the module to be identified inside the organization

Importing Modules

A Ballerina module can be imported into a Ballerina program using the following syntax:

```
import <organization>/<module_name> [as <identifier>]
```

After a module is imported, you can use its identifier as a means of accessing the data and functionality exposed by the module to the outside. This is done by using the syntax `identifier:<symbol>`, where the `symbol` can be things such as constants, functions, and objects.

The module identifier is either derived or explicitly provided. The default derived identifier is generated by the last part of the module name. That is, if the module name has its identifier separated by dot (.) characters, only the last section is used as the module identifier. For example, let's check the following imports:

```
import ballerina/io;
import ballerinax/java.jdbc;
```

The module from the first import is referenced using the derived identifier `io`, since it is the module name and its name is not divided using a period. The second imported module is accessed by the derived identifier `jdbc`. Since its module name `java.jdbc` is separated by periods, the last section of it is used as the imported module's identifier. Now, the symbols inside these modules can be accessible using references such as `io:println()` and `jdbc:TYPE_NUMERIC`.

An explicitly provided imported module identifier works by the user providing the identifier to be used in referencing the module in the `import` statement itself. Let's take the following code snippet:

```
import ballerina/io as console;
import ballerina/lang.'int as ints;
...
console:println(ints:fromString("123"));
```

Here, we have provided the explicit identifiers for the modules `ballerina/io` and `ballerina/lang.'int` as `console` and `ints`, respectively. Specially for the module `lang.'int`, the explicit identifier is easier to use, compared to the quoted identifier used as the module name there.

Dependencies and Versions

Each time you import a module into your program, it becomes a dependency to your program. This dependency is associated with our program by using a specific version of that module. If you do not provide an explicit dependency version, the compiler will look up the latest compatible version of the module to use the module with your program.

The explicit module dependency version can be provided using the `Ballerina.toml` file in your project. This means you cannot provide a module-level dependency version if you are using a single source file Ballerina program.

```
[dependencies]
"wso2/twitter" = "0.9.26"
"laf/zip" = "0.1.3"
```

As shown, in the `dependencies` section in `Ballerina.toml`, you can have key-value entries for each module dependency and its version.

Java Dependencies

In certain situations, it is required to bundle Java libraries as dependencies, which are also represented as `.jar` files. This would be required when we are using the `ballerinax/java.jdbc` module, which is used for database access from Ballerina. In this situation, a database driver is required for each separate database server type. This must be packaged as a dependency in the module that requires the driver.

For example, if you are using a MySQL database, a dependency similar to the following should be added in the `Ballerina.toml` file:

```
[platform]
target = "java8"

[[platform.libraries]]
path = "/home/laf/mysql-connector-java-8.0.18.jar"
modules = ["module1", "module2"]
```

The properties under `platform` and `platform.libraries` provides information such as the target platform version, the path to the dependency file, and a list of modules that this dependency should be applied to.

In the case of specifying multiple dependencies, the `[[platform.libraries]]` section can be repeated to add more entries. For example, the following configuration adds the MySQL and MSSQL JDBC drivers as dependencies to the `module1` and `module2` modules, respectively.

```
[platform]
target = "java8"

[[platform.libraries]]
path = "/home/laf/mysql-connector-java-8.0.18.jar"
modules = ["module1"]

[[platform.libraries]]
path = "/home/laf/mssql-jdbc-7.4.1.jre8.jar"
modules = ["module2"]
```

Ballerina database programming will be covered in detail in Chapter 10.

Adding Modules to a Project

A module is represented as a directory in the `src` directory of a project. A new module can be added to a project using the `ballerina add <module_name>` command. Let's add a few modules to the `calculator` project we created earlier.

```
$ ballerina add calfunctions
Added new ballerina module at 'src/calfunctions'

$ ballerina add calparser
Added new ballerina module at 'src/calparser'

$ ballerina add calapp
Added new ballerina module at 'src/calapp'
```

We've now added three new modules to the project: `calfunctions`, `calparser`, and `calapp`. With this, the new modules belong to the same organization and have the same version as mentioned in the current project's `Ballerina.toml`.

The `calfunctions` module is responsible for implementing the algorithms required for the calculator projects, and `calparser` will pass the calculator requests entered by a user as a string. These two modules will be used as dependencies in the `calapp` module to define the entry point to the program.

The following illustrates the directory structure after the modules are added to the project:

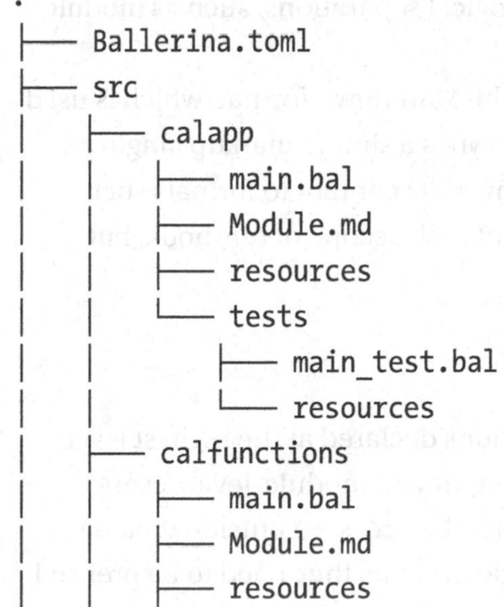

```
.
├── Ballerina.toml
├── src
│   ├── calapp
│   │   ├── main.bal
│   │   ├── Module.md
│   │   ├── resources
│   │   └── tests
│   │       ├── main_test.bal
│   │       └── resources
│   ├── calfunctions
│   │   ├── main.bal
│   │   ├── Module.md
│   │   ├── resources
```

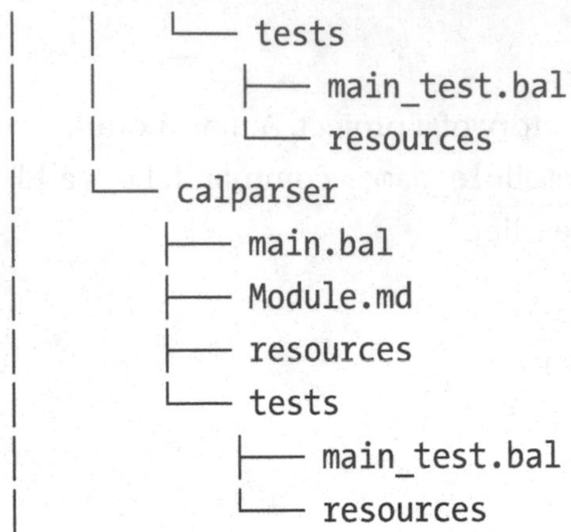

```
│   │   └── tests
│   │       ├── main_test.bal
│   │       └── resources
│   └── calparser
│       ├── main.bal
│       ├── Module.md
│       ├── resources
│       └── tests
│           ├── main_test.bal
│           └── resources
```

The directory structure that is created contains templates for the modules. The `main.bal` file represents the module code, and it contains a `resources` directory for storing any module-specific resources. There is also a special directory named `tests`, which contains the tests for the module. The `test` directory also has a separate `resources` directory for its operations.

The source `.bal` file inside the modules does not need to have a specific name; rather, it just needs the extension `.bal`. Therefore, all the Ballerina source code in this directory and any subdirectories (excluding tests/resources) will be considered as part of the current module.

Even though the source code files and directory structure do not have any effect on the module definition, as a best practice, we can further divide the module source code into multiple source files by considering additional logical separations, such as module constants, utility functions, and error handling code.

The `Module.md` file contains a description using the Markdown format, which is used as information to be shown with the module. Markdown is a simple markup language for formatting a document, which can be used to convert its content to formats such as HTML and PDF. An explanation of Markdown is out of the scope of this book, but information on this can be easily found on the Web.

Identifier Visibility in Modules

Module-level identifiers (such as variables and functions declared at the highest level in a module, i.e., not inside records, objects, and so on) have a module-level access qualifier by default. This means these identifiers cannot be accessed outside their own module. If these need to be accessible from an outside module, they need to be prefixed with the `public` access qualifier. The following shows an example of this in action:

```
public type Person record {|
    string name;
    int age;
|};

public const float PI = 3.1415;

int status = 0;

public function main() {
}
```

In the preceding code snippet, we have made the Person record have public visibility, so code outside the current module can refer to it; in addition, the const value PI and the main function are declared as public. Note that nonconstant variables cannot be made public; rather, they will only have the module-level access.

Implementing Modules

Let's perform implementations of the modules we have defined earlier for our calculator project and see how each is connected. We will be deleting the initial template source code and resource directories that were created automatically and starting over.

The main functionality of each module is as follows:

- **calfunctions**: Represents the algorithms used for the calculator, where we need to pass in the suitable input data according to the target algorithm used.
- **calparser**: Parses a given request string and returns the calculation algorithm name and the data as the output.
- **calapp**: Represents the entry point to the application; thus, it has a main function. This will start the program and prompt the user to enter a calculation request. This is like fact 10 and sort 1 10 5 3 9. This module will delegate the functionality of parsing the input string to identify the operation algorithm and the input to the calparser module, which will parse the string and give a machine-understandable representation of the input.

The result of the parsed request will now be used with the calfunctions module in order to invoke the algorithm and return and print the result to the user.

calfunctions

The `calfunctions` module is used to implement the basic algorithms used by our program. We will be implementing the following algorithms:

- **Factorial**: A factorial function, similar in functionality to the implementation we did in Chapter 2.
- **Sort**: A sort function to arrange a given list of numbers in ascending order. We will be implementing the bubble sort algorithm for this operation.

To implement the previous two operations, we will be creating a source file named `functions.bal` inside the module.

In Listing 4-2, the factorial functionality is implemented as a recursive function, where its formula can be written as `fact(n) = n * fact(n - 1); fact(1) = 1`.

Listing 4-2. functions.bal

```
public function fact(int n) returns int {
    if n <= 1 {
        return 1;
    } else {
        return n * fact(n - 1);
    }
}

public function sort(int[] input) returns int[] {
    int i = 0;
    boolean swapped;
    while i < input.length() - 1 {
        int j = 0;
        swapped = false;
        while j < input.length() - i - 1 {
            if (input[j + 1] < input[j]) {
                int temp = input[j];
                input[j] = input[j + 1];
                input[j + 1] = temp;
                swapped = true;
            }
```

```
            j += 1;
        }
        if !swapped {
            break;
        }
        i += 1;
    }
    return input;
}
```

Recursion

A recursive function is a function that calls itself again (directly or indirectly) in its own implementation. The call to itself will have a different input compared to the input it got originally. Without this behavior, the recursive function will be doing the same thing always, and its execution will not end. Also, in the same way, a recursive function must have a base condition that it will converge into. This is the case in the previous implementation at line 2, where it checks if the input equals 1, and if so, it returns a constant value immediately, without doing the recursive call again.

Recursion vs. Iteration

Recursive functions make it easy to model certain problems easily, since some solutions can be explained easily with this approach and, thus, can be implemented in the same way. Note that we now have a recursive implementation of the factorial algorithm and also as an iterative implementation in Chapter 2. In the same way, any recursive function can be implemented in an iterative approach. This is an important aspect, because the recursive function may not be the best approach for implementing algorithms sometimes. Even though it is comparatively simpler to implement, it has the inherent property that, for each recursive function call, there is a certain amount of additional memory allocated for each active call for storing function parameters and returns, and for a large input, which executes a large number of recursive calls, this can end up in an out-of-memory situation. This issue does not appear in an iterative approach, since an individual loop iteration itself does not require any additional memory allocations.

Bubble Sort

The sort operation implements the bubble sort algorithm, which simply compares two nearby numbers to see whether the second number is smaller than the first, and if so, those two values are swapped in the array. This is repeated through the whole array, from start to finish, and at the end, the last element will contain the largest value. Basically, these operations are repeated until all the biggest elements are moved to the right side of the array. The algorithm also has an optimization where it holds a flag to see whether there have been any swaps throughout a run through the array; if not, the whole array is already sorted, and we return immediately with the result.

calparser

The `calparser` module is used to pass a request string from the user and turn it into an algorithm + data representation to be used by the application to invoke the algorithms in `calfunctions`.

The module consists of two source files, `constants.bal` and `parser.bal`, as shown in Listing 4-3 and Listing 4-4.

Listing 4-3. constants.bal

```
public const ERROR_INVALID_REQUEST = "INVALID_REQUEST";
public const ALGO_FACT = "FACT";
public const ALGO_SORT = "SORT";
```

Listing 4-4. parser.bal

```
import ballerina/stringutils;
import ballerina/lang.'int as ints;

public type Algorithm ALGO_FACT|ALGO_SORT;

public type Request record {
    Algorithm algorithm;
    int[] data;
};

public function parseRequest(string request) returns Request|error {
```

```
    string trimReq = request.trim();
    if trimReq.startsWith("fact ") {
        return { algorithm: ALGO_FACT, data:
                 check parseArray(trimReq.substring(5)) };
    } else if trimReq.startsWith("sort ") {
        return { algorithm: ALGO_SORT, data:
                 check parseArray(trimReq.substring(5)) };
    } else {
        return error(ERROR_INVALID_REQUEST);
    }
}

function parseArray(string data) returns int[]|error {
    int[] result = [];
    string[] entries = stringutils:split(data, " ");
    foreach var entry in entries {
        var item = ints:fromString(entry);
        if item is int {
            result.push(item);
        } else {
            return error(ERROR_INVALID_REQUEST);
        }
    }
    return result;
}
```

The primary functionality of `calparser` is exposed through the `parseRequest` function, which takes in a string value; this string value represents an input from a user, and the function converts it to a value of the `Request` record. If there is any issue with the input data from the user, an error value is returned.

The types and functions related to error handling will be covered in detail in Chapter 5.

calapp

The `calapp` module contains the entry point to the program, with the definition of a public `main` function. This module imports both the `calparser` and `calfunctions` modules to implement the functionality it requires.

In Listing 4-5, we can see how the other two modules, calparser and calfunctions, are imported and used in order to delegate their specific functionality to each of them. And the main application coordinates the functionality between the modules to implement the overall functionality.

Listing 4-5. app.bal

```
import ballerina/io;
import laf/calparser;
import laf/calfunctions;

public function main() returns error? {
    string input = io:readln("Enter calculator request: ");
    var result = check execRequest(input);
    io:println("Result: ", result);
}

public function execRequest(string input) returns any|error {
    calparser:Request request = check calparser:parseRequest(input);
    if request.algorithm == calparser:ALGO_FACT {
        return calfunctions:fact(request.data[0]);
    } else if request.algorithm == calparser:ALGO_SORT {
        return calfunctions:sort(request.data);
    } else {
        return error("Unknown algorithm");
    }
}
```

Building Modules

We have now implemented the source code for the modules in the project; now it's time to build the project.

The project consists of three modules. We can build the modules one by one, or we can build all the modules at once. A specific module can be built with the following command:

```
ballerina build [-c] <module_name>
```

If the module on its own is not executable, you need to pass the -c switch to the compiler to only compile the module code and not create an executable .jar file. The compiler will only compile the source code and will create an intermediary file known as a BALO (Ballerina Object) file. This file simply contains the compiled result of the given source files, and it has not combined the dependencies to create a final executable.

In this manner, we can execute the final command to build the calparser and calfunctions modules, as shown in the following code:

```
$ ballerina build -c calparser
Compiling source
        laf/calparser:0.1.0

Creating balos
        target/balo/calparser-2019r3-any-0.1.0.balo

Running tests
        laf/calparser:0.1.0
        No tests found

$ ballerina build -c calfunctions
Compiling source
        laf/calfunctions:0.1.0

Creating balos
        target/balo/calfunctions-2019r3-any-0.1.0.balo

Running tests
        laf/calfunctions:0.1.0
        No tests found
```

Now the calapp module can also be built, but without the -c flag.

```
$ ballerina build calapp
Compiling source
        laf/calapp:0.1.0

Creating balos
        target/balo/calapp-2019r3-any-0.1.0.balo
```

```
Running tests
      laf/calapp:0.1.0
      No tests found

Generating executables
      target/bin/calapp.jar
```

The preceding command has built an executable file because of it having a program entry point defined in its code. Even simply building `calapp` will build the other modules automatically if they are not already built, since they have been identified as required dependencies with the `import` statements.

If we want to build all the modules in a project at once, we can use the following command:

```
ballerina build -a
```

The previous command will build all the modules and will also create the final executable if there is a module with a program entry point.

Running an Application

An application can be run in two approaches. After you have built the module that has the program entry point, you can execute the following command to run its executable:

```
ballerina run <executable_file>
```

This is the most preferred approach and should be the only approach followed in a production environment.

Our calculator project is finally run with the following command:

```
$ ballerina run target/bin/calapp.jar
Enter calculator request: fact 14
Result: 87178291200

$ ballerina run target/bin/calapp.jar
Enter calculator request: sort 54 593 03 95 915 94 125 35
Result: 3 35 54 94 95 125 593 915
```

A project executable can also be run by directly executing the `ballerina run <module_name>` command. This will build the executable and run it at the same time.

```
$ ballerina run calapp
Compiling source
      laf/calapp:0.1.0

Creating balos
      target/balo/calapp-2019r3-any-0.1.0.balo

Generating executables
      target/bin/calapp.jar

Running executables

Enter calculator request: fact 7
Result: 5040
```

You have now seen how a multimodule Ballerina project can be created, built, and executed. In the upcoming sections, we will talk more about making sure our code is understandable and follows a consistent style.

Documentation

Documentation is a crucial aspect of programming, because we need to communicate to the outside world what our code is providing as functionality and how it is supposed to be used. This is the job of any documentation system in a programming language.

The Ballerina documentation system is built-in technology in the Ballerina platform. Ballerina has defined a documentation syntax to be used in describing Ballerina language constructs and also provides the tools to generate the documentation content.

A source code construct is generally documented using the following syntax:

```
# <description>
# ...
# + <param/field> - <description>
#
# ...
# + <param/field> - <description>
# ...
# + return - <description>
```

The syntax to be used is based on Markdown, called Ballerina Flavored Markdown (BFM). With this format, we can provide richer formatting support to our code documentation.

Let's update our `calculator` project use case to add documentation to its main modules, which expose its functionality to the general public.

```
# Calculates the factorial of the given number.
#
# + n - The input number
# + return - The factorial of the given number
public function fact(int n) returns int { ...

# Sort the given integer array in ascending order.
#
# + input - The input values to be sorted
# + return - The sorted values of the input
public function sort(int[] input) returns int[] { ...
```

The preceding documentation sections are used to define the public functions of the `calfunctions` module.

In the same manner, we can document other aspects such as the record type.

```
# This represents the decoded calculator request from a user.
#
# + algorithm - This represents the algorithm that was chosen
#               as an `Algorithm` type.
# + data - The data is the input data provided by the user for
#          the given algorithm.
public type Request record {
   Algorithm algorithm;
   int[] data;
};
```

The `Module.md` file in each Ballerina module can also be used to give additional documentation content regarding the module. This content will be combined with the Ballerina code documentation to generate the final documentation page content.

Generating Documentation

The following command can be used to generate the HTML documentation pages by processing the documentation statements inside the respective modules:

```
ballerina doc <module_name>
```

All the Ballerina modules can be processed for documentation at once using the command `ballerina doc -a`.

```
$ ballerina doc -a
Compiling source
        laf/calfunctions:0.1.0
        laf/calapp:0.1.0
        laf/calparser:0.1.0

Generating API Documentation
        target/apidocs
```

Figure 4-1 shows the generated output for the `calfunctions` module's function documentation.

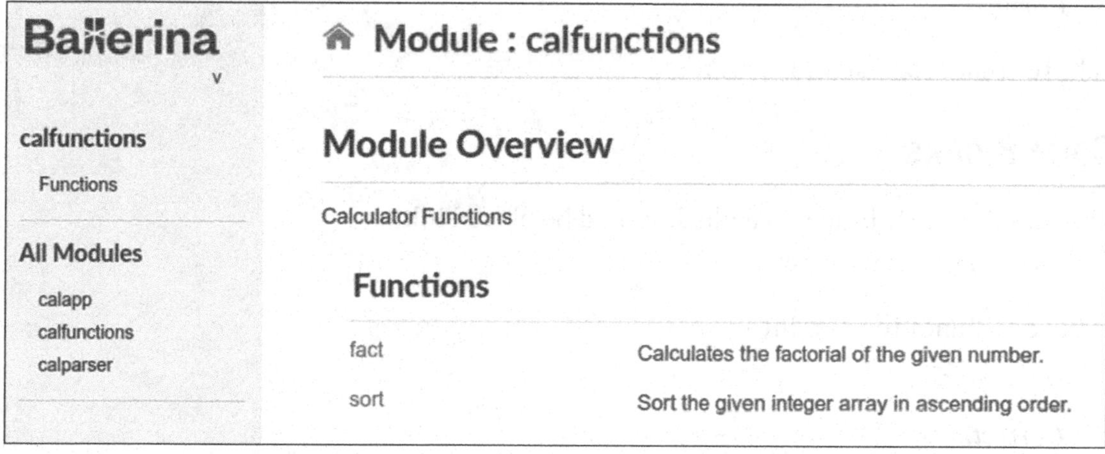

***Figure 4-1.** Generated HTML docs for the `calfunctions` module*

Coding Conventions

Ballerina programming coding conventions provide developers with general guidelines on how code should be written. This makes sure that all Ballerina code is written in a standardized manner, especially in a team environment.

The following sections highlight the most often used coding conventions in Ballerina.

Indentation and Maximum Column Size

The indentation length must be four spaces, and the source code should not use any tab characters. The maximum number of characters allowed per line is 120 characters.

Spacing: Keywords, Types, and Identifiers

The spacing between any construct such as keywords, type, and identifiers should be only a single space, not multiple.

Incorrect:

```
public   function  main() { ...
```

Correct:

```
public function main() { ...
```

Code Blocks

The opening curly braces in a block should be placed inline.

Incorrect:

```
public   function  main()
{ ...
```

Correct:

```
public function main() { ...
```

A single space should appear before the opening curly braces.

Incorrect:

```
public   function  main(){ ...
```

Correct:

```
public function main() { ...
```

Line Breaks

The code should have only one statement per line.

Incorrect:

```
int i = 0; int j = 0;
```

Correct:

```
int i = 0;
int j = 0;
```

For a full reference guide on the Ballerina coding conventions, please refer to `https://ballerina.io/learn/style-guide/`.

Testing

Testing is one of the most important aspects of computer programming. After you write some code, you need to make sure the code you've written works properly, and most importantly, you need to make sure it will continue to work properly in the future. With continuous changes applied to a programming project, by yourself or from another team member, you will not be sure if something you did has affected the correct behavior of the earlier code.

This is where automated testing comes into play. Tests make sure that we can keep a specific functionality consistent over time and that we can verify the correctness by running the tests at any time.

There are mainly two types of tests done for computer programs; these are unit testing and integration testing.

Unit Testing

Unit testing is where each lower-level module or function is separately tested, and its correctness is verified. In relation to our `calculator` project, we should have unit tests to test the functionality of individual operations found in the `calfunctions` and `calparser` modules.

The idea behind unit tests is that if we make sure the lowest-level functionality is working properly, and we can verify this, it will be easier to implement and verify the higher-level features that are built on top of the unit-level features.

Integration Testing

Integration testing is done to make sure that the lower-level modules work correctly with each other. This basically tests the module's interfaces and whether they are still compatible with each other when cooperating to build up high-level features. In our `calculator` project, a point of integration is when the `calapp` interfaces with the modules `calfunctions` and `calparser` in parsing a user request and executing a calculator operation. We should verify that the operations done by `calapp` with `calparser` and `calfunctions` remain compatible.

Ballerina Test Framework

The Ballerina test framework can be used to implement unit and integration testing.

Calculator Parser and Algorithms Testing

Let's first see how we can write the unit tests for testing the `calparser` and `calfunctions` modules.

The test code is put under the `test` directory in each module. The `ballerina/test` module provides the test assertion functions to use in test operations. Test assertions are used to notify the test framework that a given test assertion should evaluate to true, or else the test has failed. Let's look at how these test assertions are used in the `calparser` unit tests in Listing 4-6.

Listing 4-6. parser_tests.bal

```
import ballerina/test;

@test:Config{}
function testParse1() returns error? {
    Request req = check parseRequest("sort 3 2 1");
    test:assertEquals(req.algorithm, ALGO_SORT);
    int[] rx = [3, 2, 1];
```

```
    test:assertEquals(req.data, rx);
}

@test:Config{}
function testParse2() returns error? {
    Request req = check parseRequest("sort 1");
    test:assertEquals(req.algorithm, ALGO_SORT);
    int[] rx = [1];
    test:assertEquals(req.data, rx);
}

@test:Config{}
function testParse3() returns error? {
    Request req = check parseRequest("fact 14");
    test:assertEquals(req.algorithm, ALGO_FACT);
    int[] rx = [14];
    test:assertEquals(req.data, rx);
}

@test:Config{}
function testParse4() returns error? {
    var res = parseRequest("fact");
    if res is error {
        test:assertTrue(true);
    } else {
        test:assertTrue(false);
    }
}

@test:Config{}
function testParse5() returns error? {
    var res = parseRequest("sort");
    if res is error {
        test:assertTrue(true);
    } else {
```

```
        test:assertTrue(false);
    }
}

@test:Config{}
function testParse6() returns error? {
    var res = parseRequest("sort a b 10");
    if res is error {
        test:assertTrue(true);
    } else {
        test:assertTrue(false);
    }
}

@test:Config{}
function testParse7() returns error? {
    var res = parseRequest("run 1 2 40");
    if res is error {
        test:assertTrue(true);
    } else {
        test:assertTrue(false);
    }
}
```

The test assertion `assertEquals` is used to check whether a given expected result is equal to a result retrieved by the test. If this evaluates to `false`, the test will fail. In the same manner, the test assertion `assertTrue` is used to give a Boolean expression that should evaluate to `true`; if not, the assertion will have failed, along with the test.

In these tests, our main target is to check all the execution paths of the module functionality. This will make sure all the possible logic executed in our functionally is covered in the unit tests. These include checking edge cases as well, such as 0 and 1 for the size input length, and any other parameter where the internal implementation may do some special operations.

Also, it is important to test for failure scenarios. As part of the contract of the module's functions, if there is any invalid input, it must return a proper error, without succeeding with wrong values. This is critical to the application's behavior, and the tests should cover all these scenarios. Such failure test cases are shown in `testParse4`, `testParse5`, `testParse6`, and `testParse7`, which are testing for invalid payloads and invalid algorithms.

In the same manner, we should write unit tests for `calfunctions` to test the correct behavior of its algorithm implementations.

Calculator App Testing

In this section, we will test the overall application functionality; thus, this is an integration test between `calparser`, `calfunctions`, and `calapp`.

Listing 4-7 demonstrates how integration tests evaluate the functionality of the module `calapp`, which implements its features using the integration between the `calparser` and `calfunctions` modules.

Listing 4-7. app_tests.bal

```
import ballerina/test;

@test:Config{}
function testApp1() returns error? {
    any result = check execRequest("sort 3 2 1");
    int[] rx = [1, 2, 3];
    test:assertEquals(result, rx);
}

@test:Config{}
function testApp2() returns error? {
    any result = check execRequest("fact 3");
    test:assertEquals(result, 6);
}

@test:Config{}
function testApp3() returns error? {
    any result = check execRequest("sort 59");
```

```
    int[] rx = [59];
    test:assertEquals(result, rx);
}

@test:Config{}
function testApp4() {
    any|error result = execRequest("sort");
    if result is error {
        test:assertTrue(true);
    } else {
        test:assertTrue(false);
    }
}

@test:Config{}
function testApp5() {
    any|error result = execRequest("fact");
    if result is error {
        test:assertTrue(true);
    } else {
        test:assertTrue(false);
    }
}
```

The primary function of these tests is to check whether the integration between the modules is functioning properly and whether their own functionality is invoked correctly. Therefore, it is not the responsibility of the integration tests to verify the unit tests' functionality again, with a large number of tests to go through all the low-level combinations. For example, in the integration tests, we do not have to try all the possible `sort` combinations to see whether the underlying `sort` operation is implemented properly. This operation was already covered by the `sort` unit tests. In the integration tests, we only test the interface between the higher-level `calapp` and the connection to the modules that provide the low-level functionality. At this point, if we prove that we can reach the sort operation from the integration test and we get a correct result, we should be able to safely say we will get the same correct results for other inputs as well, since the different input combinations have already been verified in the unit tests.

Sharing and Reuse

So far, we have seen how to use Ballerina modules on a local computer. But Ballerina provides a mechanism where we can share our modules with external users as well. This is done using a central module repository called Ballerina Central. This also allows us to conveniently reuse these modules for our different projects.

Using Ballerina Central, we can browse the existing modules that are available for use. This is possible using the ballerina tool or from the web UI, which can be reached at http://central.ballerina.io.

The command ballerina search <query> can be used to search for modules in Ballerina Central. For example, let's do a search for modules related to *email*.

```
$ ballerina search email

Ballerina Central
=================

|NAME                   | DESCRIPTION                                 | DATE           | VERSION |
|-----------------------| --------------------------------------------| ---------------| --------|
|wso2/twilio            | Connects to Twilio from Ballerina.          | 2019-09-09-Mon | 0.8.31  |
|wso2/gmail             | Connects to Gmail from Ballerina.           | 2019-10-02-Wed | 0.10.1  |
|wso2/sfdc46            | Connects to Salesforce from Ballerina.      | 2019-10-02-Wed | 0.10.1  |
|hemikak/smtp           | SMTP Library to send Emails.                | 2019-11-08-Fri | 2.0.1   |
|wso2/salesforce_to_m...| Template for Salesforce to MySQL using Ba...| 2019-10-22-Tue | 1.1.1   |
|ldclakmal/committer    | Generates WSO2 Committer Report from Ball...| 2019-10-30-Wed | 1.0.0   |
|wso2/amazons3_service  | Demonstrates on connecting to Amazon S3     | 2019-10-04-Fri | 1.0.1   |
|hirantha/firebase_auth | Connects to Firebase Auth from Ballerina.   | 2019-10-20-Sun | 0.1.3   |

$ ballerina pull hemikak/smtp
hemikak/smtp:2.0.1 [central.ballerina.io -> home repo]
                   [==========>] 500919/500919
```

After a module search, we can pull a specific module to the local module cache by running the `ballerina pull <module>` command. Note that even if we don't perform this step beforehand, when we import this module, and at compile time, it will be automatically pulled from Ballerina Central.

Publishing Modules

To publish our Ballerina modules, we first need to register at Ballerina Central. It provides multiple login options, and we can automatically sign in using a Google or GitHub account.

After the login, we will be presented with a screen similar to the one shown in Figure 4-2.

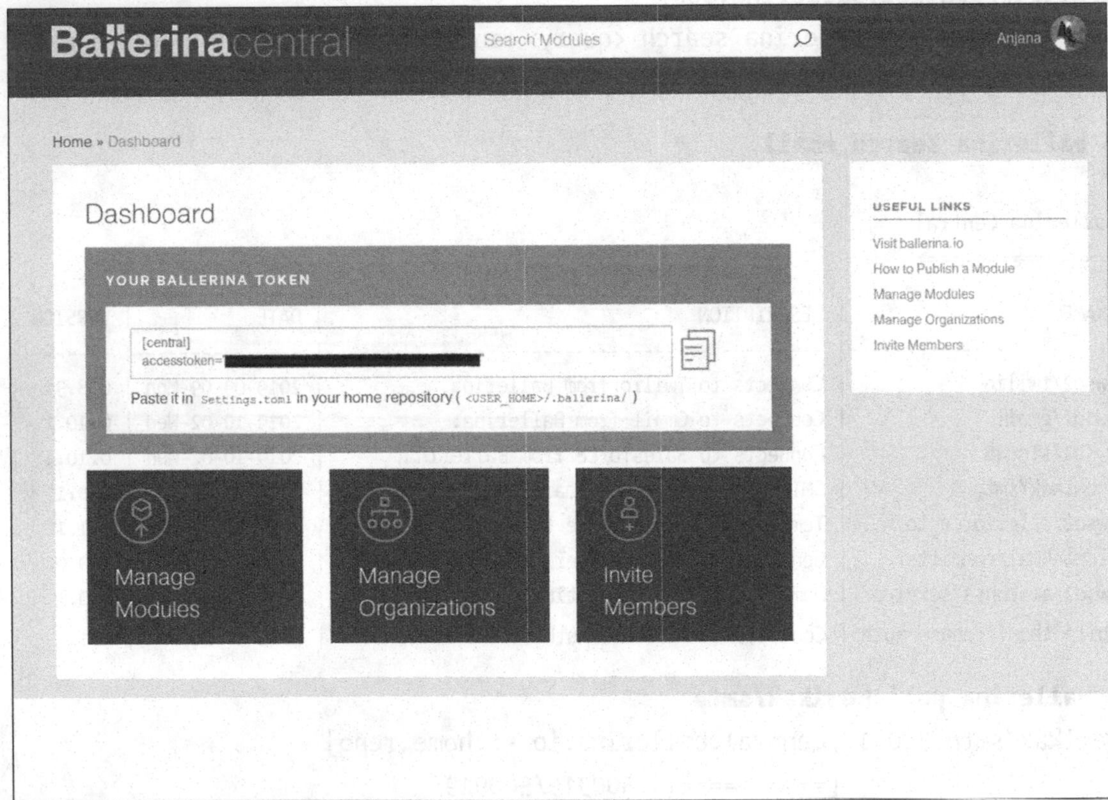

Figure 4-2. *Ballerina Central, Dashboard*

As per the instructions given on the page, we need to copy the Ballerina token and paste it inside <USER_HOME>/.ballerina/Settings.toml.

In the next step, we need to create a new organization by clicking Manage Organization, as shown in Figure 4-3.

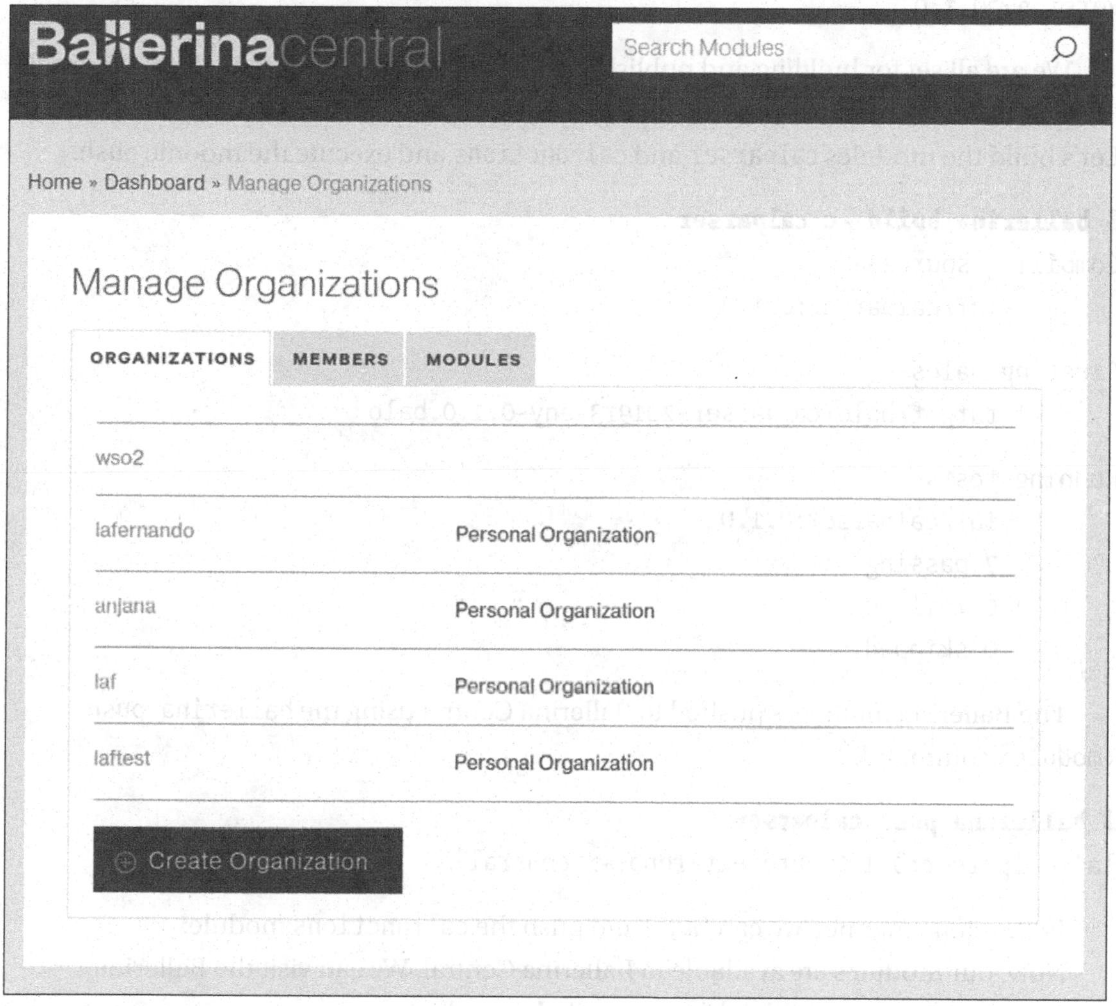

***Figure 4-3.** Ballerina Central, Manage Organizations page*

Here, we can create an organization that we would like to use to publish our modules. The name of the organization we create here should match the organization name we put in the Ballerina project's Ballerina.toml file.

Now, let's update the Ballerina.toml file in our calculator project with the newly created organization.

```
[project]
org-name="laf"
version="0.1.0"
```

We are all set for building and publishing the Ballerina modules to Ballerina Central.

The Ballerina modules must be built before they can be pushed to Ballerina Central. Let's build the modules calparser and calfunctions and execute the module push.

```
$ ballerina build -c calparser
Compiling source
        laf/calparser:0.1.0

Creating balos
        target/balo/calparser-2019r3-any-0.1.0.balo

Running tests
        laf/calparser:0.1.0
        7 passing
        0 failing
        0 skipped
```

The Ballerina module is pushed to Ballerina Central using the ballerina push <module> command.

```
$ ballerina push calparser
laf/calparser:0.1.0 [project repo -> central]
```

In the same manner, we can build and push the calfunctions module.

Now, our modules are available in Ballerina Central. We can visit the Ballerina Central web interface and check our uploaded modules.

As shown in Figure 4-4, the Ballerina Central Dashboard shows that the laf/calparser and laf/calfunctions modules have just been updated and that they are available for anyone else to use in their own Ballerina projects.

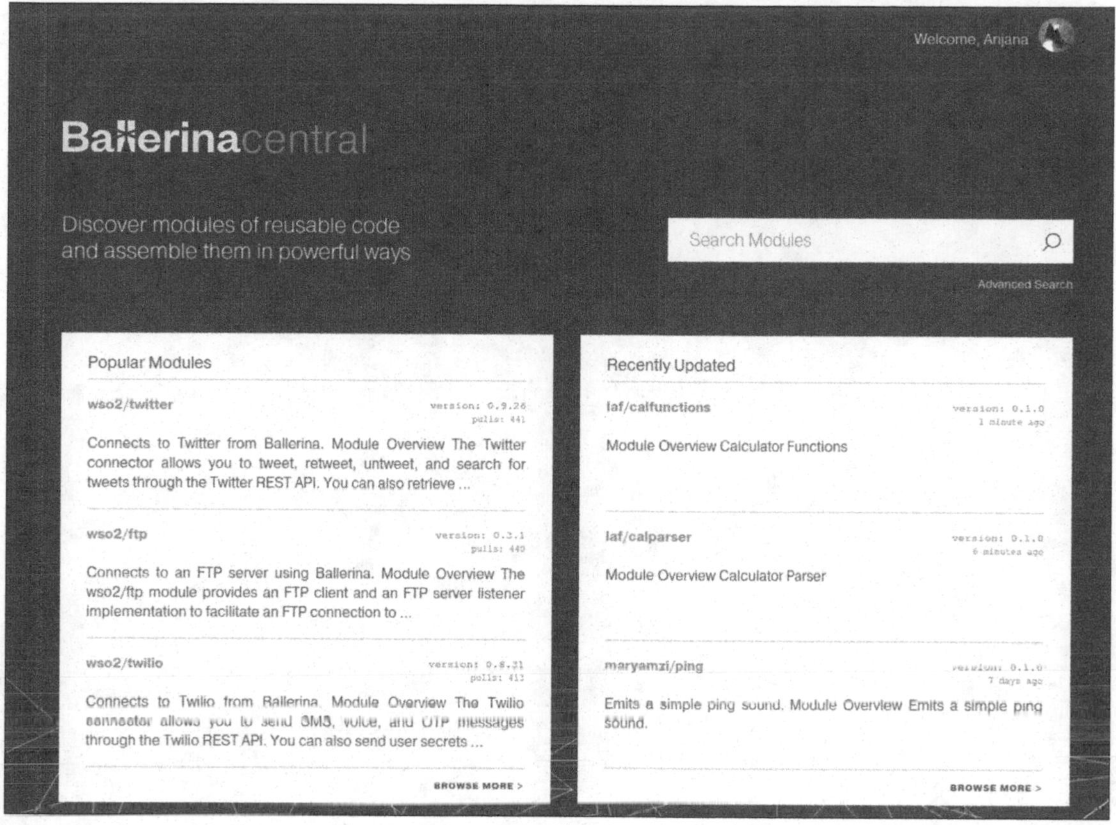

Figure 4-4. *Ballerina Central, Ballerina modules pushed*

Summary

In this chapter, we learned how Ballerina projects and modules work, how to import external dependencies, and the difference between creating single source file programs and full multimodule applications. Documentation plays an important part in communicating the functionality to the external user, while coding conventions make sure that a general set of best practices is maintained in a common code base. The most crucial aspect of programming is testing. Ballerina provides rich functionality to write unit and integration tests. It is vital that you make it a habit to design automated tests, along with the main business logic, to ensure the intended functionality will continue to work in the future.

We finished the chapter by showing you how to push your modules to Ballerina Central in order to encourage module sharing and reuse.

CHAPTER 5

Error Handling

When writing computer programs, sometimes your program does not execute with the behavior that you were expecting. This can be because of human errors, such as entering incorrect input, or because of environmental issues, such as network communication failures. It can even be because of issues with how the program logic was written. We call these scenarios generated in the program *errors*, and we call the act of anticipating these errors and taking appropriate actions *error handling*.

You know some errors that can happen in your program; that is, your program will be ready to face those scenarios that deviate from what you want the program to do. For example, your program should be able to recover when receiving invalid user input to do some calculations. It may simply be a case of presenting an error message to the user and asking her to re-enter the values.

The other type of errors are the ones that are not generally expected in your program, so the program does not really have a way to handle these errors and recover. An example is an out-of-memory situation when trying to allocate some memory to store some data. These are potentially fatal situations, because the program will not handle the error explicitly or try to recover from it. This can even result in early or abnormal termination of the program.

Let's start by checking how we can react to the error situations we are faced with.

Reacting to Errors

In this section, we will learn how to work with operations that could end in an error situation. We demonstrated some error handling in earlier chapters, when we showed how to convert a string to a number. Let's look at this scenario again in Listing 5-1.

A. Fernando and L. Warusawithana, *Beginning Ballerina Programming*,
https://doi.org/10.1007/978-1-4842-5139-3_5

Listing 5-1. num_errors.bal

```
import ballerina/io;
import ballerina/lang.'int as ints;

public function main() {
    string input = io:readln("Input: ");
    int|error val = ints:fromString(input);
    if val is error {
        io:println("Reason: ", val.reason());
        io:println("Detail: ", val.detail());
        io:println("Stacktrace: ", val.stackTrace().callStack);
        io:println("ToString: ", val.toString());
    } else {
        io:println(val);
    }
}
```

```
$ ballerina run num-errors.bal
Input: abc
Reason: {ballerina/lang.int}NumberParsingError
Detail: message='string' value 'abc' cannot be converted to 'int'
Stacktrace: callableName=fromString moduleName=ballerina.lang_int.int
fileName=int.bal lineNumber=53 callableName=main moduleName=num-errors
fileName=num-errors.bal lineNumber=6
ToString: error {ballerina/lang.int}NumberParsingError message='string'
value 'abc' cannot be converted to 'int'
```

Here, the `input` variable has a specific string value, but we cannot be sure if it will actually be a representation of a number. So, when we call `ints:fromString`, it expects the passed-in argument to contain a string representation of an integer; if so, it will return the integer value of that, or else, it will return an `error` value saying that it cannot convert the string to an integer.

The previous scenario shows a general pattern in error handling, where the function in question will return a union type with the successful execution value type and the error type combined. So, when processing the result, you will do a type test on the value and take appropriate actions for the successful value type and the error type. All errors in Ballerina are based on the built-in type `error`. This error type consists of the following structure:

- **Error reason**: This identifies the category of the error and is accessed with the `reason()` function.
- **Error detail**: This provides additional information on the error as a record and is accessed with the `detail()` function. It contains two optional fields, `message` and `cause`, with the types `string` and `error`, respectively. The execution output in Listing 5-1 shows the field `message`, which provides extended information related to the error situation.
- **Stacktrace**: The stack trace contains a snapshot of the call stack when the error condition happened. The call stack is basically information about each active function call that has occurred at this point in time. The stack trace is accessed using the `stackTrace()` function, which provides a value of type `CallStack`, which in turn contains a field called `callStack`. The `callStack` variable is an array of type `CallStackElement`. A single `CallStackElement` value contains the information of a single function call in the call stack. The fields of the `CallStackElement` are as follows:
    - **`callableName`**: The function name executed
    - **`moduleName`**: The module the function lives in
    - **`fileName`**: The file name where the source code resides
    - **`lineNumber`**: The location in the function where the execution is done in relation to the source file

The execution output of the sample in Listing 5-1 shows each of the previous aspects of the error value returned. Using this information, we can get additional insights into the error situation and take any necessary actions going forward.

In the preceding scenario, a possible way of handling the error would be to simply give the error message and terminate the program, as we have done in Listing 5-1.

Or, in the case that the user has given an invalid input, we can retry the operation, as demonstrated in Listing 5-2.

Listing 5-2. num_errors_retry.bal

```
import ballerina/io;
import ballerina/lang.'int as ints;

public function main() {
    while true {
        string input = io:readln("Input: ");
        int|error val = ints:fromString(input);
        if val is error {
            io:println("Invalid input, please enter again");
            continue;
        } else {
            io:println(val);
            break;
        }
    }
}
```

```
$ ballerina run num-errors-retry.bal
Input: abc
Invalid input, please enter again
Input: 150
150
```

Here, we are simply trying to recover from a possible problematic situation by prompting the user to re-enter the value and try again. This is a common pattern we practice in many places. For example, in network communication, because of its inherent unreliability in physical equipment and connections over distances, we follow strategies such as network timeouts, retries, and circuit breakers to provide a smoother experience to the end user. Chapter 9 will provide more details on network programming.

We have now covered the general operations of error handling. Now let's see how we can also create our own code that can generate such error scenarios when necessary.

Creating Your Own Errors

In this section, we will look at how we can create our own custom error types and how to use them.

Creating Custom Error Types

A new error type is defined in the following manner:

```
type ErrorType error<ErrorReason[, ErrorDetail]>;
```

Here, we have defined the error type `ErrorType`, with the error reason of type `ErrorReason`, as well as the error detail of type `ErrorDetail`. An error type is defined by providing these two types.

- **Error reason**: This represents a subtype of `string`, which represents the error category. This value is returned when invoking the error's `reason()` function. When creating error types in specific Ballerina modules, it is recommended to use the module qualified error reason string, which has the following format: `{org-name/module-name}identifier`.
- **Error detail**: This is a record type that provides additional details of the error. This is the type of the value that is returned with the error's `detail()` function. This type should belong to the `ballerina/lang.error:Detail` record type, which is defined as follows:

  ```
  record {|
     string message?;
     error cause?;
     (anydata|error)...;
  |};
  ```

  The error detail type is optional when defining an error type, and if this type is not given, it defaults to the aforementioned type `ballerina/lang.error:Detail`.

Now that we have learned how to define an error type, let's define our own.

```
type MyErrorDetail record {|
   string message?;
   error cause?;
   string location;
|};

const MY_REASON = "MY_REASON";

type MyError error<MY_REASON, MyErrorDetail>;
```

The error type `MyError` is defined as the reason type being the singleton string type referenced using the constant `MY_REASON`, and the error detail type as `MyErrorDetail`. Here, the `MyErrorDetail` record type has an additional `location` field compared to the default `Detail` record type.

Error Subtyping

The overall type of the error is defined using the error reason type and the error detail type. The stack trace is not considered for the type of the error. So basically, when we are checking whether a particular target error value is of a specific error type, the target error reason type and the error detail type should be the same or a subtype of the corresponding types of the other error type in order for the target to be a subtype.

Creating Error Values

An error value is created using an error constructor. There are two types of error constructors.

- **Direct error constructor**: A direct error constructor is used when the error reason is given as the first argument to the constructor. The expression used to create an error value takes the following format:

  ```
  error(<reason>[, named args])
  ```

The named arguments from the second argument and onward represent the error detail structure's field names as the names of the arguments here. For this type of error constructor, there is no need for an error type to be explicitly defined beforehand, but rather an error value is directly created. If required later, we can check whether the created error value is of a specific error type. For example, a variable err with an error value, a type test can be done directly using an error type descriptor, similar to the following code:

```
if err is error<MY_REASON> {
    ....
}
```

- **Indirect error constructor**: This approach is used by directly referring to an existing error type; thus, the error reason is automatically determined. For the reason to be automatically selected, this error type must be a singleton string. Basically, if the reason is not a singleton string type, an indirect error constructor cannot be used; instead, a direct error constructor needs to be used. The expression used to create an error using the indirect error constructor takes the following format:

  ```
  <ErrorType>([named args])
  ```

  The named arguments take the same format as the one used in the direct error constructor.

Let's take a look at how we can create values to be compatible with the error type `MyError` we defined earlier.

```
error err = error(MY_REASON, location = "L1");
```

The previous line is created using the direct error constructor, where the constant string `MY_REASON` is used as the error reason, and the named argument `location` is used to represent a field with the same name in the error detail. Because of this, in accordance to our subtyping rules, the generated error value is of type `MyError`. So, this can be written in the following manner as well:

```
MyError err = error(MY_REASON, location = "L1");
```

We can also use the indirect error constructor here, since we have only a singleton type as the error reason.

```
error err = MyError(message = "invalid input", location = "L1");
```

Here, I've also given a value to the named parameter `message`, which will become a field in the error's detail record value.

Now that we know the basics of defining error types and creating values out of them, let's explore another practical usage of error handling, where we are faced with multiple error types returned from a function. See Listing 5-3.

Listing 5-3. custom_errors.bal

```
import ballerina/io;
import ballerina/math;

type MyErrorDetail record {|
    string message?;
    error cause?;
    string location;
|};

const MY_REASON1 = "MY_REASON1";
const MY_REASON2 = "MY_REASON2";

type MyError1 error<MY_REASON1, MyErrorDetail>;
type MyError2 error<MY_REASON2>;

public function main() {
    string|error result = myErrorProneFunction();
    if (result is string) {
        io:println(result);
    } else if (result is MyError1) {
        io:println("Error1: ", result);
    } else if (result is MyError2) {
        io:println("Error2: ", result);
    }
```

```
25 }
26
27 function myErrorProneFunction() returns string|error {
28     if (math:random() > 0.5) {
29         return error(MY_REASON1, message = "invalid input",
30                      location = "MyLocation");
31     } else {
32         return error(MY_REASON2, message = "invalid operation");
33     }
34 }
```

```
$ ballerina run custom_errors.bal
Error2: error MyReason2 message=invalid operation
```

```
$ ballerina run custom_errors.bal
Error1: error MyReason1 message=invalid input location=MyLocation
```

In Listing 5-3, we have defined two error types, `MyError1` and `MyError2`. Because of the function `myErrorProneFunction`, there is a chance that either one of these errors will be returned. At line 17, where we have done the function invocation, it returns either a `string` or an `error` type. The types `MyError1` and `MyError2` are subtypes of `error`, and using a type test expression, we can specifically find out which exact type the returned error value belongs to.

It is important to know how the type difference between `MyError1` and `MyError2` has happened. As mentioned, the type of an error value consists of the type of error reason and the detail. So, basically, the type uniqueness is mandated by the record type defined for the detail and the `string` subtype given as the reason.

There is a possibility that the detail structure is similar between different error types, specifically, if we simply use the default `lang.error:Detail` type as we have done with `MyError2` in the previous example. In working with such error types, only the error reason is used as the unique attribute in the error type to distinguish between each other. So, we must make sure we have unique values in the reason string when we are defining error types. We can do this by providing the reason as a module-qualified reason string (`"{org-name/module-name}identifier"`).

To prove this point, let's do a minor update to the type definitions of our earlier example.

```
const MY_REASON1 = "MY_REASON";
const MY_REASON2 = "MY_REASON";

type MyError1 error<MY_REASON1>;
type MyError2 error<MY_REASON2>;
```

Note that we've defined the error types with the default detail structure, and the error reason constant string values (`MY_REASON1,MY_REASON2`) have the same value.

Let's update our `main` function also slightly, to do independent type tests and print a value.

```
public function main() {
    string|error result = myErrorProneFunction();
    if (result is MyError1) {
        io:println("Error1: ", result);
    }
    if (result is MyError2) {
        io:println("Error2: ", result);
    }
}
```

The output of the previous code looks like this:

```
$ ballerina run custom_errors.bal
Error1: error MyReason message=invalid input location=MyLocation
Error2: error MyReason message=invalid input location=MyLocation

$ ballerina run custom_errors.bal
Error1: error MyReason message=invalid operation
Error2: error MyReason message=invalid operation
```

We can see that in each execution, the type test succeeds for both error types, since they are indeed similar types due to having the same error reason. This shows the importance of having unique strings for the error reason.

Expected vs. Unexpected Errors

Earlier we looked at errors generated from certain program logic in the code and how we can try to handle the errors by examining the error values. There are also errors that are usually not expected by the program code and the developer. For example, when our code is executing some function and we run out of main memory or hard disk space, we probably cannot continue with our execution, and our program should just quit. These types of errors are not supposed to be returned from functions, and basically they are not exposed to the developer to handle them. The mechanism of raising such errors in Ballerina is called a *panic.*

When a panic operation is executed in Ballerina, the currently executing function immediately stops and exits, and its execution jumps back to the function that called it. It keeps unwinding the function call stack in this manner until someone *traps* the error.

Error trapping is when you can explicitly signal to the program code that you would like to catch an error that has been raised using a panic operation.

A panic statement takes the following format:

```
panic <error_value>;
```

Listing 5-4 demonstrates a panic situation in action.

Listing 5-4. panic_run.bal

```
import ballerina/io;

type MyReason "CODE1"|"CODE2";

type MyErrorDetail record {|
    string message?;
    error cause?;
    string location;
|};

type MyError error<MyReason, MyErrorDetail>;

public function main() {
    string result = myErrorProneFunction();
```

```
    io:println(result);
}

function myErrorProneFunction() returns string {
    myPanicFunction();
    return "response";
}

function myPanicFunction() {
    MyError err = error("CODE1", location = "L1");
    panic err;
}
```

```
$ ballerina run panic_run.bal
error: CODE1 location=L1
        at panic:myPanicFunction(panic_run.bal:24)
           panic:myErrorProneFunction(panic_run.bal:19)
           panic:main(panic_run.bal:14)
```

Listing 5-4 contains a new function called `myPanicFunction`, which has a *panic* statement that is used to raise a panic situation with the given error. This function is called inside `myErrorProneFunction`, and even though `myErrorProneFunction` does not declare itself to return an error value now, in the runtime we still get into an error situation. This is because the panic statement executed inside `myPanicFunction` is propagated up to `myErrorProneFunction`, which in turn propagates it to the calling `main` function, where again it is sent up to the Ballerina runtime to immediately stop the execution.

At this point, you can see a log printed to the standard output, which shows the execution stack trace where it stopped the execution from each function.

Trapping Errors

The errors that are raised through the panic functionality can actually be caught, or *trapped*. You can visualize this situation as a downstream function doing a panic, with an error flying toward you. If you do not trap it, it will pass through you stopping and killing everything in its path.

You trap an error with the following syntax:

```
error|T result = trap <expression>;
```

Here, the type of the expression is T, and it is suspected to raise a panic situation through its downstream operations. For example, if this expression is a function call, this function itself may have executed a panic statement, or different actions it performed resulted in a panic, and an error is propagated upward from there.

Let's update our earlier program to trap the panic in the main function.

```
public function main() {
    string|error res = trap myErrorProneFunction();
    if res is error {
        io:println("Error: ", res);
    } else {
        io:println(res);
    }
}
```

```
$ ballerina run panic_run.bal
Error: error CODE1 location=L1
```

Figure 5-1 shows the flow with steps labeled from 1 to 5 to show how the code execution happens.

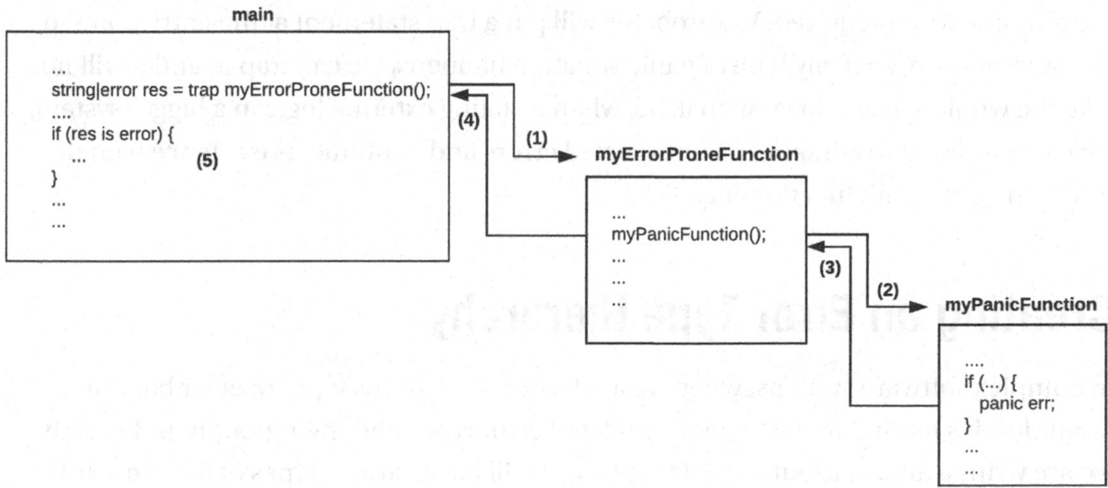

***Figure 5-1.** Error handling flow with panic/trap*

The flow starts from the main function and, in the downstream execution inside `myPanicFunction`, a panic situation occurs that triggers all the function calls to return immediately until a trap statement is met.

You probably noticed that originally the `myErrorProneFunction` call simply returned a `string` value, but now the earlier function call expression turns into a *trap* expression that makes the final type of the expression become a union type with the original function return type and an error type, i.e., `string|error`.

Is It Time to *panic*?

You may wonder when you should actually use a `panic` in your code. A panic is usually used in unrecoverable error situations when the user is not expected to handle the error. Generally, panics are rarely used; they are only commonly used in situations where you expect to work with results that have a high probability of critical errors.

For example, we usually safely assume we have enough hard disk space to temporarily store some data. But when working with the I/O library, if we get an error saying we are out of space, we usually send out a panic and stop the execution. This is probably one of the situations that we cannot recover from, and we don't expect the developers using this code to handle this scenario.

The trap functionality also works in the same context, where generally we should not be trapping the panic, but we can let it exit the full program by itself.

In some special situations, we may need to trap panic situations such as if we create a system where external users install their own code via a plug-in system and we invoke the plug-ins when required. We probably will put a trap statement at the entry point to the plug-in code, so if any type of panic situation happens, we can trap it, and it will not take the whole system down with it. So, when isolating external logic in a bigger system, we can use a trap to contain any unexpected errors and continue its existence with the rest of the program's functionality.

Creating an Error Type Hierarchy

In complex software systems, when we are faced with various types of error handling scenarios, it's natural for us to identify related error types and their groupings. Let's say we are writing an input/output (I/O) library. It will have various types of functionality, from reading/writing files to performing network operations. The error scenarios that might arise here can be grouped into certain higher-level errors, and these higher-level error themselves can get categorized again. This is a *hierarchical* error type system.

Figure 5-2 illustrates a graphical view of how these different types of errors can possibly be arranged.

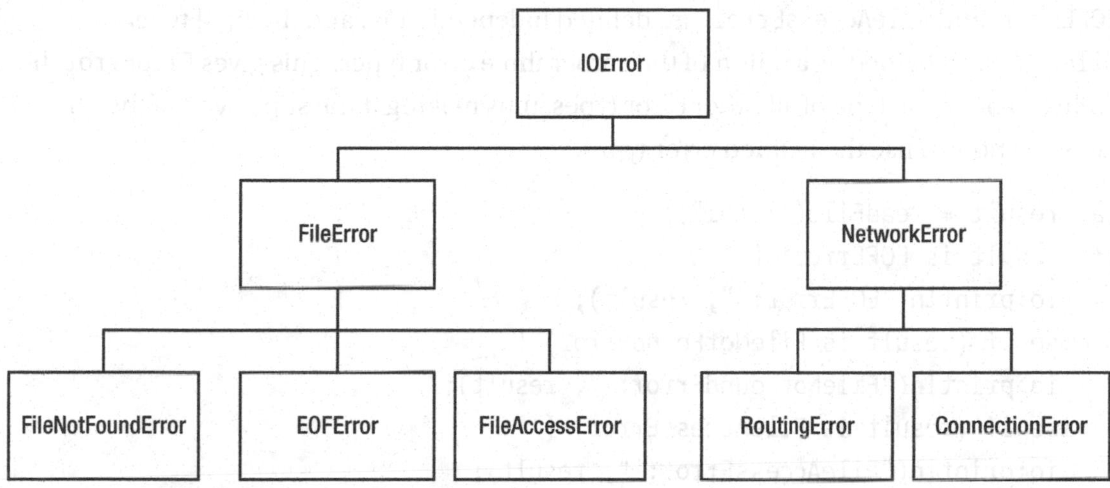

Figure 5-2. *Type hierarchy for I/O errors*

Figure 5-2 shows how the type hierarchy defines where a child node represents a subtype of the parent node's type. Basically, the types `FileNotFoundError`, `EOFError`, and `FileAccessError` are of type `FileError`. And in this way, the types `FileError` and `NetworkError` belong to `IOError`. Since `IOError` is the root of the whole tree, it is the supertype of all the types below it. The general idea here is the deeper you go into the hierarchy, the more specific the error is. For example, with `FileError` being a child of `IOError`, and thus a subtype, it says, "I'm an error that happened due to a file-based error, but I'm still fundamentally an I/O error."

So, how can we model these types in code to show this relationship? This is done by simply using union types to group error types together and to create new higher-level error types.

```
const FILE_NOT_FOUND_ERROR = "FILE_NOT_FOUND_ERROR";
type FileNotFoundError error<FILE_NOT_FOUND_ERROR>;

const EOF_ERROR = "EOF_ERROR";
type EOFError error<EOF_ERROR>;
```

```
const FILE_ACCESS_ERROR = "FILE_ACCESS_ERROR";
type FileAccessError error<FILE_ACCESS_ERROR>;

type FileError FileNotFoundError|EOFError|FileAccessError;
```

In the previous code snippet, the first three error types, `FileNotFoundError`, `EOFError`, and `FileAccessError`, are defined independently, and the final type, `FileError`, is defined as a union of the earlier three error types. This gives `FileError` the ability to be of the type of all other error types, thus making it the supertype of the others. Let's see how to use the defined error types.

```
var result = readFile("file1");
if (result is EOFError) {
    io:println("EOFError: ", result);
} else if (result is FileNotFoundError) {
    io:println("FileNotFoundError: ", result);
} else if (result is FileAccessError) {
    io:println("FileAccessError: ", result);
}

result = writeFile("file2", "data");
if (result is FileError) {
    io:println("FileError: ", result);
}
```

The `readFile` and `writeFile` functions can return either `FileNotFoundError`, `EOFError`, or `FileAccessError`. After the `readFile` operation, we are checking for a specific error type and trying to reach them individually. But in the `writeFile` operation, we don't care what the exact file-related error is; we just want to know if it's a general `FileError`. Because of the error type hierarchy, if `writeFile` returns any subtype of `FileError`, we will be able to detect it there.

Let's define our error types to extend up to the `IOError` level as well.

```
const ROUTING_ERROR = "ROUTING_ERROR";
type RoutingError error<ROUTING_ERROR>;

const CONNECTION_ERROR = "CONNECTION_ERROR";
type ConnectionError error<CONNECTION_ERROR>;
```

```
type NetworkError RoutingError|ConnectionError;
type IOError FileError|NetworkError;
```

Now we have defined the full type hierarchy shown in Figure 5-1, and we can create any arbitrary error type hierarchy by following a similar approach.

Error Handling Case Study: Connected Banking

In this section, we'll demonstrate end-to-end error handling functionality by creating a system similar to a real-world use case. Here, we will be implementing a connected banking scenario. For this, we will be creating a software system that implements several features used by customers. The main features are the following:

- Automated teller machine (ATM) functionality
  - Look up account balance
  - Withdraw money
- Online banking
  - Look up account balance
  - Transfer money

These features share lot of general functionality that can be reused via a shared component. These are mainly the following actions:

- Query account balance
- Debit account
- Credit account

Using these features as a base, we can implement all the functionality needed for our connected banking scenario. A basic design goal is to delegate the high-level functionality to the common set of available features. This is where we end up with a *layered architecture.*

Figure 5-3 shows how different functioning units are layered on top of each other.

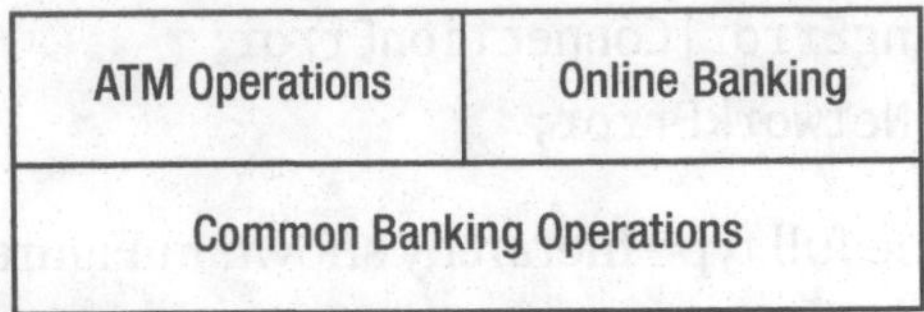

Figure 5-3. *Connected banking layered architecture*

At the bottom level, we have the common banking operations, which provide the base functionality, and on top of that, we have other specific operations that are implemented using the functionality in the lower layers. The general concept of a layered architecture is that more advanced features are built on top of a general set of functionality provided by a lower layer. In this manner, we are encouraged to design for reusability and separation of concerns.

With the general design done, let's look at how each component in our system is implemented. In our sample implementation, to represent each component, we will be implementing a Ballerina object to encapsulate the respective functionality. Here, we will specifically look at the common banking operations and the online banking layer implementations. Note that in a more real-world implementation, these functionalities would probably be implemented as their own network service. Writing services will be covered in Chapter 9.

Common Banking Operations

This component represents the basic operations implemented by the banking solution. These operations will be used by other higher-level components to implement more specialized and advanced scenarios.

Listing 5-5 shows what the object definition and its usage looks like.

Listing 5-5. connected_banking.bal (Common Banking Operations)

```
import ballerina/io;
import ballerina/time;

const INVALID_ACCOUNT_NUMBER = "INVALID_ACCOUNT_NUMBER";
const INSUFFICIENT_ACCOUNT_BALANCE = "INSUFFICIENT_ACCOUNT_BALANCE";

type AccountMgtErrorReason INVALID_ACCOUNT_NUMBER |
```

```
                                INSUFFICIENT_ACCOUNT_BALANCE;

type AccountMgtErrorDetail record {|
    string message?;
    error cause?;
    int time;
    string account;
|};

type AccountMgtError error<AccountMgtErrorReason,
                               AccountMgtErrorDetail>;

public type AccountManager object {

    private map<decimal> accounts = { AC1: 1500.0, AC2: 2550.0 };

    public function getAccountBalance(string accountNumber)
                                     returns decimal|AccountMgtError {
        decimal? result = self.accounts[accountNumber];
        if result is decimal {
            return result;
        } else {
            return error(INVALID_ACCOUNT_NUMBER,
                         time = time:currentTime().time,
                         account = accountNumber);
        }
    }

    public function debitAccount(string accountNumber, decimal amount)
                                returns AccountMgtError? {
        decimal? result = self.accounts[accountNumber];
        if result is decimal {
            decimal balance = result - amount;
            if (balance < 0.0) {
                return error(INSUFFICIENT_ACCOUNT_BALANCE,
```

```
                    time = time:currentTime().time,
                    account = accountNumber);
        } else {
            self.accounts[accountNumber] = balance;
        }
    } else {
        return error(INVALID_ACCOUNT_NUMBER,
                    time = time:currentTime().time,
                    account = accountNumber);
    }
}

public function creditAccount(string accountNumber, decimal amount)
                                returns AccountMgtError? {
    decimal? result = self.accounts[accountNumber];
    if result is decimal {
        self.accounts[accountNumber] = result + amount;
    } else {
        return error(INVALID_ACCOUNT_NUMBER,
                    time = time:currentTime().time,
                    account = accountNumber);
    }
}

};

public function main() {
    AccountManager am = new;
    decimal|error r1 = am.getAccountBalance("AC1");
    decimal|error r2 = am.getAccountBalance("AC2");
    decimal|error r3 = am.getAccountBalance("AC3");
    io:println("AC1 Balance: ", r1);
    io:println("AC2 Balance: ", r2);
    io:println("AC3 Balance: ", r3);
    error? err = am.debitAccount("AC1", 1000);
```

```
    if (err is error) {
        io:println("AC1 Debit Error: ", err);
    }
    err = am.creditAccount("AC2", 1000);
    if (err is error) {
        io:println("AC2 Credit Error: ", err);
    }
    io:println("AC1 Balance: ", am.getAccountBalance("AC1"));
    io:println("AC2 Balance: ",  am.getAccountBalance("AC2"));
    err = am.debitAccount("AC1", 1000);
    if (err is error) {
        io:println("AC1 Debit Error: ", err);
    }
}
```

```
$ ballerina run connected_banking.bal
AC1 Balance: 1500.0
AC2 Balance: 2550.0
AC3 Balance: error INVALID_ACCOUNT_NUMBER time=1573197078846 account=AC3
AC1 Balance: 500.0
AC2 Balance: 3550.0
AC1 Debit Error: error INSUFFICIENT_ACCOUNT_BALANCE time=1573197078858
account=AC1
```

The code in Listing 5-5 represents the functionality exposed as common banking operations. This functionality is mainly encapsulated in the object `AccountManager`. This object contains the operations `getAccountBalance`, `debitAccount`, and `creditAccount`.

The following error handling scenarios are covered in the account management component:

- Invalid account number provided for bank operations
- Insufficient funds in account for withdrawals

The error representation is done by the new error type defined as `AccountMgtError`. This contains a union type called `AccountMgtErrorReason` for the error reason, representing the invalid account number and insufficient funds states.

For the demonstration here, a few bank account details are hard-coded into the AccountManager object. In a real-world solution, the accounts would be loaded from a database.

Now let's move on to the higher-level layers implemented on top of the common banking operations.

Online Banking

These operations are implemented for users connecting through the Internet. The bank's systems are designed to have a separate component to serve the web requests, which in turn depend on the common banking operations to get its operations done.

Let's look at how this functionality is implemented in code (Listing 5-6).

Listing 5-6. connected_banking.bal (Online Banking Operations)

```
type OnlineBanking object {

    private AccountManager accountMgr;

    public function __init(AccountManager accountMgr) {
        self.accountMgr = accountMgr;
    }

    public function lookupAccountBalance(string accountNumber)
                                   returns decimal|AccountMgtError {
        return self.accountMgr.getAccountBalance(accountNumber);
    }

    public function transferMoney(string sourceAccount,
                                   string targetAccount,
                                   decimal amount)
                                   returns AccountMgtError? {
        AccountMgtError? err = self.accountMgr.debitAccount(
                                   sourceAccount, amount);
        if (err is error) {
            return err;
```

```
        }
        err = self.accountMgr.creditAccount(targetAccount, amount);
        if (err is error) {
            return err;
        }
    }

};

public function main() {
    AccountManager am = new;
    OnlineBanking olBank = new(am);
    error? err = olBank.transferMoney("AC1", "AC2", 500.0);
    if (err is error) {
        io:println("AC1->AC2 Transfer Error: ", err);
    }
    io:println("AC1 Balance: ", olBank.lookupAccountBalance("AC1"));
    io:println("AC2 Balance: ", olBank.lookupAccountBalance("AC2"));
    err = olBank.transferMoney("AC1", "AC2", 1500.0);
    if (err is error) {
        io:println("AC1->AC2 Transfer Error: ", err);
    }
}
```

```
$ ballerina run connected_banking.bal
AC1 Balance: 1000.0
AC2 Balance: 3050.0
AC1->AC2 Transfer Error: error INSUFFICIENT_ACCOUNT_BALANCE
time=1573198735855 account=AC1
```

Listing 5-6 shows the additional code required when implementing the online banking component of the full system. The OnlineBanking object contains a reference to the AccountManager object, which provides the base functionality for the banking functionality.

The sample run of the functionality in the `main` function shows how to transfer funds between accounts and print their account balances. The last statements simulate the scenario of doing an account transfer, where the source account does not have enough funds to complete the transfer. Because of this, the online banking component returns the error `INSUFFICIENT_ACCOUNT_BALANCE {time:1560401037681, account:"AC1"}`.

This is basically the exact error returned from a `debitAccount` call in the `AccountManager` object. But from the context of the function `transferMoney`, we probably could have given a better error message, saying something similar to `Money Transfer Failed` and also giving more contextual information, such as the source and target account numbers and the transfer amount. This contextual information is important, because it is better to return the error in relation to the overall functionality you are doing. Listing 5-7 demonstrates how we can update our code to do this.

Listing 5-7. connected_banking.bal (Improved Error Handling)

```
type OnlineBankingTransferErrorDetail record {|
    string message?;
    AccountMgtError cause;
    string sourceAccount;
    string targetAccount;
    decimal amount;
|};

const OB_TRANSFER_ERROR = "ONLINE_BANKING_TRANSFER_ERROR";

type OnlineBankingTransferError error<OB_TRANSFER_ERROR,
                                OnlineBankingTransferErrorDetail>;

type OnlineBanking object {

    private AccountManager accountMgr;

    public function __init(AccountManager accountMgr) {
        self.accountMgr = accountMgr;
    }

```

```
    public function lookupAccountBalance(string accountNumber)
                                     returns decimal|AccountMgtError {
        return self.accountMgr.getAccountBalance(accountNumber);
    }

    public function transferMoney(string sourceAccount,
                                  string targetAccount,
                                  decimal amount)
                                  returns OnlineBankingTransferError? {
        AccountMgtError? err = self.accountMgr.debitAccount(
                                  sourceAccount, amount);
        if err is error {
            return error(OB_TRANSFER_ERROR,
                            sourceAccount = sourceAccount,
                            targetAccount = targetAccount,
                            amount = amount, cause = err);
        }
        err = self.accountMgr.creditAccount(targetAccount, amount);
        if err is error {
            return error(OB_TRANSFER_ERROR,
                            sourceAccount = sourceAccount,
                            targetAccount = targetAccount,
                            amount = amount, cause = err);
        }
    }

};
```

$ ballerina run connected_banking.bal

```
AC1 Balance: 1000.0
AC2 Balance: 3050.0
AC1->AC2 Transfer Error: error ONLINE_BANKING_TRANSFER_ERROR
sourceAccount=AC1 targetAccount=AC2 amount=1500.0 cause=error INSUFFICIENT_
ACCOUNT_BALANCE time=1573203411294 account=AC1
```

Listing 5-7 contains the additional error type definitions required for the online banking operations scenario, as well as the updated `transferMoney` function, to intercept the downstream error returned from the common banking operations and create a new more context-specific error from the `transferMoney` function.

In the output, you can see that the error message is now more relevant from the view of the online banking operations component, since it gives a specific error that is more meaningful for its situation, and with the required contextual information. The contextual information here includes the bank accounts involved in the transactions and the amount. Also, it encapsulates the root error that caused this error; thus, from that information, we can gain more insights into what actually caused the current error. As we can see here, the root case is having an insufficient account balance in one of the given accounts.

Error Chaining

As we observed in our connected banking case study, we showed how to display information about the current error by adding the reason for it as the `cause` field in our error detail record. This practice is called *error chaining*. In each layer of our system, we create a new error to capture the context in that environment and store a reference to the error that *caused* the error in the downstream logic. So now, in this way, starting from the final error structure, we are able to navigate through the cause error values and reach the root error that started the chain. This is useful in debugging and to gather all the information related to what took place along the path to the final error scenario.

Figure 5-4 visualizes an error chaining scenario of a bank transfer that has failed with an error. It shows how a bank transfer error has occurred because of an account debit error, which in turn was caused because of a database access error.

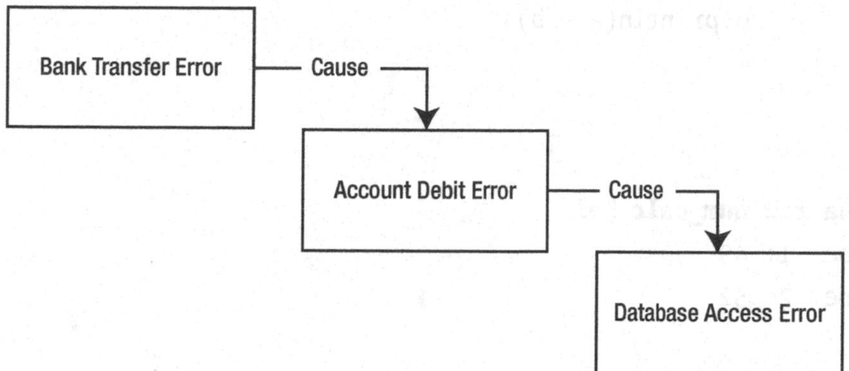

Figure 5-4. *Error chaining pattern*

check and checkpanic

The check and checkpanic expressions are convenience features that can be used in error handling scenarios. The check keyword can be used in front of any sub-expression that can return an error, and if the sub-expression results in an error at runtime, the check expression will make the current function return immediately with this error value.

Let's see how a possible scenario can be implemented with or without the check expression. Listing 5-8 shows how to read in multiple integer values from the user and do some processing.

Listing 5-8. num_calc.bal

```
import ballerina/io;
import ballerina/lang.'int as ints;

public function main() returns @tainted error? {
    error|int a = ints:fromString(io:readln("Enter number 1: "));
    if (a is error) {
        return a;
    } else {
        error|int b = ints:fromString(io:readln("Enter number 2: "));
        if (b is error) {
            return b;
        } else {
```

```
13              io:println(a + b);
14          }
15      }
16 }
```

```
$ ballerina run num_calc.bal
Enter number 1: 49
Enter number 2: 52
101
```

```
$ ballerina run num_calc.bal
Enter number 1: 15
Enter number 2: ABC
error: {ballerina/lang.int}NumberParsingError message='string' value 'ABC' cannot be converted to 'int'
```

In line 5 of Listing 5-8, the `ints:fromString` function returns the union type `int|error`. So, in every call, we must check whether there is a number conversion error and continue with the following operations. Basically, each time we simply check whether the result value is an error; if so, we return the error from the function. There is a shorter way to do this, which is by using the check expression. Let's update our code to do this.

Listing 5-9. num_calc.bal (Updated with the check Keyword Usage)

```
import ballerina/io;
import ballerina/lang.'int as ints;

public function main() returns @tainted error? {
    int a = check ints:fromString(io:readln("Enter number 1: "));
    int b = check ints:fromString(io:readln("Enter number 2: "));
    io:println(a + b);
}
```

The code in Listing 5-9 produces the same functionality as the earlier code but is more concise.

We can also use `checkpanic` in place of `check` to generate a panic, which will result in not needing to have the function return an error type. Instead, the error in question will be propagated to the calling function as a panic situation.

Summary

In this chapter, we looked at error handling techniques and patterns—one of the most important factors when designing and developing software. A good error handling strategy comes with a good design of your code. So, as a best practice, always design your code design and structure with the error handling aspects before writing any code. This will make sure you have an effective error handling strategy and a consistent behavior throughout your application.

CHAPTER 6

Concurrency

Concurrency is a broad topic in computer science, usually referring to a process that occurs simultaneously with one or more processors. *Asynchronous*, *parallel*, *threaded*, and *workers* are some key terms you may have heard related to concurrency. Some people think all of these terms mean the same thing, but there are some differences among these terms.

In this chapter, we are not going to discuss deep theory, approaches to building concurrent models, correctness of logic, practical issues, and so on. Rather, we will look at how we can use Ballerina to build concurrent programs that execute much faster than sequential programs.

Threads and Processes

When we want to have a scalable solution, we want to run the same program in multiple processes. Each process should have its own isolated space such as separate memory, counters, heap, and so on. This isolation is important because if one process is corrupted, it will not affect any other process. But sometimes these processes need to communicate with each other in order to coordinate some tasks. In such situations, these processes will use communication techniques such as sockets, pipelines, and channels to communicate with each other.

A single machine has a limited number of CPUs and cores. When we are running multiple process, the operating system should have a way to allocate CPU cycles for each process. In general, an OS uses threads to schedule CPU allocations with running processes. A process can be allocated to a single thread or to multiple threads, as illustrated in Figure 6-1.

A. Fernando and L. Warusawithana, *Beginning Ballerina Programming*,
https://doi.org/10.1007/978-1-4842-5139-3_6

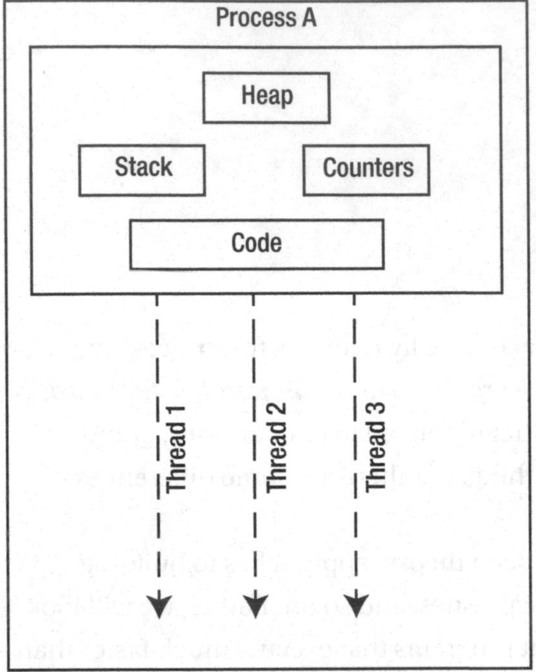

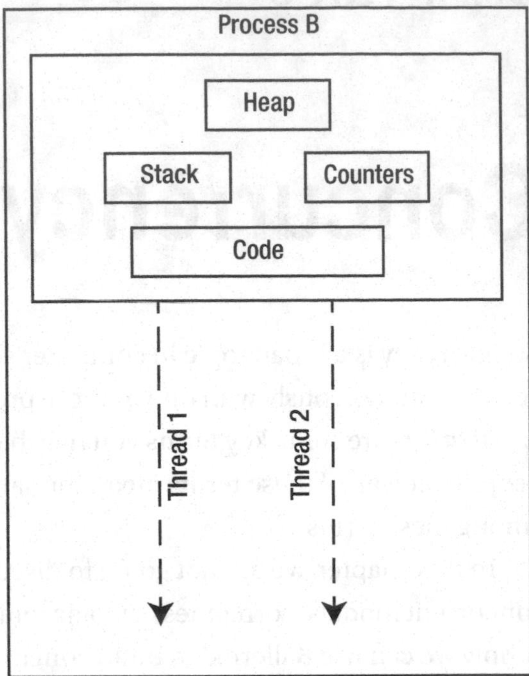

Figure 6-1. *Threads and processes*

Having a shared address space such as a heap, stack, or counter will help threads to communicate. But this comes with a cost, because it can lead to issues such as data corruption and synchronization. Each stack in the threads has an allocated size; in general, this is 2 MB. This limits the number of threads on a single machine. Having uncontrolled threads can eat up all the machine memory.

Concurrency and Parallelism

In many cases, people can't clearly distinguish the difference between concurrency and parallelism. There are various ways to define these two terms, but we like to describe concurrency as a way for a developer to write a piece of code so that it will run in parallel. This means concurrency is a property of the code, but parallelism is a property of how the code is executed.

When we write a piece of code, it will consist of a set of tasks that will execute and return a single result or a set of results. Sometimes these tasks can be independently run, but sometimes these tasks need to be coordinated to produce a result. As developers, we want to write our code to run in an optimal way and return results fast. Writing this code to execute concurrently is the best way to accomplish returning a fast result because independent tasks will always run parallel in multi threaded computer. See Figure 6-2.

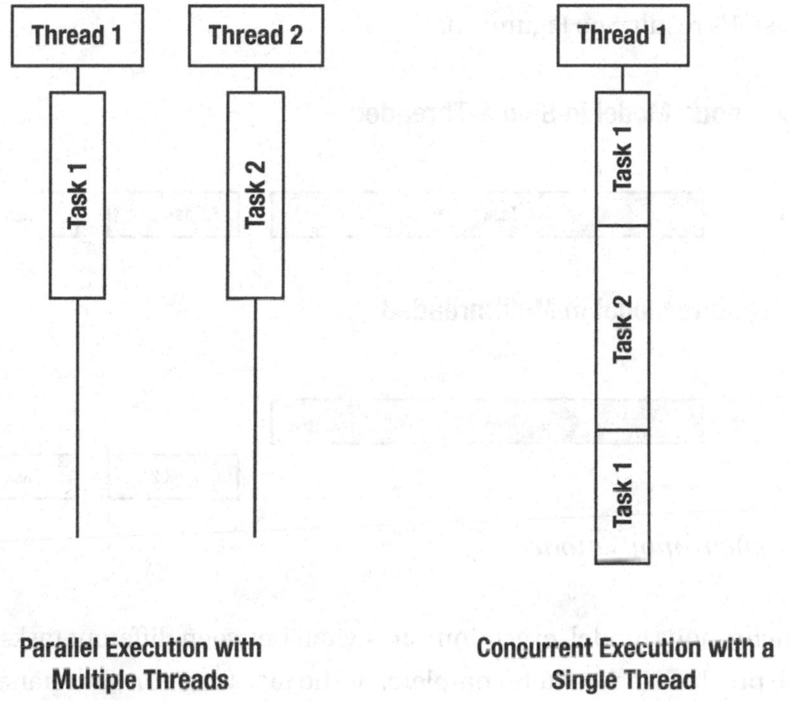

Figure 6-2. *Concurrency vs. parallelism*

Parallelism is one way to have multiple threads working on different tasks at the same time. But it's not the only way. If the computer has a single thread, it will execute our code by doing task switching, which works like this: Task 1 works up to a certain point, then the thread working on it stops and switches over to task 2; that thread works on task 2 for a while and then switches back to task 1. Sometimes the thread yields, and sometimes the scheduler does this. If the time slices are small enough, it may appear to the user that both things are being run in parallel, even though they're actually being processed in serial by multitasking threads.

To recap, we are not writing parallel programs, but we are writing concurrent programs with the hope of executing them in parallel. In a single-CPU (thread) environment, concurrency happens with tasks executing over the same time period via context switching. In other words, at a particular time period, only a single task gets executed. In a multicore environment, concurrency can be achieved via parallelism in which multiple tasks are executed simultaneously.

Synchronous and Asynchronous

Let's review the synchronous and asynchronous models. In a synchronous program, tasks are executed one after the other. This kind of execution is important if task 2 depends on task 1's result. See Figure 6-3.

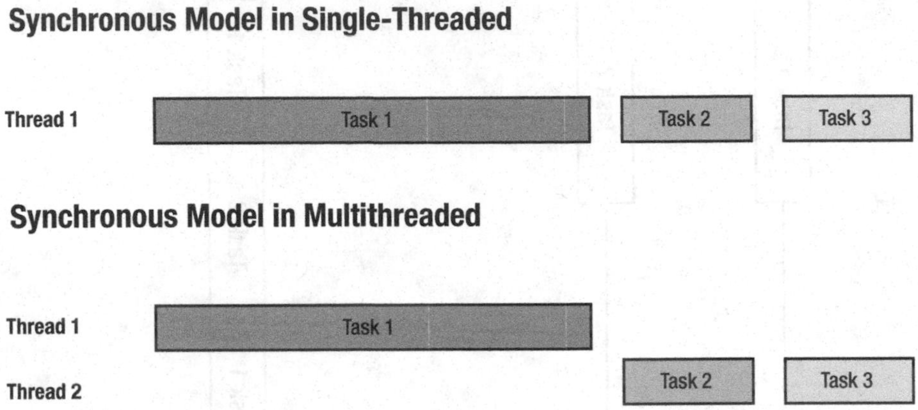

Figure 6-3. *Synchronous model*

In an asynchronous model, execution can switch between different tasks without waiting for the previous task to fully complete, or the tasks can run simultaneously, as shown in Figure 6-4.

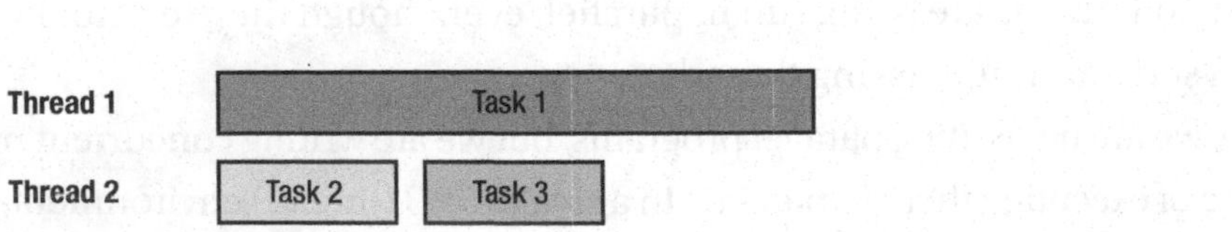

Figure 6-4. *Asynchronous model*

The synchronous and asynchronous programming models help us to achieve concurrency.

The asynchronous programming model in a multithreaded environment is a way to achieve parallelism.

Multitasking

Multitasking is a common feature of modern computer operating systems. The main motivation of multitasking is to fully utilize the computer hardware; when a task is waiting for some external events such as input/output to complete, the CPU can still be utilized for another task. When the CPU is switching from one task to another, it is required to save its state (partial results, memory contents, and computer register contents), load the saved state of another task, and transfer control to it. We call this *context switching*. This context switch can be handled in two different ways.

- The scheduler decides when to context switch, and threads do not decide when to run and are forced to share the CPU (called *preemptive multitasking*).
- Each thread decides how long it keeps the CPU, and once running, the thread decides how long to keep the CPU and when to give it up so another thread can use it (called *cooperative multitasking*).

Operating systems schedule threads either preemptively or cooperatively. In general, almost all modern operating systems support preemptive multitasking in the operating system kernel, by initiating context switching to satisfy the scheduling policy's priority constraint; thus, all processes will get some amount of CPU time at any given time.

Cooperative multitasking (also known as nonpreemptive) was used in early operating systems (Windows 95, Power PC) where the operating system never initiated a context switch from a running process to another process.

Scheduling can be done at the kernel level or at the user level. The difference between the user level and the kernel level depends on the privilege level within the system; it may also be used to distinguish whether a task is currently preemptible.

Kernel thread scheduling is typically uniformly done preemptively. The term *lightweight thread* refers to cooperatively scheduling user threads to kernel mechanisms for scheduling onto kernel threads.

Coroutines

Coroutines are lightweight threads that use cooperative multitasking by allowing execution to be suspended and resumed. This means that coroutines provide concurrency but not parallelism. Coroutines are well-suited for implementing components such as cooperative tasks, exceptions, event loops, iterators, and infinite lists. Many modern programming languages have included a coroutine-style thread to achieve concurrency and asynchronous programming.

Understanding the Ballerina Concurrency Model

Ballerina's concurrency model supports both threads and coroutines. A Ballerina program is executed on one or more threads. A thread may run on a separate core simultaneously with other threads or may be preemptively multitasked with other threads onto a single core.

A strand is not bound exclusively to a single operating system thread, but rather, it uses a full nonblocking policy, where it will never block an executing thread if it is not actively using it. Instead, all the strands belonging to a particular thread are cooperatively multitasked. A strand can yield, and then the runtime scheduler can suspend execution of the strand and switch its thread to execute another strand.

This is controlled by the scheduler in Ballerina, which coordinates the worker executions with the physical threads. For example, I/O operations such as HTTP calls will release the physical threads, and only after the I/O response is available will the strand resume.

This behavior creates a more natural programming environment for the developer, so the developer does not have to explicitly consider nonblocking I/O handling semantics. Also, this style of physical thread allocation is efficient and lowers the number of context switches that optimize CPU allocations.

There are two language constructs in Ballerina whose execution causes the creation of new strands. They are called *worker declaration* and *start-action*.

Asynchronous Programming

The keyword `start` causes the following function or method invocation to be executed on a new strand and run asynchronously. The arguments for the function or method call are evaluated on the current strand. A start-action returns a value of a basic type called `future` immediately.

```
01  future<int> f1 = start verySlowFunction();
02  int result = anotherFunction(f1);
03  _ = wait f1;
```

Line 1 asynchronously calls the `verySlowFunction` function, and line 2 passes the value of the `future` variable and calls its results later. Line 3 waits for the future called `f1` to finish.

This future can be used to get the result of the target function call, by using the `wait` instruction, or it can control operations such as `isDone`, `isCancelled`, and `cancel` to check for the running status of the asynchronous call. Or it can cancel asynchronous call if needed.

```
01 future<()> f2 = start countInfinity();
02 f2.cancel();
```

Line 1 calls the `countInfinity()` function, which runs forever in asynchronous mode. Line 2 cancels the asynchronous execution.

In asynchronous calls, `wait` has the same behavior as using a normal function call and waiting for the result. That is, in the successful scenario, it will eventually return the result value of the target function, and if it throws an error, the `await` statement will throw the same error to the caller. Therefore, the asynchronous call can be adapted to your code easily, without needing to consider any other complexities. See the following sample code block:

```
future<http:Response | error> f3 = start clientEndpoint->
get("/get?test=123");
http:Response | error response = wait f3;
if (response is http:Response) {
    io:println(response.getJsonPayload());
} else {
    io:println(response.reason());
}
```

Workers

Workers in Ballerina allow developers to delegate their tasks to parallel running executions.

A function always has a single default worker, which is unnamed.

Let's look at the program shown in Listing 6-1.

Listing 6-1. main.bal

```
import ballerina/io;
public function main() {
    io:print("Hello");
}
```

When we run the previous program, it will execute in a single default unnamed worker.

The strand for the default worker is the same as a strand of the worker on which the function was called. When a function is called, the current worker becomes inactive, and a default worker for the called function is started. The program shown in Listing 6-2 initially starts with a strand of the default unnamed worker of the `main()` function, and in line 4, when we call `world()`, the default unnamed worker of `main()` becomes inactive and starts the unnamed worker of the `world()` function in the same strand.

Listing 6-2. main_with_fn.bal

```
01 import ballerina/io;
02 public function main() {
03     io:print("Hello");
04     world();
05     io:print("!\n");
06 }
07 function world (){
08     io:print(" World");
09 }
```

```
$ ballerina run main_with_fn.bal
Hello World!
```

When the default worker terminates, the function returns to its caller. Thus, only one worker in each strand is active at any given time. If the default worker terminates normally, then its termination value provides the return value of the function.

In the previous sample program, we are calling the `world()` function inside the main function, and since both `main()` and `world()` have only default unnamed workers, it will execute in a single stand.

The named worker in Ballerina allows developers to delegate their tasks to parallel running executions because each named worker runs on its own new strand.

The code shown in Listing 6-3 defines a main function with two workers in it. These workers will be executed concurrently when the function is invoked.

Listing 6-3. workers_iteration1.bal

```
import ballerina/io;

public function main() {
    //io:println("Worker execution started");

    worker w1 {
            // Calculate sum(n)
            int n = 10000000;
            int sum = 0;
            foreach var i in 1...n {
             sum += i;
            }
           io:println("w1: sum of first ", n, " positive numbers = ", sum);
    }

   worker w2 {
            // Calculate sum(n^2)
            int n = 10000000;
            int sum = 0;
            foreach var i in 1...n {
             sum += i * i;
            }
```

```
23          io:println("w2: sum of squares of first ", n,
24          " positive numbers = ", sum);
25      }
26
27      // _ = wait {w1, w2};
28
29      // io:println("Worker execution finished");
30  }
```

Let's run `workers_iteration1.bal`.

```
$ ballerina run workers_iteration1.bal
w1: sum of first 10000000 positive numbers = 50000005000000
w2: sum of squares of first 10000000 positive numbers = 1291990006563070912
```

Let's remove the comment from line 4 and line 29 and run the code.

```
$ ballerina run workers_iteration2.bal
Worker execution started
Worker execution finished
w1: sum of first 10000000 positive numbers = 50000005000000
w2: sum of squares of first 10000000 positive numbers = 1291990006563070912
```

Now you can see that line 4 and line 29 executed and printed before the two workers print the sum of `n` and the sum of `n` squares. This is because if explicit workers are not mentioned within worker blocks, the function code will belong to a single unnamed default worker.

If you want to wait for both workers to get printed sums before line 29 gets printed, you can uncomment line 27, (`_ = wait {w1, w2};`), which makes it wait before it executes.

```
$ ballerina run workers_iteration2.bal
Worker execution started
w1: sum of first 10000000 positive numbers = 50000005000000
w2: sum of squares of first 10000000 positive numbers = 1291990006563070912
Worker execution finished
```

Workers with Interaction

As discussed, workers help to do things concurrently. Sometimes these workers need to interact each other to complete a given task. In Ballerina, worker-to-worker interaction happens via message passing. This message passing happens over asynchronous communication channels. A worker is never in a block state until the message is delivered unless if you use a synchronous send (by using `()` `send`). `flush` also can be used to guarantee that all asynchronous messages sent to a given worker are successful. If both `send` and `flush` synchronous messaging failed, a worker will be returned with an error. On the other side, if a receiver is not received, it will be returned with a panic.

The message parsing between workers is done using worker send and receive instructions, which basically consist of the format `variable -> worker_name` and `worker_name <- variable`, respectively, as shown in Listing 6-4.

Listing 6-4. worker_interaction.bal

```
import ballerina/io;
import ballerina/runtime;

public function main() {
    worker w1 {
        int iw1 = 50;
        float kw1 = 7.67;
        [int, float] x1 = [iw1, kw1];
        x1 -> w2;
        io:println("[w1 -> w2] iw1: ", iw1, " kw1: ", kw1);

        json jw1 = {};
        jw1 = <- w2;
        string jStr = jw1.toString();
        io:println("[w1 <- w2] jw1: ", jStr);
        io:println("[w1 ->> w2] iw1: ", iw1);

        () send = iw1 ->> w2;

        io:println("[w1 ->> w2] successful!!");
```

```

        io:println("[w1 -> w3] kw1: ", kw1);
        kw1 -> w3;
        kw1 -> w3;
        kw1 -> w3;

        io:println("Waiting for worker w3 to fetch messages..");

        error? flushResult = flush w3;
        io:println("[w1 -> w3] Flushed!!");
    }

    worker w2 {
        int iw2;
        float kw2;
        [int, float] vW1 = [0, 1.0];
        vW1 = <- w1;
        [iw2, kw2] = vW1;
        io:println("[w2 <- w1] iw2: ", iw2 , " kw: ", kw2);

        json jw2 = { "greet": "Hello World" };
        io:println("[w2 -> w1] jw2: ", jw2);
        jw2 -> w1;

        int lw2;
        runtime:sleep(5);
        lw2 = <- w1;
        io:println("[w2 <- w1] lw2: ", lw2);
    }

    worker w3 {
        float mw;

        runtime:sleep(50);
        mw = <- w1;
```

```
56         mw = <- w1;
57         mw = <- w1;
58         io:println("[w3 <- w1] mw: ", mw);
59     }
60
61     wait w1;
62 }
```

Let's run worker-interaction.bal, as shown here:

```
$ ballerina run worker_interaction.bal
[w2 <- w1] iw2: 50 kw: 7.67
[w1 -> w2] iw1: 50 kw1: 7.67
[w2 -> w1] jw2: greet=Hello World
[w1 <- w2] j: greet=Hello World
[w1 ->> w2] iw1: 50
[w2 <- w1] lw2: 50
[w1 ->> w2] successful!!
[w1 -> w3] kw1: 7.67
Waiting for worker w3 to fetch messages..
[w3 <- w1] mw: 7.67
[w1 -> w3] Flushed!!
```

Line 9 sends messages asynchronously to worker `w2`. This message contains a tuple value with member types of `int` and `float`. In line 39, worker `w2` receives a message from worker `w1`. Our program output prints the corresponding values.

On line 43, `w2` sends a JSON message asynchronously to worker `w1`, and on line 13, `w1` receives the `w2` JSON value. The program output on lines 3 and 4 prints this message passing.

On line 18, `w1` sends messages synchronously to worker `w2`. Worker `w1` will wait until worker `w2` receives the message. A synchronous send returns `nil` if the message was successfully sent or returns an error or panics based on the receiving worker's state. On line 47, `w2` receives the message sent synchronously from worker `w1`.

On lines 23, 24, and 25, `w1` sends messages asynchronously to worker `w3`, and on lines 55, 56, and 57, `w3` receives `w1` messages. Line 29 flushes all messages sent asynchronously to worker `w3`. The worker will halt here until all messages are sent or until worker `w3` fails.

Ballerina's underlying language semantics were designed by modeling how independent parties communicate via structured interactions. Subsequently, every Ballerina program can be displayed as a sequence diagram of its flow with endpoints, including synchronous and asynchronous calls. To view the sequence diagram of a Ballerina file, click the diagram icon in the top-right corner of your VS Code editor.

Figure 6-5 shows the generated sequence diagram from our program.

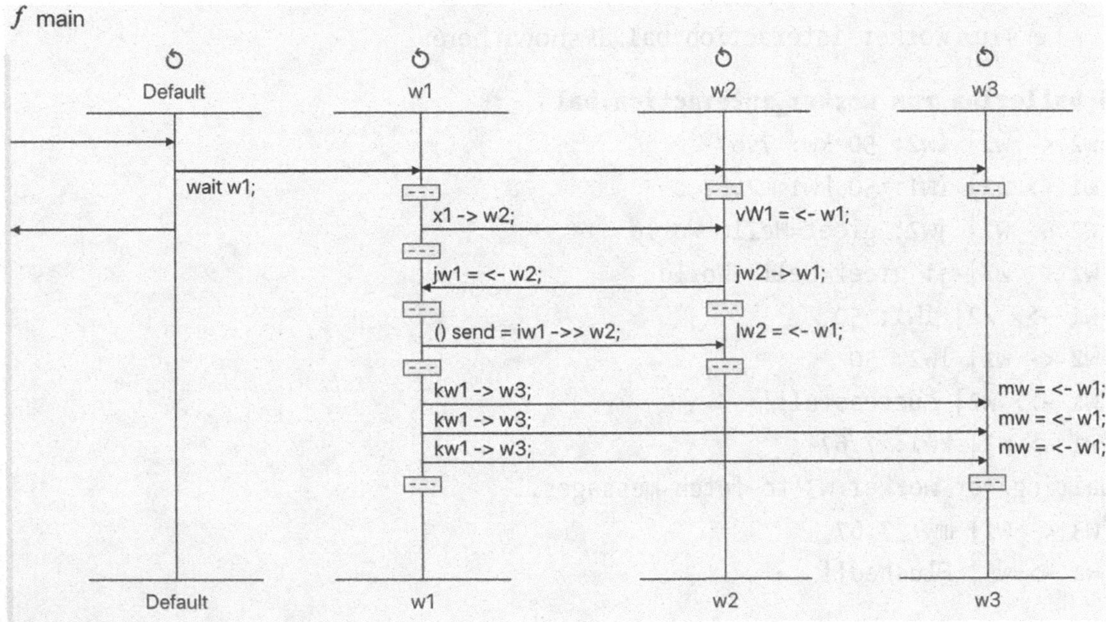

***Figure 6-5.** Sequence diagram of worker interaction*

The message parsing between workers is done in a way that every "worker send" should contain a corresponding "worker receive" in the receiving worker in the same order. This is to make sure that there is always a matching send/receive pair and to avoid the possibility of deadlocks.

Fork Statement

In the previous section, you learned about workers. Workers are allowed to be defined only at the root level of a function. For example, you can't define a worker inside an `if/then` block. But sometimes you might need to use these workers at a different level like other statements. The `fork` statement is allowed to use workers in such situations.

These workers will be visible as futures outside of a `fork` block. By default, these workers will work asynchronously, and you can use `wait` for these workers to return. You can only send `anydata` variables from one fork worker to another worker. `anydata` is a special type of all pure values other than errors.

Note that `anydata` allows structures whose members are errors. Thus, the type `anydata|error` is the supertype of all pure types. The type `anydata` is equivalent to the union of `() | boolean | int | float | decimal | string | (anydata|error)[] | map<anydata|error> | xml | table`.

Listing 6-5 shows an example.

Listing 6-5. fork.bal

```
import ballerina/io;

public function main() {

    fork {
        worker w1 returns [int, string] {
            int i = 23;
            string s = "Colombo";
            io:println("[w1] i: ", i, " s: ", s);
            // Return of worker `w1`.
            return [i, s];
        }

        worker w2 returns float {
            float f = 10.344;
            io:println("[w2] f: ", f);
            // Return of worker `w2`.
            return f;
        }
    }

    record{ [int, string] w1; float w2; } results = wait {w1, w2};

    var [iW1, sW1] = results.w1;
```

```
25    var fW2 = results.w2;
26    io:println("[main] iW1: ", iW1, " sW1: ", sW1, " fW2: ", fW2);
27 }
```

```
$ ballerina run fork.bal
[w1] i: 23 s: Colombo
[w2] f: 10.344
[main] iW1: 23 sW1: Colombo fW2: 10.344
```

On line 5, the `fork` block allows you to spawn (*fork*) multiple workers within any execution flow of a Ballerina program. On line 22, workers are visible outside the `fork` block as futures. The `wait-action` will wait for both workers `w1` and `w2` to finish. In this case, `wait-action` waits for multiple futures (`w1`, `w2`), returning the result as a record.

```
multiple-wait-action := wait { wait-field (, wait-field)* }
wait-field :=
  variable-name
  | field-name : wait-future-expr
```

A `multiple-wait-action` is evaluated by evaluating each `wait-future-expr` resulting in a value of type `future` for each `wait-field`. The `multiple-wait-action` then performs a wait operation on all of these futures. If all the wait operations complete normally, then it constructs a record with a field for each `wait-field`, whose name is the `field-name` and whose value is the result of the wait operation. If any of the wait operations complete abruptly, then the `multiple-wait-action` completes abruptly.

When `wait-action` waits for a single future, resulting in a value of basic type future. Here's an example:

```
single-wait-action := wait wait-future-expr
```

Sometimes `wait-action` can be used with a set of future values. Here's an example:

```
alternate-wait-action := wait wait-future-expr (| wait-future-expr)+
```

The `alternate-wait-action` then performs a wait operation on all of the members of this set. As soon as one of the wait operations completes normally with a nonerror value `v`, the `alternate-wait-action` completes normally with the result `v`. If all the wait operations complete normally with an error, then it completes normally with the result e, where e is the result of the last wait operation to complete. If any of the wait operations complete abruptly before the `alternate-wait-action` completes, then the `alternate-wait-action` completes abruptly.

Fork Variable Access

In general, we have two types of variables, namely, value type variables and reference type variables. As an example, `string`, `int`, `float`, and `byte` are value type variables, and `map`, `json`, `xml`, and `record` are reference type variables. But when you are using `fork`, all variables are passed into the workers as a reference to the original data. Therefore, if you update the value of these variables within a worker, the value gets updated for the entire function. Let's look at an example in Listing 6-6.

Listing 6-6. fork_variable.bal

```
import ballerina/io;

public function main() {
    int i = 100;
    string s = "WSO2";
   map<string> m = { "name": "Bert", "city": "New York", "postcode": "10001"};

    string name = <string> m["name"];
    string city = <string> m["city"];
    string postcode = <string> m["postcode"];

    io:println("[value type variables] before fork: " +
                    "value of integer variable is [", i, "] ",
                    "value of string variable is [", s, "]");

    io:println("[reference type variables] before fork: value " +
      "of name is [", name , "] value of city is [", city, "] value of " +
      "postcode is [", postcode, "]");
```

```

    fork {
        worker W1 {
            i = 23;
            m["name"] = "Moose";

            fork {
                worker W3 {
                    string street = "Wall Street";
                    m["street"] = street;

                    i = i + 100;
                }
            }

            wait W3;
        }

        worker W2 {
            s = "Ballerina";
            m["city"] = "Manhattan";
        }
    }

    _ = wait {W1, W2};

    io:println("[value type variables] after fork: " +
               "value of integer variable is [", i, "] ",
               "value of string variable is [", s, "]");

    name = <string> m["name"];
    city = <string> m["city"];
    string street = <string> m["street"];
    io:println("[reference type variables] after fork: " +
               "value of name is [", name,
```

```
54                  "] value of city is [", city, "] value of street is
                     [", street,
55                  "] value of postcode is [", postcode, "]");
56 }
```

```
$ ballerina run fork_variable.bal
>[value type variables] before fork: value of integer variable is [100]
value of string variable is [WSO2]
>[reference type variables] before fork: value of name is [Bert] value of
city is [New York] value of postcode is [10001]
>[value type variables] after fork: value of integer variable is [123]
value of string variable is [Ballerina]
>[reference type variables] after fork: value of name is [Moose] value of
city is [Manhattan] value of street is [Wall Street] value of postcode is
[10001]
```

The in-scope variables can be accessed by the workers inside the `fork` block. For example, variable `i` defined in line 4 can be accessed by the forked workers. Lines 22 and 23 change the value of the integer variable `i` and change the value of the `map` variable `m` within worker `W1`. Now, here's an example:

```
i = 23
M["name"] = "Moose"
```

In the `fork` block and in `W3`, change the value of the `map` variable `m` and change the value of the integer variable `i`. Here's an example:

```
i = 123
    m["name"] = "Moose"
    m["street"] = "Wall Street"
```

Note that line 34 waits for worker `W3` to finish. Then lines 38 and 39 within the `W2` block change the value of the `string` variable `s` and change the value of the `map` variable `m`.

Here's an example:

```
i = 123
m["name"] = "Moose"
m["street"] = "Wall Street"
m["city"] = "Manhattan"
s = "Ballerina"
```

Note that line 43 waits for both workers `W1` and `W2` to finish. If you looked at the final output of our program, the value type variables have changed since the original variables are passed on to the workers. Also, the internal content of the reference type variables has been updated since they are passed in as a reference to the workers.

Summary

In this chapter, we discussed the concepts of concurrency, parallelism, threads, and processes. Then we learned how to write effective concurrent programs by using Ballerina.

Next, we will look at how we can perform I/O operations by using Ballerina.

CHAPTER 7

Files and I/O

Computers are useless if they don't have input/output (I/O) capabilities. Almost all the work done by a computer requires some input, performs some processing, and returns some output. I/O capabilities are computing facilities to provide user input/output, data storage and retrieval, and network access capabilities in the computer system. To generalize, there are four types of I/O devices.

- Input devices such as keyboards and mice
- Output devices such as screens and printers
- Both input and output devices such as networks and touchscreens
- Storage such as disks

All the I/O operations of programs are not directly performed with these devices; rather, the devices require I/O services from the operating system. Therefore, I/O instructions are privileged and can be initiated only by the operating system.

There are two ways to handle I/O operations.

- Programmed I/O
- Direct memory access

Programmed I/O

Programmed I/O consists of the data transfers initiated by a CPU. Normally I/O devices have their own special interface that is used to connect with the CPU. We call them *driver software* (I/O module), and it controls access to the registers or memory on a device.

A. Fernando and L. Warusawithana, *Beginning Ballerina Programming*,
https://doi.org/10.1007/978-1-4842-5139-3_7

Programmed I/O requires the CPU to constantly monitor the I/O devices. First, the CPU issues a command and then waits for I/O operations to be complete. Since the CPU is much faster than the I/O operation, the CPU has to wait a long time for the I/O operation to be ready to transmit data. While the CPU is just waiting, it needs to repeatedly check the status of the I/O module. As a result, the performance of the entire system is severely degraded.

On some systems, after the CPU issues commands to the I/O module, without waiting to get the result, the CPU proceeds with its normal work until interrupted by the I/O device on completion of its work. We call this *interrupt-initiated I/O*.

Direct Memory Access

In direct memory access (DMA), data is transferred between the I/O device and the memory without any CPU involvement. Direct memory access needs special hardware called a *DMA controller* (DMAC) that manages the data transfers. It is important to avoid conflicts between the CPU and the I/O module writing to memory. DMA is well-suited for high-speed data transfers (e.g., disk transfers, video I/O devices, etc.).

Ballerina I/O Module

File reading and input/output are the most common operations performed in any programming language. In this chapter, we will see how to use the `ballerina/io` module to handle files and I/O operations (see Figure 7-1).

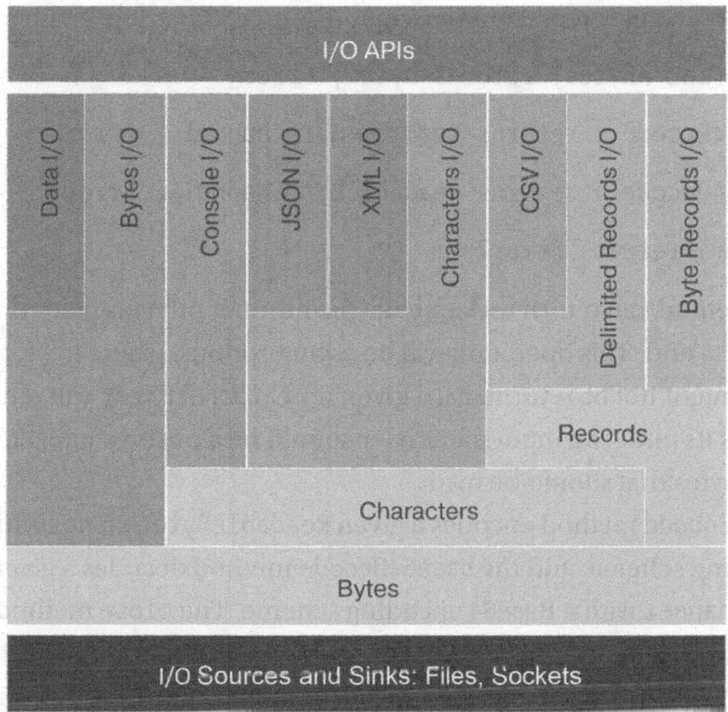

***Figure 7-1.** Ballerina I/O module*

The Ballerina I/O module is designed to support input and output operations via channels in a canonical way, either in a blocking or nonblocking manner. Let's try to understand a few primitives.

Channels

A channel represents an I/O source or sink of some bytes, characters, or records that are opened for reading or writing, respectively. There are a few channel types in Ballerina, namely, byte channels, character channels, record channels, and data channels.

Byte Channels

The most primitive channel is the `ByteChannel`, which reads and writes 8-bit bytes. The Ballerina I/O module has two main `ByteChannels`.

ReadableByteChannel represents an input resource. It has four main methods.

- read (int nBytes) returns byte | Error
- base64Encode() returns ReadableByteChannel | Error
- base64Decode() returns ReadableByteChannel | Error
- close() returns Error?

The read method can return the content (the number of bytes read) or an error if the file reaches its end. This operation will be asynchronous, where the total number of required bytes might not be returned at a given time. io:EofError will return once the channel reaches its end. The input parameter should be a positive integer. It represents the number of bytes that should be read.

The base64Encode method encodes a given ReadableByteChannel with a Base64 encoding scheme, and the base64Decode method decodes a given ReadableByteChannel with a Base64 encoding scheme. The close method closes a given ReadableByteChannel.

WritableByteChannel represents an output resource, and it has two main methods.

- write (byte content, int offset) returns int | Error
- close() returns Error?

The write method writes bytes to a given output resource. This operation will be asynchronous; write might return without writing all the content. It has two parameters: content (the block of bytes that should be written) and offset (which is the offset to start).

Let's write some sample code to do a file copy by using ReadableByteChannel and WritableByteChannel. See Listing 7-1.

Listing 7-1. file-copy-byte.bal

```
import ballerina/io;
import ballerina/log;

function copy(io:ReadableByteChannel src,
                   io:WritableByteChannel dst) returns error? {

    while (true) {
```

```
        byte[]|io:Error readByte = src.read(1000);
        if (readByte is io:EofError) {
            break;
        } else if (readByte is error) {
            return <@untained> readByte;
        } else {

            int writePointer = 0;
            while (writePointer < readByte.length()) {
                var writeByteCount = dst.write(readByte, writePointer);
                if (writeByteCount is error) {
                    return writeByteCount;
                } else {
                    writePointer = writePointer + writeByteCount;
                }
            }
        }
    }
    return;
}

function close(io:ReadableByteChannel|io:WritableByteChannel ch) {
    abstract object {
        public function close() returns error?;
    } channelResult = ch;
    var cr = channelResult.close();
    if (cr is error) {
        log:printError("Error occurred while closing the channel: ", err = cr);
    }
}

public function main() returns error? {
    string srcPath = "./photo.jpg";
    string dstPath = "./photoCopy.jpg";
```

```
42      io:ReadableByteChannel srcCh = check io:openReadableFile(srcPath);
43      io:WritableByteChannel dstCh = check io:openWritableFile(dstPath);
44      io:println("Start to copy files from " + srcPath + " to " +
        dstPath);
45      var result = copy(srcCh, dstCh);
46      if (result is error) {
47          log:printError("error occurred while performing copy ",
            err = result);
48      } else {
49          io:println("File copy completed. The copied file is located at " +
50                         dstPath);
51      }
52      close(srcCh);
53      close(dstCh);
54 }
```

```
$ ballerina run file-copy-byte.bal
Start to copy files from ./photo.jpg to ./photoCopy.jpg
File copy completed. The copied file is located at ./photoCopy.jpg
```

Line 4 defines a function to copy content from the source channel to a destination channel. On line 7, the `while` loop reads all the content from the source and copies it to the destination. On line 8, the operation attempts to read a maximum of 1,000 bytes and returns with the available content, which could be < 1000.

I/O requires you to deal with channels and file descriptors, which need to be closed properly, to avoid unnecessary open socket connections and file handers. Line 29 defines a function to close a given readable or writable byte channel.

Using a byte channel is the lowest level of I/O, so if you are reading or writing character data, the best approach is to use a character channel. Other channel types are built on top of the byte channel.

Character Channels

The `CharacterChannel` is used to read and write characters. A charset encoding is specified when creating the `CharacterChannel`. The Ballerina I/O module has two main `CharacterChannels`.

ReadableCharacterChannel represents a channel that can be used to read characters. It has four main methods and a constructor.

- Constructor __init(ReadableByteChannel byteChannel, string charset)
- read (int numberOfChars) returns string | Error
- readJson() returns json | Error
- readXml() returns xml | Error
- close() returns Error?

The constructor has two parameters: ReadableByteChannel and the character set, which would be used to encode/decode given bytes to/from characters.

The read methods will attempt read up to numberOfChars (an input parameter; the number of characters that should be read) characters from the channel and return content that is read. io:EofError will return once the channel reaches its end and will return an error if any other error occurred. The readJson method reads the JSON from the given channel's return JSON string or returns an error if any error occurred. The readXml method reads XML from the given channel and returns XML or an error if any error occurred. The close method closes a given character channel or returns an error if any error occurred.

WritableCharacterChannel represents a channel that can be used to write characters. It has four main methods and a constructor.

- Constructor __init(WritableByteChannel bChannel, string charset)
- write (string content, int startOffset) returns int | Error
- writeJson (json content) returns Error?
- writeXml (xml content) returns Error?
- close() returns Error?

The constructor has two parameters, bChannel as WritableByteChannel and charset as a string, which would be used to encode given bytes to characters. The write method writes a given sequence of characters taking two input parameters: the input content that should be written, and startOffset, which is the number of characters that should be offset when writing content. The writeJson method writes a json taking content as a json parameter and return an error if an error occurred while writing. The writeXml method writes a given XML taking content as a XML parameter and return error if an error occurred while writing. The close method closes a given WritableCharacterChannel channel or returns an error if any error occurred.

Listing 7-2 shows a sample program that reads content from a text file, appends the additional string, and writes the content. We are going to use the following text file and add “my name is” in between the greeting and the name and write to sampleResponse.txt:

sample.txt --

```
Hello Ballerina!
```

Listing 7-2. file-copy-character.bal

```
import ballerina/io;
import ballerina/log;

function process(io:ReadableCharacterChannel src,
                 io:WritableCharacterChannel dst) returns error? {
    string intermediateCharacterString = " my name is ";
    string greetingText = check src.read(5);
    string name = check src.read(15);
    var writeCharResult = check dst.write(greetingText, 0);
    var writeCharResult1 = check dst.write(intermediateCharacterString, 0);
    var writeCharResult2 = check dst.write(name, 1);
    return;
}

function closeRc(io:ReadableCharacterChannel ch) {
    var closer = ch.close();
    if (closer is error) {
        log:printError("Error occurred while closing the channel: ", err = closer);
```

```
    }
}

function closeWc(io:WritableCharacterChannel ch) {
    var closer = ch.close();
    if (closer is error) {
        log:printError("Error occurred while closing the channel: ", err
        = closer);
    }
}

public function main() returns error? {
    io:ReadableByteChannel readableFieldResult =
            check io:openReadableFile("./sample.txt");
    io:ReadableCharacterChannel sourceChannel = new(readableFieldResult,
    "UTF-8");
    io:WritableByteChannel writableFileResult =
            check io:openWritableFile("./sampleResponse.txt");
    io:WritableCharacterChannel destinationChannel =
            new(writableFileResult, "UTF-8");
    io:println("Started to process the file.");
    var result = process(sourceChannel, destinationChannel);
    if (result is error) {
        log:printError("error occurred while processing charactors ",
        err = result);
    } else {
        io:println("File processing completed");
    }
    closeRc(sourceChannel);
    closeWc(destinationChannel);
}
```

```
$ ballerina run file-copy-character.bal
Started to process the file.
File processing complete.
```

Line 7 reads characters from the source channel, and line 9 writes characters to the destination channel. The function `closeRc` closes the readable character channel, and the function `closeWc` closes the writable character channel.

Let's see how we can handle JSON I/O. JSON I/O is implemented at the top of the character channel.

JSON I/O

Listing 7-3 demonstrates how to read JSON content from a file and how to write JSON content to a file using the character channel `readJson()` and `writeJson()` of the I/O API.

Listing 7-3. json-io.bal

```
import ballerina/io;
import ballerina/log;

function closeRc(io:ReadableCharacterChannel rc) {
    var result = rc.close();
    if (result is error) {
        log:printError("Error occurred while closing character stream",
                        err = result);
    }
}

function closeWc(io:WritableCharacterChannel wc) {
    var result = wc.close();
    if (result is error) {
        log:printError("Error occurred while closing character stream",
                        err = result);
    }
}

function write(json content, string path) returns @tainted error? {
    io:WritableByteChannel wbc = check io:openWritableFile(path);
    io:WritableCharacterChannel wch = new(wbc, "UTF8");
    var result = wch.writeJson(content);
    closeWc(wch);
```

```
    return result;
}

function read(string path) returns @tainted json|error {
    io:ReadableByteChannel rbc = check io:openReadableFile(path);
    io:ReadableCharacterChannel rch = new(rbc, "UTF8");
    var result = rch.readJson();
    closeRc(rch);
    return result;
}

public function main() {
    string filePath = "./sample.json";
    json j1 = { "Store": {
        "@id": "AST",
        "name": "Anne",
        "address": {
            "street": "Main",
            "city": "94"
        },
        "codes": ["4", "8"]
    }
    };
    io:println("Preparing to write json file");
    var wResult = write(j1, filePath);
    if (wResult is error) {
        log:printError("Error occurred while writing json: ", err =
            wResult);
    } else {
        io:println("Preparing to read the content written");
        var rResult = read(filePath);
        if (rResult is error) {
            log:printError("Error occurred while reading json: ",
                                err = rResult);
        } else {
```

```
59              io:println(rResult);
60          }
61      }
62 }
```

```
$ ballerina run json-io.bal
Preparing to write json file
Preparing to read the content written
{"Store":{"@id":"AST", "name":"Anne", "address":{"street":"Main",
"city":"94"}, "codes":["4", "8"]}}
```

First, we define two functions to close the readable channel and the writable channel, respectively, in lines 4 and 12.

In line 20, we define the JSON write function to write the provided `json` to the specified path. In that function, first we create a writable byte channel from the given path in line 21, and then in line 22, we derive the character channel from the byte channel.

Line 28 reads a `json` value from the specified path. Line 29 creates a readable byte channel from the given path, and line 30 derives the character channel from the byte channel.

For both the `write` and `read` function signatures, we use the `@tainted` annotation to tag these return values as tainted because these variables populate values from outside files. If we use path variable in another expression without marking them explicitly as untainted (or clean), that second variable is now also marked as suspicious. This kind of analysis is important to prevent SQL injection (such as direct commands into an SQL database or the host computer operating system), path manipulation, file manipulation, unauthorized file access, and unvalidated redirect (open redirect). Since a taint check is done at the compiler stage, the programmer can then redesign the program to erect a safe wall around the dangerous input.

You can find out more details about using the `tainted` and `untainted` operations in Chapter 9.

On lines 38 to 46, we have defined the sample JSON inline. On line 49 we write some sample JSON to the file and then handle any errors if they occur. On line 54, we read the JSON file we have written and print to console.

In the same way, we can write a program to handle XML content from a file by using the character channel of the I/O API. We will leave that to you to try as an exercise.

Record Channels

The Ballerina record channel is derived on top of the character channel, which is derived on top of the byte channel. The Ballerina record channel supports I/O for delimited records. The Ballerina I/O module has two main `RecordChannels`.

`ReadableTextRecordChannel` represents a channel that will allow it to read. It has three main methods and a constructor.

- `Constructor __init (ReadableCharacterChannel charChannel, string fs, string rs, string fmt)`
- `hasNext() returns boolean`
- `getNext() returns string | Error`
- `close() returns Error?`

The constructor has four parameters. `charChannel` is a `ReadableCharacterChannel` that will point to the input/output resource, the `fs` string is a field separator (this could be a regex), the `rs` string is record separator (this could be a regex), and the `fmt` string.

The `hasNext` method checks whether there's a record left to be read and returns true if so. The `getNext` method gets the next record from the input/output resource and returns a string set of fields included in the record or returns an error if any error occurred. The `close` method closes a given record channel and returns an error if the record channel could not be closed properly.

`WritableTextRecordChannel` represents a channel that will allow us to write records through a given `WritableCharacterChannel`. It has two main methods and a constructor.

- `Constructor __init (WritableCharacterChannel characterChannel, string fs, string rs, string fmt)`
- `write (string textRecord) returns Error?`
- `close() returns Error?`

The constructor has four parameters. `characterChannel` is `WritableCharacterChannel`, which will point to the input/output resource; the `fs` string is a field separator (this could be a regex); the `rs` string is record separator (this could be a regex); and the `fmt` string is XXX.

The `write` method writes records to a given output resource. The `textRecord` parameter is a list of fields to be written and returns an error if the records cannot be written properly. The `close` method closes a given record channel and returns an error if the record channel cannot be closed properly.

Let's find out some details by using the sample program shown in Listing 7-4.

Listing 7-4. record-io.bal

```
import ballerina/io;
import ballerina/log;

function getReadableRecordChannel(string filePath, string encoding, string rs,
                    string fs) returns @tainted (io:ReadableTextRecordChannel)|error {
    io:ReadableByteChannel byteChannel = check io:openReadableFile(filePath);
    io:ReadableCharacterChannel characterChannel = new(byteChannel, encoding);
    io:ReadableTextRecordChannel delimitedRecordChannel = new(characterChannel,
                                     rs = rs,
                                     fs = fs);
    return delimitedRecordChannel;
}

function getWritableRecordChannel(string filePath, string encoding, string rs,
                    string fs) returns @tainted (io:WritableTextRecordChannel)|error {
    io:WritableByteChannel byteChannel = check io:openWritableFile(filePath);
    io:WritableCharacterChannel characterChannel = new(byteChannel, encoding);
    io:WritableTextRecordChannel delimitedRecordChannel = new(characterChannel,
```

```
                                      rs = rs,
                                      fs = fs);
    return delimitedRecordChannel;
}

function process(io:ReadableTextRecordChannel srcRecordChannel,
                 io:WritableTextRecordChannel dstRecordChannel) returns error? {
    while (srcRecordChannel.hasNext()) {
        string[] records = check srcRecordChannel.getNext();
        var result = check dstRecordChannel.write(records);
    }
    return;
}

function closeRc(io:ReadableTextRecordChannel rc) {
    var closeResult = rc.close();
    if (closeResult is error) {
        log:printError("Error occurred while closing the channel: ",
                err = closeResult);
    }
}

function closeWc(io:WritableTextRecordChannel wc) {
    var closeResult = wc.close();
    if (closeResult is error) {
        log:printError("Error occurred while closing the channel: ",
                err = closeResult);
    }
}

public function main() returns error? {
    string srcFileName = "./sample.csv";
    string dstFileName = "./sampleResponse.txt";
    io:ReadableTextRecordChannel srcRecordChannel =
```

```
55      check getReadableRecordChannel(srcFileName, "UTF-8", "\\r?\\n",
        ",");
56      io:WritableTextRecordChannel dstRecordChannel =
57      check getWritableRecordChannel(dstFileName, "UTF-8", "\r\n", "|");
58      io:println("Start processing the CSV file from " + srcFileName +
59                 " to the text file in " + dstFileName);
60      var result = process(srcRecordChannel, dstRecordChannel);
61      if (result is error) {
62          log:printError("An error occurred while processing the records: ",
63                      err = result);
64      } else {
65          io:println("Processing completed. The processed file is located
            in ",
66                          dstFileName);
67      }
68      closeRc(srcRecordChannel);
69      closeWc(dstRecordChannel);
70 }
```

On line 4, the `getReadableRecordChannel` function returns a `ReadableTextRecordChannel` from a given file location. The encoding is a character representation (i.e., UTF-8 ASCCI) of the content in the file. The `rs` parameter defines a record separator (e.g., a new line), and the `fs` parameter is a field separator (e.g., a comma). On line 8, we create a readable character channel from the readable byte channel to read content as text. On line 9, we convert the readable character channel to a readable record channel to read the content as records.

On lines 15 to 24, the `getWritableRecordChannel` function returns a `WritableTextRecordChannel` from a given file location.

On line 26, the function processes the `.cxv` file and writes content back as text with the | delimiter. On line 28, we read all the records from the provided file until there are no more records.

We have defined `closeRc` and `closeWc` to close the readable text record channel and close the writable channel, respectively.

The main function, on line 54, passes the record separator of the `.csv` file as a new line and passes the field separator as a comma (,). Line 56 passes the record separator of the text file as a new line and the field separator as a pipe (|).

When you run this program, you can see the following output:

```
$ cat sample.csv
MATH,Mathematics,Mathematic,CAS,Department
MUS,Music,Music,CAS,Department
PHY,Physics,Physics,CAS,Department
PSY,Psychology,Psychology,CAS,Department
$ ballerina run record-io.bal
Start processing the CSV file from ./sample.csv to the text file in ./
sampleResponse.txt
Processing completed. The processed file is located in ./sampleResponse.txt
$ cat sampleResponse.txt
MATH|Mathematics|Mathematic|CAS|Department
MUS|Music|Music|CAS|Department
PHY|Physics|Physics|CAS|Department
PSY|Psychology|Psychology|CAS|Department
CHEM|Chemistry|Chemistry|CAS|Department
```

File and File Path Modules

The Ballerina `File` module offers a rich set of functionality for reading, writing, and manipulating files and directories. The `File` module ships with the Ballerina standard library, and you can import the file module by using `import ballerina/file`.

The file path provides the utility functions for manipulating the file path in a way that is compatible with the target operating system. You can import the file path module by using `import ballerina/filepath`.

The following sample shows the functionalities of the file and file path modules:

```
import ballerina/file;
import ballerina/filepath;
import ballerina/io;

public function main() {

    io:println("Current directory: " + file:getCurrentDirectory());

```

```
    string|error createDirResults = file:createDir("foo");
    if (createDirResults is string) {
        io:println("Created directory path: " + createDirResults);
    }

    string|error createFileResults = file:createFile("test.txt");
    if (createFileResults is string) {
        io:println("Created file path: " + createFileResults);
    }

    file:FileInfo|error fileInfoResults = file:getFileInfo("test.txt");
    if (fileInfoResults is file:FileInfo) {
        io:println("File name: " + fileInfoResults.getName());
        io:println("File size: " + fileInfoResults.getSize().
        toString());
        io:println("Is directory: " + fileInfoResults.isDir().
        toString());
        io:println("Modified at " +
                        fileInfoResults.getLastModifiedTime().
                        toString());
    }

    boolean fileExists = file:exists("test.txt");
    io:println("test.txt file exists: " + fileExists.toString());

    string filePath = checkpanic filepath:build("foo", "bar", "test.
    txt");
    error? copyDirResults = file:copy("test.txt", filePath, true);
    if (copyDirResults is()) {
        io:println("test.txt file is copied to new path " + filePath);
    }

    string newFilePath = checkpanic filepath:build("foo", "test.txt");
    error? renameResults = file:rename("test.txt", newFilePath);
    if (renameResults is()) {
```

```
        io:println("test.txt file is moved to new path " + newFilePath);
    }

    string tempDirPath = file:tempDir();
    io:println("Temporary directory: " + tempDirPath);

    file:FileInfo[]|error readDirResults = file:readDir("foo");

    error? removeResults = file:remove(newFilePath);

    if (removeResults is()) {
        io:println("Remove file at " + newFilePath);
    }

    removeResults = file:remove("foo", true);
    if (removeResults is()) {
        io:println("Remove foo directory with all child elements.");
    }
}
```

```
$ ballerina run file.bal
Compiling source
    file.bal

Generating executables
Running executables

Current directory: /Users/lakmal/ballerina-book/chapter-7
Created file path: /Users/lakmal/ballerina-book/chapter-7/test.txt
File name: test.txt
File size: 0
Is directory: false
Modified at time=1571870431000 zone=id=Z offset=0
test.txt file exists: true
test.txt file is moved to new path foo/test.txt
```

```
Temporary directory: /var/folders/rm/j_mxzqmx5kvfv7g210vjnzkr0000gn/T/
Remove file at foo/test.txt
Remove foo directory with all child elements.
```

Summary

In this chapter, we studied how to handle file reading and input/output operations by using the `ballerina/io`, `ballerina/file`, and `ballerina/filepath` modules. Next, we will study the basics of computer networks, distributed programming concepts, and distributed architectures. We will also learn how to write distributed applications by using Ballerina.

CHAPTER 8

Programming the Network

In previous chapters, we learned how to write programs by using different language constructs. Those programs run on one machine. But modern applications interact with many other external systems. These systems can be databases, SaaS applications, APIs, or other dependent programs that are running in different processes or sometimes on different machines. Therefore, we need to write programs to interact with external systems, and these interactions mainly happen over the computer network.

In the first part of this chapter, we will focus on understanding a few basic terms and technologies of computer networking, and then we will focus on writing applications with network interactions. We can think of these applications as network-distributed applications.

The Basics of Computer Networks

A computer network is used to connect multiple devices in order to send and receive data. Computer networks have evolved rapidly over the past two decades, and in today's world, almost all electronic devices are connected to one or more other devices.

Distributed applications communicate each other components in a certain way to complete a common task. This communication is going through a stack of protocol layers. The communication between these layers is defined by the protocol.

ISO OSI Protocol

The Open System Interconnection (OSI) model defines a networking framework for implementing protocols in seven layers. This model has influenced the design of distributed applications and many practical implementations like TCP/IP, which was used to build the Internet.

A. Fernando and L. Warusawithana, *Beginning Ballerina Programming*,
https://doi.org/10.1007/978-1-4842-5139-3_8

OSI defines seven layers, each of which has unique functionality and bridges the communication from the software program to the hardware layer. The layers can transmit over different physical mediums such as wire or wireless. Figure 8-1 shows these seven layers.

For more information, see `https://en.wikipedia.org/wiki/OSI_model`.

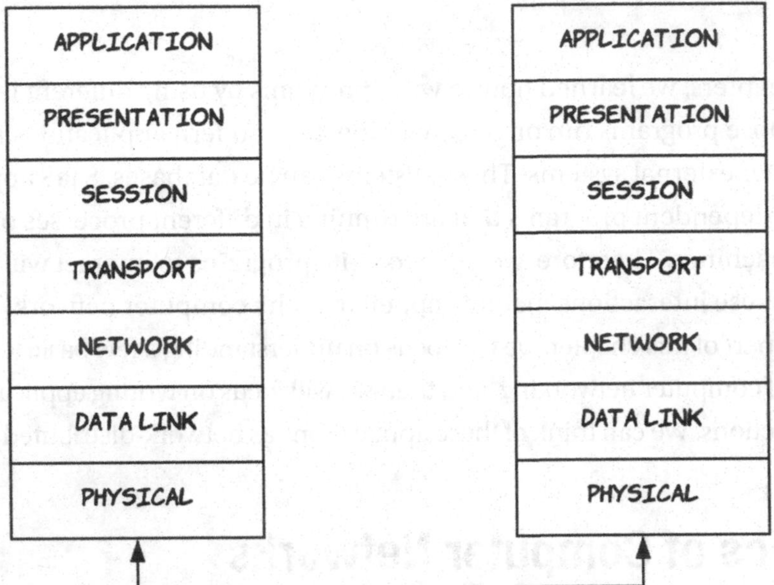

Figure 8-1. *OSI protocol stack*

Layer 1: Physical Layer

The Physical layer converts the digital bits into electrical, radio, or optical signals.

Layer 2: Data Link Layer

The Data Link layer defines the protocol to establish and terminate a connection between two physically connected devices.

Layer 3: Network Layer

The Network layer provides switching and routing technologies.

Layer 4: Transport Layer

The Transport layer provides end-to-end data transfer from a source to a destination host while maintaining the quality of service functions.

Layer 5: Session Layer

The Session layer establishes, manages, and terminates the connections between the local and remote applications.

Layer 6: Presentation Layer

This layer provides independence from data representation by translating between application and network formats.

Layer 7: Application Layer

This layer interacts with software applications that implement a communication component.

TCP/IP Protocol

The Defense Advanced Research Projects Agency (DARPA) came up with an implementation called the Internet protocol suite, and it is what the Internet was built on top of. It is commonly known as TCP/IP because the foundational protocols in the suite are the Transmission Control Protocol (TCP) and the Internet Protocol (IP). Figure 8-2 shows the TCP/IP model.

For more information, see `https://en.wikipedia.org/wiki/Internet_protocol_suite`.

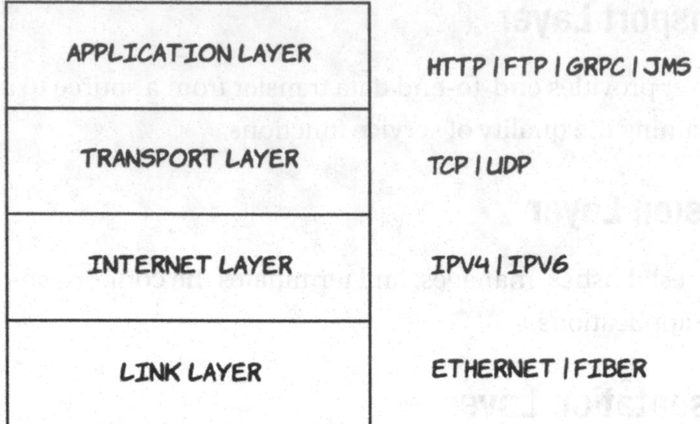

Figure 8-2. *TCP/IP protocol*

Link Layer

The Link layer defines the networking methods within the scope of the local network link on hosts communicating without intervening routers.

Internet Layer

The Internet layer is concerned with addressing and routing packets so that they can cross interconnecting networks to arrive at a remote location on a remote network.

Transport Layer

This layer provides a channel for the communication needs of applications. UDP is the basic transport layer protocol, providing an unreliable datagram service. TCP provides flow control, connection establishment, and reliable transmission of data.

Application Layer

The application layer set the scope within applications, or processes and create user data and communicate this data to other applications on another or the same host. This is the layer where all higher-level protocols are defined, such as HTTP, FTP, SSH, GRPC, etc.

Packet Encapsulation

Communication between layers in the stack takes place by sending packet data from one layer to the next layer. Every layer will add administrative information into the header of the packet that is received from the layer above as the packet is passed down. From the receiving side, the receiver will use the relevant header for administrative purpose and remove relevant header and pass the rest to the upper layer.

For example, the HTTP protocol has the packet encapsulation shown in Figure 8-3 to communicate over the network.

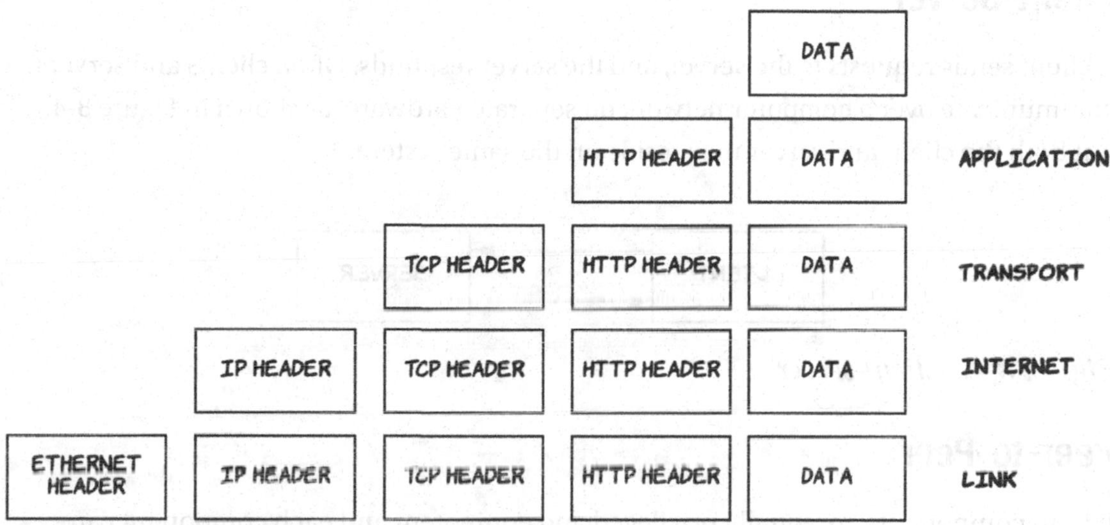

Figure 8-3. *HTTP protocol*

Connection Models

There are two main connection models, namely, connection-oriented and connectionless, used to communicate between two machines.

Connection-oriented is where a session is established before any useful data can be transferred and where a stream of data is delivered in the same order as it was sent. TCP is a connection-oriented protocol.

In a connectionless protocol, no session is created, and messages are sent independently of each other. UDP is a connectionless protocol.

Distributed Computing Architectures

There are four main architectures for distributed computing.

- Client-server
- Peer-to-peer
- Three-tier
- N-tier

Client-Server

A client sends requests to the server, and the server responds. Often clients and servers communicate over a computer network on separate hardware, as shown in Figure 8-4, but both the client and server may reside on the same system.

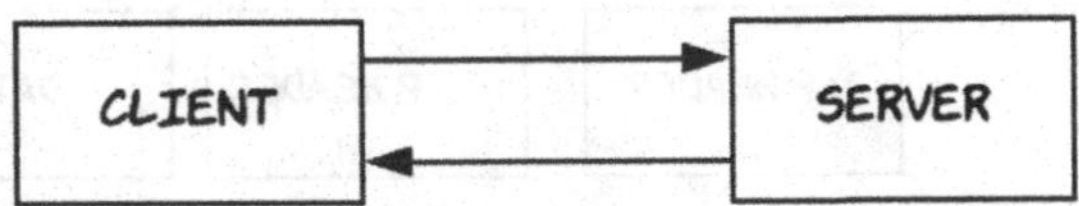

Figure 8-4. *Client-server*

Peer-to-Peer

If both components are equally privileged and equipotent and each component can initiate or respond to a message, then that system is called a *peer-to-peer* system (see Figure 8-5).

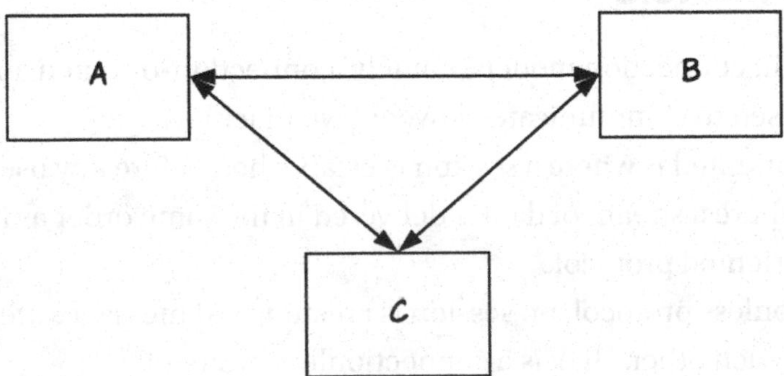

Figure 8-5. *Peer-to-peer*

Three-Tier

A three-tier architecture is a client-server model in which the user interface, business logic, data storage, and access are developed and maintained as independent components. Most web applications are three-tier. Figure 8-6 illustrates this three-tiered model.

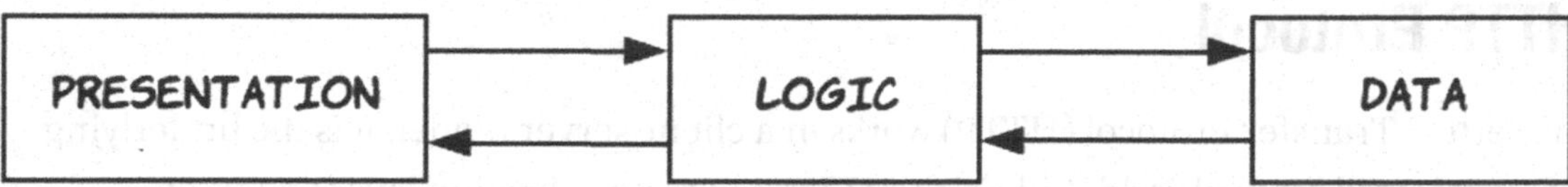

Figure 8-6. *Three-tier*

N-tier

The n-tier architecture provides a model by which developers can create flexible and reusable components. This disaggregation helps components to individually scale. Modern microservice architecture is a good example of the n-tier architectural pattern.

Communication Flows

In the previous section, we learned how distributed components communicate with each other under different architectural patterns. Now let's look at how data flow can be organized between these components.

Synchronous Communication

Synchronous communication can be defined as real-time communication between two people. One party will send a message and then block, waiting for a reply. For this type of communication, both the sender and the receiver need to be active at the same time.

Asynchronous Communication

In asynchronous communication, one party will send a message, and without waiting for a reply, they will carry out the rest of the work. When the reply eventually comes, it is handled.

Streaming Communication

In streaming communication, inputs arrive as continuous data stream messages. Video and audio data are normally sent as streams.

Publisher/Subscriber Communication

In a publisher/subscriber system, interested parties can subscribe to a topic while another party sends data to it. Twitter is a good example of a large-scale publisher/subscriber system.

HTTP Protocol

Hypertext Transfer Protocol (HTTP) works in a client-server model. It is the underlying protocol used by the World Wide Web. HTTP is in the application layer on top of TCP/IP (see Figure 8-2). It is a stateless protocol because each command is executed independently, without any knowledge of the commands that came before it.

Endpoint and Service

A network endpoint is an Internet-capable program on a TCP/IP network. In distributed programs, all the components that are accessible to communicate to other parties are endpoints. In a general network, an endpoint can be represented by a Uniform Resource Locator (URL).

As an example, the URL `http://www.example.org:8080/bar/foo.html#bar` contains the following information:

- The protocol used to access the resource (e.g., `http`)
- The location of the server (whether by IP address or domain name, e.g., `www.example.org`)
- The port number on the server (optional; e.g., `8080`)
- The location of the resource in the directory structure of the server (path; e.g., `/bar/foo.html`)
- A fragment identifier (optional; e.g., `#bar`)

The programs that handle the real business logic are called the *service*, and this service can be exposed to the rest of the world via an endpoint. These services can be implemented by using different protocols such as HTTP, WebSockets, gRPC, and so on.

So far, we have focused on HTTP and gRPC protocol-based sample service implementations and interactions.

Writing Network-Distributed Programs

In the previous section, we learned about some important distributed computing concepts. Now let's look at how we can write network-distributed programs by using Ballerina. Figure 8-7 illustrates how a Ballerina abstraction interacts with the network.

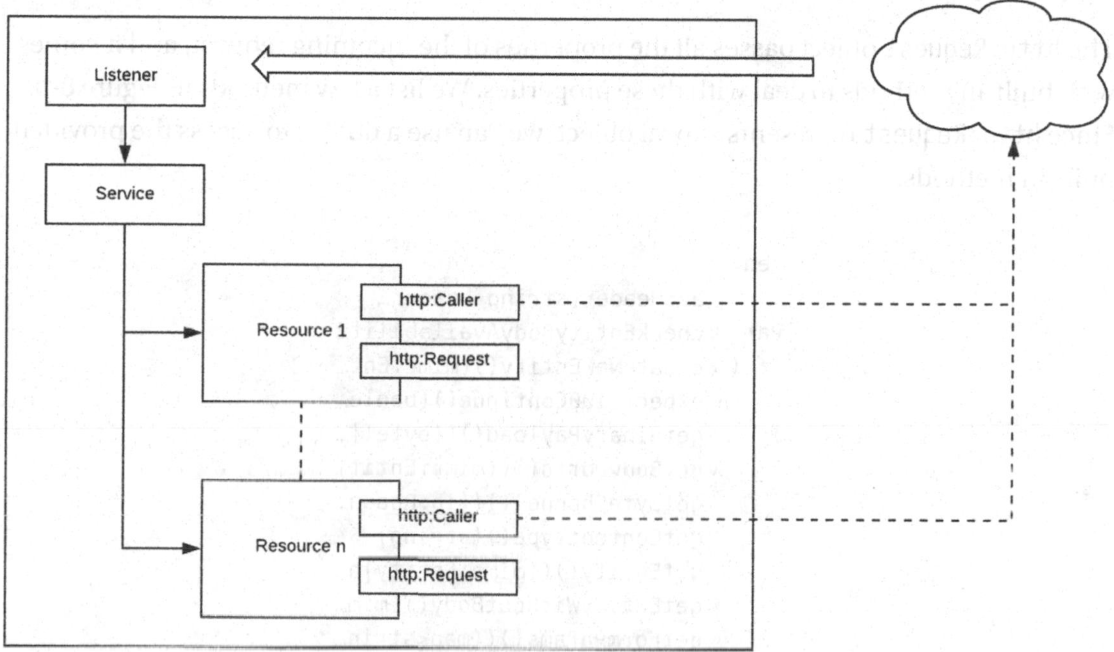

Figure 8-7. Ballerina network abstractions

Unlike other programming languages, Ballerina introduces fundamental, new abstractions of services, resource functions, and listeners to bring networking into the language.

Listener

Listeners provide the interface between the network and services. A listener object receives network messages from a remote process according to some protocol and translates the received messages into calls on the resource methods of service values that have been attached to the listener object.

It is up to the listener object to determine how this translation happens; the type of the listener object thus constrains the type of a service that can be attached to the listener.

Service/Resource

In Ballerina, `service` represent collections of network-accessible entry point call 122 resource functions.

http:Request Object

The `http:Request` object passes all the properties of the incoming request, and it comes with built-in methods to deal with these properties. We list a few methods in Figure 8-8. Since `http:Request` represents a local object, we can use a dot (`.`) to access the provided built-in methods.

```
req.
    addHeader(string header…
var checkEntityBodyAvailabilit…
if ( createNewEntity()(mime:Ent…
    expects100Continue()(boole…
}   getBinaryPayload()((byte[]…
    getBodyParts()((mime:Entit…
    getByteChannel()((io:Reada…
    getContentType()(string)
    getEntity()((mime:Entity|h…
    getEntityWithoutBody()(mim…
    getFormParams()((map<strin…
    getHeader(string headerNam…
```

Figure 8-8. *HTTP request object*

http:Caller Object

The `http:Caller` object is where we can interact and send back the response that is calling this resource function. Since `http:Caller` is representing the caller, which is remote to the resource function, it is a remote interaction, and we can invoke it by using the `->` notation, as shown in Figure 8-9.

```
var result = caller->
if (result is error)   acceptWebSocketUpgrade(m…
    log:printError("   accepted((http:Response|st…
}                      cancelWebSocketUpgrade(int…
                       continue()((()|http:Generi…
                       created(string uri, (http:…
                       ok((http:Response|string|x…
                       promise(http:PushPromise p…
                       pushPromisedResponse(http:…
                       redirect(http:Response res…
                       respond((http:Response|str…
```

Figure 8-9. *HTTP caller object*

Simple HTTP Service

Let's write a simple HTTP service with Ballerina. See Listing 8-1.

Listing 8-1. hello_world_service.bal

```
01 import ballerina/http;
02 import ballerina/log;
03
04 listener http:Listener httpListener = new(9090);
05
06 service hello on httpListener {
07     resource function sayHello(http:Caller caller, http:Request req) {
08         var result = caller->respond("Hello, World!\n");
09         if (result is error) {
10             log:printError("Error sending response", err = result);
11         }
12     }
13 }
```

The `ballerina/http` module will provide all the necessary functionality required to write a complete HTTP service. You can see that on line 1 we have imported the `ballerina/http` module.

On line 4, we define the `http:Listener` object, and on line 6, we define the HTTP service as a first-class construct. On line 7, resource functions are defined, and the caller (who is invoking this resource function) and the incoming request are passed as arguments.

Interactions over the network are denoted by the arrow operator (`->`) to differentiate from normal function calls. Line 8 is a network call, and it sends a response back to the caller. In Ballerina, the unreliability of the network is not ignored, and calls over the network can return an error in addition to the actual response. Lines 9, 10, and 11 log the error in the case of a failure.

Figure 8-10 is autogenerated when the code shown in Listing 8-1 is executed.

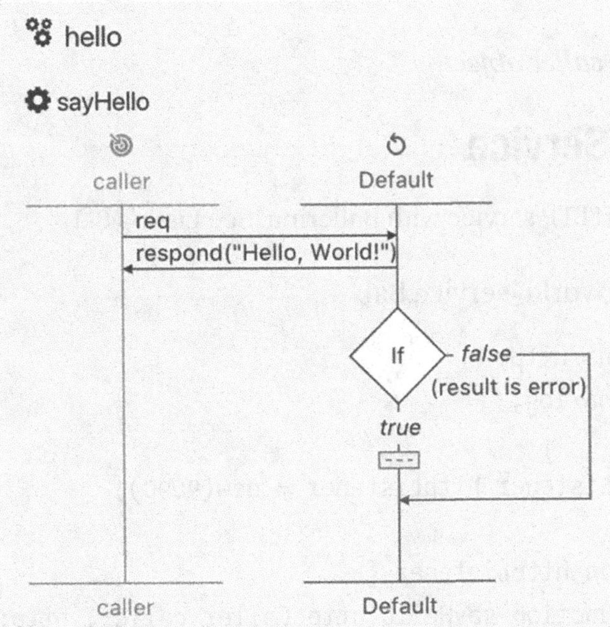

***Figure 8-10.** Sequence diagram of the "Hello, World!" program*

Let's run our "Hello, World!" service program. We can use the following command in our Terminal window, and it will start the Ballerina service:

```
$ ballerina run hello_world_service.bal
[ballerina/http] started HTTP/WS listener 0.0.0.0:9090
```

As shown in previous printed logs, our sample program is listening on port 9090. We can open a web browser and type the following URL, or we can use the `curl` command to access this service. (`curl` is a software program that can be used as a command-line tool to invoke a network endpoint using various protocols.)

```
$ curl http://localhost:9090/hello/sayHello
> Hello, World!
```

The service responded with “Hello, World!” You may notice that we used `/hello/sayHello` in the request path. This is because we have not set any specific path in our program, and we can access the resource with the service name and the resource name.

Let’s see how we can extend the same “Hello, World!” sample to handle the HTTP request object and alter the HTTP service to work with different HTTP methods using the example shown in Listing 8-2.

Listing 8-2. hello_world_extended_service.bal

```
import ballerina/http;
import ballerina/log;

@http:ServiceConfig {
    basePath: "/"
}
service hello on new http:Listener(9090) {

    @http:ResourceConfig {
        path: "/",
        methods: ["POST"]
    }
    resource function sayHello(http:Caller caller, http:Request req) {

        http:Response res = new;

        var payload = req.getTextPayload();

        if (payload is error) {
            log:printError("Error retrieving request", err = payload);
        } else {
            var result = caller->respond("Hello, " + <@untainted>
            payload + "!\n");
```

```
23             if (result is error) {
24                 log:printError("Error sending response", err = result);
25             }
26         }
27     }
28 }
```

Ballerina uses annotations to provide additional metadata about a particular construct. The `http` module in the Ballerina standard library provides a set of annotations. Annotations can be attached to various language constructs such as functions, services, and types. In this sample, we have used an annotation attached to the `service function` (lines 4 to 6) and the `resource function` (lines 9 to 12).

On lines 4 to 6, we have used the `@http:ServiceConfig` annotation to set the HTTP service to listen to the / (root) base path instead of using the service name (e.g., `/hello/` in Listing 7-1). We have only used `basePath` property in our sample, but Ballerina supports all the properties that are listed in Table 8-1.

***Table 8-1.** @http:ServiceConfig Supported Annotation Properties*

Field Name	Data Type	Default Value	Description
endpoints	http:Listener[]	[]	An array of endpoints the service would be attached to
host	String	b7a.default	Domain name of the service
basePath	String		Service base path
compression	http:CompressionConfig	{}	The status of compression
chunking	AUTO|ALWAYS|NEVER	CHUNKING_AUTO	Configures the chunking behavior for the service
cors	http:CorsConfig	{}	The cross-origin resource sharing configurations for the service
versioning	http:Versioning	{}	The version of the service to be used
authConfig	http:ListenerAuthConfig?	{}	Authentication configurations for securing the service

On lines 9 to 12 in Listing 8-2, we have used the `@http:ResourceConfig` annotation to set a few properties attached to the resource function `sayHello`. In this sample, we have set the path property as / (root) and changed the HTTP method to listen to POST.

With this change, now our sample service can be accessed by using `http://localhost:9090/` because both the base path and the path are set to /. The `sayHello` resource now listens only to the HTTP POST method instead of listening to all HTTP methods.

The properties listed in Table 8-2 are supported in the `@http:ResourceConfig` annotation.

Table 8-2. *`@http:ResourceConfig` Supported Annotation Properties*

Field Name	Data Type	Default Value	Description
methods	string[]	[]	The array of allowed HTTP methods.
Path	String		The path of the resource.
Body	String		Inbound request entity body name that is declared in the signature.
consumes	string[]	[]	The media types that are accepted by resource.
produces	string[]	[]	The media types that are produced by resource.
Cors	http:CorsConfig	{}	The cross-origin resource sharing configurations for the resource. If not set, the resource will inherit the CORS behavior of the enclosing service.
webSocket Upgrade	http:WebSocket UpgradeConfig?	()	Annotation to define HTTP to WebSocket upgrade.
authConfig	http:Listener AuthConfig?	()	Authentication configs to secure the resource.

In Listing 8-2, on line 17, we read the request object and extract the payload as a string by using the `req.getTextPayload()` method. This method can return either an error or the text payload. We have handled the error case separately in lines 19 and 20. On line 22, we append the payload to the response. You might notice that we have used the `<@untainted> payload` when appending the payload, and this will be discussed in detail in Chapter 9.

Let's run our sample program.

```
$ ballerina run hello_world_extended_service.bal
[ballerina/http] started HTTP/WS listener 0.0.0.0:9090
```

We can use following command to access our service:

```
$ curl -X POST -d "Ballerina" http://localhost:9090/
> Hello, Ballerina!
```

Use Case: HTTP RESTful Service

REST stands for Representational State Transfer, which is an architectural style for developing web services. Web services that conform to the REST architectural style are called RESTful web services and primarily use the following HTTP verbs (or *methods*, as they are properly called), which correspond to create, read, update, and delete (or CRUD) operations, respectively:

- GET requests retrieve resource representation/information only.
- POST methods are used to create a new resource in the collection of resources.
- PUT APIs are primarily to update existing resources.
- DELETE APIs are used to delete resources.
- PATCH requests are to make partial updates on a resource.

REST is not dependent on any protocol, but almost every RESTful service uses HTTP as its underlying protocol. RESTful services are considered lightweight, maintainable, and scalable compared to other services. They are also popular in modern API-oriented application development.

To understand how you can build a RESTful web service using Ballerina, let's consider a real-world use case of an order management scenario in an online retail application. The following are all the functionalities in the order management system:

- Create an order
- Retrieve an order
- Update an order
- Delete an order

Now, let's model these functionalities in a RESTful service. We can use different HTTP methods and header values to model this in a proper RESTful service.

Create Order: To place a new order, use an HTTP POST request that contains order details and then send the request to the `http://localhost:9090/order` endpoint. If the request is successful, the service should respond with a 201 Created HTTP response that has the location header pointing to the newly created resource like `http://localhost:9090/order/123456`. Figure 8-11 illustrates this.

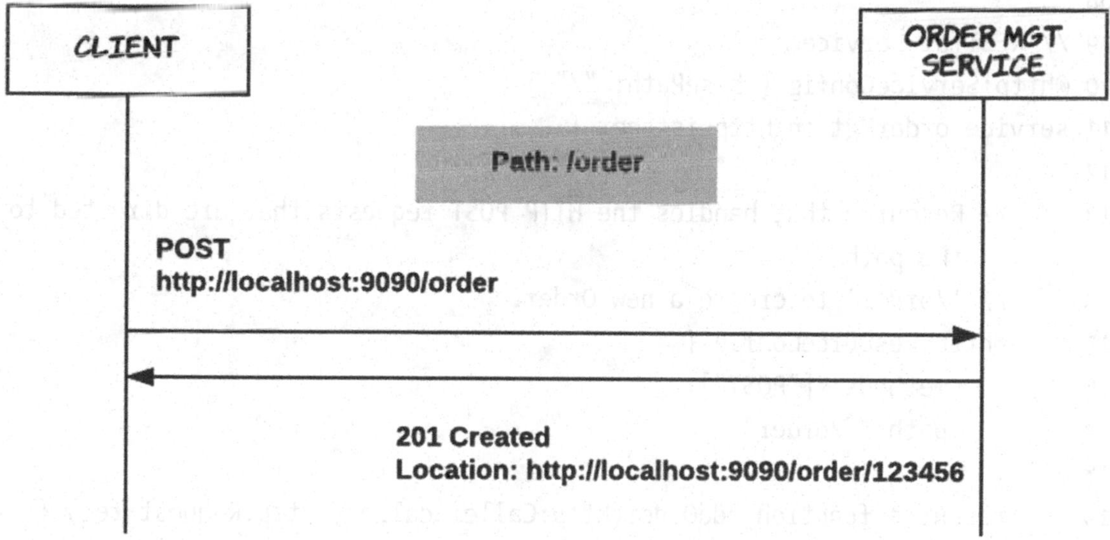

***Figure 8-11.** Sequence diagram of "create order" functionality*

We can start by defining a Ballerina HTTP service for the order management service (`orderMgt`). The `orderMgt` service can comprise multiple resources where each resource is responsible for a specific order management functionality. First, we will implement the "create order" functionality.

For the sample implementation shown in Listing 8-3, we will assume the following:

- Order details will be sent as a JSON object with the following structure:

  '{ "Order": { "ID": "100500", "Name": "XYZ", "Description": "Sample order."}}'

- Orders are stored as an in-memory map.

Listing 8-3. order_mgt_service.bal (Create Order Resource Function)

```
import ballerina/http;
import ballerina/log;

listener http:Listener httpListener = new(9090);

// Order management is done using an in-memory map.
map<json> ordersMap = {};

// RESTful service.
@http:ServiceConfig { basePath: "/" }
service orderMgt on httpListener {

    // Resource that handles the HTTP POST requests that are directed to the path
    // '/order' to create a new Order.
    @http:ResourceConfig {
        methods: ["POST"],
        path: "/order"
    }
    resource function addOrder(http:Caller caller, http:Request req) {
        http:Response response = new;
        var orderReq = req.getJsonPayload();
        if (orderReq is json) {
            json | error idJ = orderReq.Order.ID;
            if idJ is error {
```

```
25                log:printError("Error extracting order ID", err = idJ);
26            } else {
27                string orderId = idJ.toString();
28                ordersMap[orderId] = orderReq;
29                // Create response message.
30                json payload = { status: "Order Created.", orderId:
                  orderId };
31                response.setJsonPayload(<@untainted> payload);
32                // Set 201 Created status code in the response message.
33                response.statusCode = 201;
34                // Set 'Location' header in the response message.
35                // This can be used by the client to locate the newly
                     added order.
36                response.setHeader("Location",
37                    "http://abc.retail.com:9090/ordermgt/order/" + orderId);
38            }
39        } else {
40            response.statusCode = 400;
41            response.setPayload("Invalid payload received");
42        }
43        // Send response to the client.
44        var result = caller->respond(response);
45        if (result is error) {
46            log:printError("Error sending response", err = result);
47        }
48    }
49 }
```

In line 19, we have defined an `addOrder` resource function to handle the "create order" functionality. On lines 15 to 18, we set the path to `/order` and the HTTP method to `POST` to fulfill our "create order" functionality in the RESTful service. With this configuration, the "create order" resource can be accessed by the `http://localhost:9090/order` URL with a `POST` request.

With our previous assumption, we are expecting order details as a JSON object. On line 21, we process the request object, extract the JSON value by using the `req.getJsonPayload()` method, and assign the value into the `orderReq` variable. `req.getJsonPayload()` can return either an error or a JSON value. On lines 22 to 39, we have set the business logic for order creation, and on lines 39 to 42 we are handling the error case.

Unlike other programming languages, Ballerina is able to process JSON data with native functions without importing third-party libraries. On line 23, we pass through the JSON structure, read the order ID JSON value, and then cast it to a string on line 27 and assign it to the `orderId` variable.

In this sample code, we are storing orders in an in-memory map (on line 7, defined the in-memory map), and on line 28 we have assigned JSON to a map by using `orderId` as the key.

In this sample, we are sending a JSON payload with the response to the caller. Since Ballerina can handle JSON natively, on line 30 we have defined our response as a JSON payload. On line 20, we have initialized the `response` variable as an `http:Response` object, and on line 31, we have attached our defined JSON payload to the response.

In the success case of a "create order" function, we need to set the correct HTTP status code and headers. Line 33 sets the HTTP status code to 201, and line 36 sets the HTTP header with the correct location redirect URL.

On lines 40 and 41, we have set the HTTP status code to 400 and set the payload with the relevant error message to the response object to handle the error case. On lines 44 and 47, we send the response back to caller.

Now we can run and test the "create order" functionality of our RESTful service.

```
$ ballerina run order_mgt_service.bal
[ballerina/http] started HTTP/WS listener 0.0.0.0:9090

$ curl -v -X POST -d \
   '{ "Order": { "ID": "100500", "Name": "XYZ", "Description": "Sample
   order."}}' \
   "http://localhost:9090/order" -H "Content-Type:application/json"

Output :
< HTTP/1.1 201 Created
< Content-Type: application/json
< Location: http://localhost:9090/order/100500
```

```
< content-length: 46
< server: ballerina/0.991.0

{"status":"Order Created.","orderId":"100500"}
```

Retrieve Order: To retrieve order details, we send an HTTP GET request to the appropriate URL that includes the order ID, as shown in Figure 8-12.

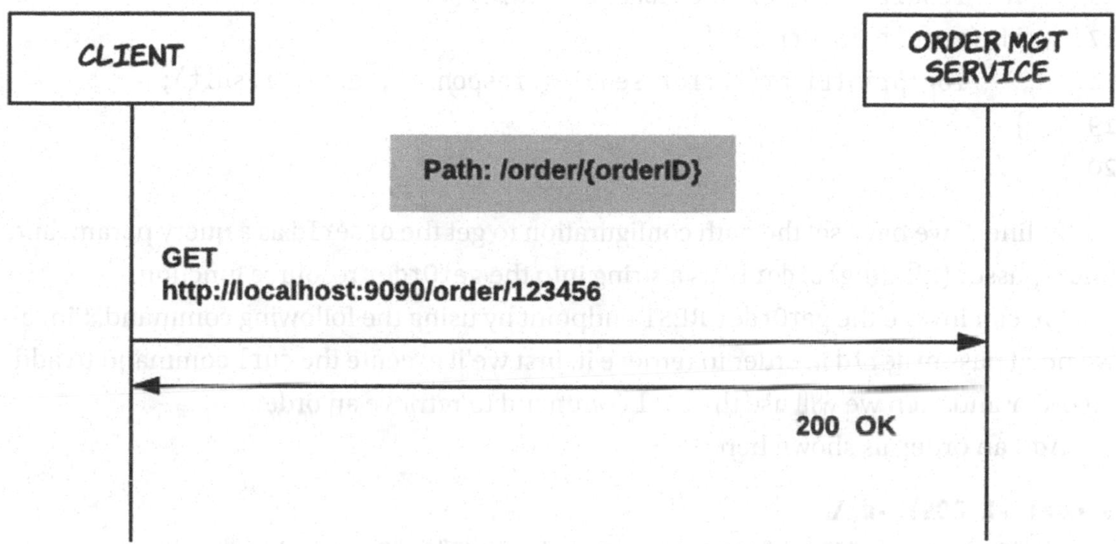

Figure 8-12. *Sequence diagram of the "Retrieve Order"*

In Listing 8-4, we'll extend the same code with the "retrieve order" functionality.

Listing 8-4. order_mgt_service.bal (Get Order Resource Function)

```
@http:ResourceConfig {
    methods: ["GET"],
    path: "/order/{orderId}"
}
resource function getOrder(http:Caller caller, http:Request req, string orderId) {
    // Find the requested order from the map and retrieve it in JSON format.
    json? payload = ordersMap[orderId];
    http:Response response = new;
    if (payload == null) {
```

```
10          payload = "Order : " + orderId + " cannot be found.";
11      }
12
13      // Set the JSON payload in the outgoing response message.
14      response.setJsonPayload(<@untainted> payload);
15     // Send response to the client.
16     var result = caller->respond(response);
17     if (result is error) {
18         log:printError("Error sending response", err = result);
19     }
20 }
```

In line 3, we have set the path configuration to get the `orderId` as a query param, and line 5 passes (binding) `orderId` as a string into the `getOrder` resource function.

We can invoke the `getOrder` REST endpoint by using the following command. Since we need pass `orderId` in order to retrieve it, first we'll execute the `curl` command to add an order and then we will use the `curl` command to retrieve an order.

Add an order, as shown here:

```
$ curl -X POST -d \
   '{ "Order": { "ID": "100500", "Name": "XYZ", "Description": "Sample
   order."}}' \
   "http://localhost:9090/order" -H "Content-Type:application/json"
{"status":"Order Created.","orderId":"100500"}
```

Retrieve an order, as shown here:

```
$ curl "http://localhost:9090/order/100500"

 Output :
 >  {"Order":{"ID":"100500","Name":"XYZ","Description":"Sample order."}}
```

Update Order: To update an existing order, send an HTTP PUT request with content for the order update. Listing 8-5 shows a sample skeleton code block. You can try to fill in the implementation of "update order" as an exercise.

Listing 8-5. Update Order Resource Function

```
@http:ResourceConfig {
    methods: ["PUT"],
    path: "/order/{orderId}"
}
resource function updateOrder(http:Caller caller, http:Request req,
string orderId){
    // Implementation
}
```

Delete Order: To delete an existing order, send an HTTP DELETE request to the `http://localhost:9090/order/` endpoint. A sample skeleton code block is shown in Listing 8-6. You can try to fill in the implementation of "delete order" as an exercise.

Listing 8-6. Delete Order Resource Function

```
@http:ResourceConfig {
  methods: ["DELETE"],
  path: "/order/{orderId}"
}
resource function deleteOrder(http:Caller caller, http:Request req, string
orderId) {
  // Implementation
}
```

HTTP Client

In our previous example, we used `curl` commands to invoke our HTTP service. The `curl` command is an HTTP client program. We can write a Ballerina program to invoke these HTTP services instead of using `curl`. The HTTP client endpoint can be used to connect to and interact with an external HTTP server.

Let's write a simple program to call our Listing 8-1 program instead of using the `curl` command; see Listing 8-7.

Listing 8-7. http_client.bal for Invoking an HTTP Service via the GET Method

```
01 import ballerina/http;
02 import ballerina/io;
03 http:Client clientEndpoint = new("http://localhost:9090");
04
05 public function main() {
06
07     var response = clientEndpoint->get("/hello/sayHello");
08
09     if (response is http:Response) {
10         var msg = response.getTextPayload();
11         if (msg is string) {
12             io:println(msg);
13         } else {
14             io:println("Invalid payload received:" , msg.reason());
15         }
16     } else {
17         io:println("Error when calling the backend: ", response.reason());
18     }
19 }
```

Line 3 defines a new `http:client` with the backend URL we want to interact with. Line 7 was configured to send a GET request to the specified endpoint. Since we are doing a network call, the `response` can be either `http:Response` or an error. Therefore, on lines 16 to 18 we handle the error case. Since the backend returns a `String`, line 10 retrieves a `String` value from the response. Retrieving a `String` value also can return an error, so lines 13 to 15 handle the error case.

We can use an HTTP POST method to send data enclosed in the body of the request message to the HTTP server. In Ballerina, you can create an `http:Request` object and set various types of payload as the body of the request message. See Listing 8-13, where we can set `BinaryPayload, TestPayload, XMLPayloads, JsonPayloads,` and many more. See Figure 8-13.

```
// Initializes a request.
http:Request req = new;
req.set
    setBinaryPayload(byte[]…
    setBodyParts(mime:Entity[]…
    setByteChannel(io:Readable…
    setContentType(string cont…
    setEntity(mime:Entity e)
    setFileAsPayload(string fi…
    setHeader(string headerNam…
    setJsonPayload(json payloa…
    setPayload((string|xml|jso…
    setTextPayload(string payl…
    setXmlPayload(xml payload,…
    addHeader(string headerNam…
```

Figure 8-13. *http:Request object set options*

After we are done with our HTTP message body, we can use the `clientEndpoint->post` method to post our request to the HTTP server.

```
response = clientEndpoint->post("/path/", req);
```

Let's write a simple program to call our Listing 8-2 program instead of using the `curl` command. See Listing 8-8.

Listing 8-8. http_client.bal for Invoking an HTTP Service via a POST Method

```
import ballerina/http;
import ballerina/io;
http:Client clientEndpoint = new("http://localhost:9090");

public function main() {

    http:Request req = new();
    req.setTextPayload("Ballerina");
    var response = clientEndpoint->post("/", req);

    if (response is http:Response) {
        var msg = response.getTextPayload();
        if (msg is string) {
```

```
            io:println(msg);
        } else {
            io:println("Invalid payload received:" , msg.reason());
        }
    } else {
        io:println("Error when calling the backend: ", response.reason());
    }
}
```

In the same way, we can use PUT and DELETE requests. Depending on the backend requirements, we can define custom HTTP request headers and an HTTP request payload and pass it to the backend.

gRPC Service

gRPC is a modern, open source remote procedure call (RPC) framework initially developed at Google and now widely used in distributed computing. It uses HTTP/2 (a major revision of the HTTP network protocol) for transport protocol buffers (a method of serializing structured data) as the interface description language, and it provides features such as authentication, bidirectional streaming and flow control, blocking or nonblocking bindings, and cancellation and timeouts.

gRPC enables client and server applications to communicate transparently. In gRPC, a client application can directly call methods of a server application that is on a different machine as if it were a local object. On the server side, the server implements and runs a gRPC server to handle client calls. On the client side, the client has a stub that provides the same methods as the server.

Let's use the same real-world use case that we used in a RESTful service and implement a gRPC service. Figure 8-14 illustrates all the functionalities of the `order_mgt` gRPC service that we need to build.

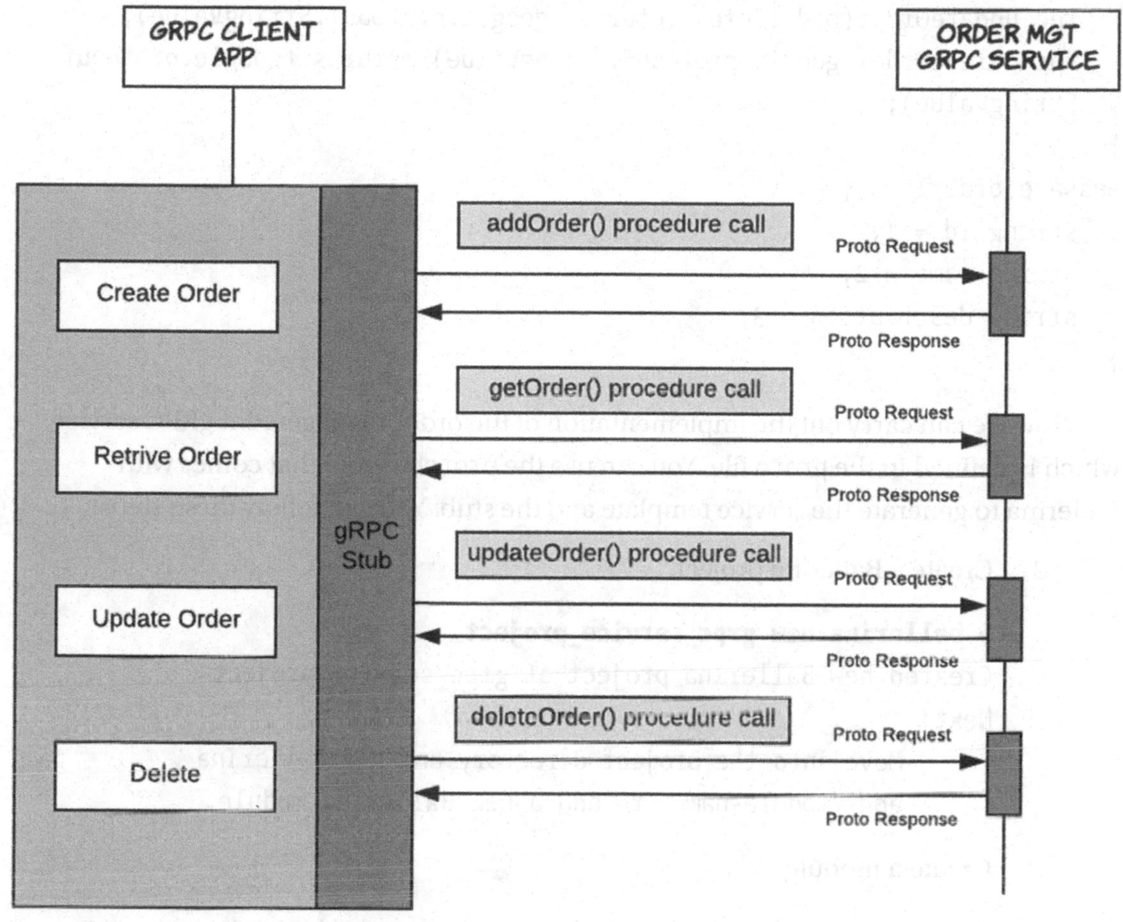

Figure 8-14. *gRPC order management service*

In Listing 8-9, we'll create the `protobuf` definition for our order management service.

Listing 8-9. orderMgt.proto (Protobuf Definition for Order Management Service)

```
syntax = "proto3";
package grpc_service;
import "google/protobuf/wrappers.proto";
service orderMgt {
   rpc addOrder(orderInfo) returns (google.protobuf.StringValue);
   rpc getOrder(google.protobuf.StringValue) returns (google.protobuf.
   StringValue);
```

```
    rpc updateOrder(orderInfo) returns (google.protobuf.StringValue);
    rpc deleteOrder(google.protobuf.StringValue) returns (google.protobuf.
    StringValue);
}
message orderInfo {
    string id = 1;
    string name = 2;
    string description = 3;
}
```

Now we can carry out the implementation of the order management gRPC service, which is defined in the proto file. You can use the protobuf tool that comes with Ballerina to generate the service template and the stub. You can follow these steps:

1. Create a Ballerina project.

   ```
   $ ballerina new grpc_service_project
   Created new Ballerina project at grpc_service_project
   Next:
           Move into the project directory and use ballerina
           add <module-name> to add a new Ballerina module.
   ```

2. Create a module.

   ```
   $ cd grpc_service_project
   $ ballerina add order_mgt
   Added new ballerina module at 'src/order_mgt'
   ```

3. Delete main.bal and copy and copy orderMgt.proto into the order_mgt module folder.

4. Go into the order_mgt module folder and run the Ballerina grpc tool from the autogenerated source file.

   ```
   $ ballerina grpc --input orderMgt.proto --output
   grpc_service --mode service
   > Downloading protoc executor file - protoc-osx-x86_64.exe
   > Download successfully completed. Executor file path
   -  /var/folders/rm/j_mxzqmx5kvfv7g210vjnzkr0000gn/T/
   protoc-osx-x86_64.exe
   ```

```
> Successfully extracted library files.
> Successfully generated ballerina file.
```

Now, you should see two new files inside the grpc_service directory, namely, orderMgt_sample_service.bal, which is a sample gRPC service, and orderMgt_pb.bal, which is the gRPC stub.

We can extend the orderMgt_sample_service.bal file with the business logic to handle order management functionalities, as shown in Listing 8-10.

Listing 8-10. Generated orderMgt_sample_service.bal

```
import ballerina/grpc;

listener grpc:Listener ep = new (9000);

service orderMgt on ep {

  resource function addOrder(grpc:Caller caller, orderInfo value) {
      // Implementation goes here.
      // You should return a string
  }
  resource function getOrder(grpc:Caller caller, string value) {
      // Implementation goes here.
      // You should return a string
  }
  resource function updateOrder(grpc:Caller caller, orderInfo value) {
      // Implementation goes here.
      // You should return a string
  }
  resource function deleteOrder(grpc:Caller caller, string value) {
      // Implementation goes here.
      // You should return a string
  }
}
```

Listing 8-11 demonstrates the implementation of the addOrder and getOrder resource functionalities.

Listing 8-11. gRPC addOrder Resource Function

```
01    resource function addOrder(grpc:Caller caller, orderInfo orderReq) {
02        // Add the new order to the map.
03        string orderId = orderReq.id;
04        ordersMap[orderReq.id] = orderReq;
05        // Create response message.
06        string payload = "Status : Order created; OrderID : " + orderId;
07
08        // Send response to the caller.
09        error? result = caller->send(payload);
10        result = caller->complete();
11        if (result is error) {
12            log:printError("Error from Connector: " + result.reason().
              toString());
13        }
14    }
```

In line 4, we assign order details to the in-memory map. To work with the map, we need to initialize the in-memory map as follows at the module level:

```
map<orderInfo> ordersMap = {};
```

Since we are logging the errors, we need to import the `ballerina/log` module.

You may have noticed that `orderMap` is a map of `orderInfo`. `orderInfo` is a record, and it is defined in the generated `orderMgt_pb.bal file.`

Let's add an implementation for `getOrder`, as shown in Listing 8-12.

Listing 8-12. gRPC getOrder Resource Function

```
resource function getOrder(grpc:Caller caller, string orderId) {
    string payload = "";
    error? result = ();
    // Find the requested order from the map.
    if (ordersMap.hasKey(orderId)) {
        var jsonValue = json.constructFrom(ordersMap[orderId]);
        if (jsonValue is error) {
```

```
                // Send casting error as internal error.
                result = caller->sendError(grpc:INTERNAL,
                    <string>jsonValue.detail().message);
            } else {
                json orderDetails = jsonValue;
                payload = orderDetails.toString();
                // Send response to the caller.
                result = caller->send(payload);
                result = caller->complete();
            }
        } else {
            // Send entity not found error.
            payload = "Order : '" + orderId + "' cannot be found.";
            result = caller->sendError(grpc:NOT_FOUND, payload);
        }

        if (result is error) {
            log:printError("Error from Connector: " + result.reason().
            toString());
        }
    }
```

As an exercise, you can do the implementation of the updateOrder and deleteOrder resource functionalities.

Let's see how we can implement the gRPC client and invoke our gRPC service. Run the following commands to autogenerate the client stub and a Ballerina gRPC client template:

1. Create a Ballerina project.

```
$ ballerina new grpc_client_project
Created new Ballerina project at grpc_client_project
Next:
        Move into the project directory and use ballerina
        add <module-name> to add a new Ballerina module.
```

2. Create a module.

   $ cd grpc_client
   $ ballerina add order_client
   Added new ballerina module at 'src/order_client'

3. Delete `main.bal` and copy `orderMgt.proto` into the `order_client` module folder.

4. Go into the `order_client` module folder and run the Ballerina gRPC tool to autogenerate the source file.

   $ ballerina grpc --input orderMgt.proto --output grpc_client --mode client

Now, you should see two new files inside the `grpc_client directory`, namely, `orderMgt_sample_client.bal`, which is a sample gRPC client, and `orderMgt_pb.bal`, which is the gRPC client stub.

You can use `orderMgt_sample_client.bal` file with the business logic you need to invoke your gRPC service. For example, refer to Listing 8-13, which shows an implementation to invoke the `addOrder` and `getOrder` functionalities that extend the main function that is generated by the tool. We will leave the implementation of `updateOrder` and `deleteOrder` for you as an exercise.

Listing 8-13. gRPC orderMgt_sample_client.bal

```
import ballerina/log;
import ballerina/grpc;

// This is client implementation for unary blocking scenario
public function main(string... args) {
    // Client endpoint configuration
    orderMgtBlockingClient orderMgtBlockingEp = new("http://localhost:9090");

    // Add an order
    log:printInfo("--------------------Add a new order------------------");
    orderInfo orderReq = {id:"100500", name:"XYZ", description:"Sample order."};
```

```
12      var addResponse = orderMgtBlockingEp->addOrder(orderReq);
13      if (addResponse is error) {
14          log:printError("Error from Connector: " + addResponse.reason().
            toString());
15      } else {
16          string result;
17          grpc:Headers resHeaders;
18          [result, resHeaders] = addResponse;
19          log:printInfo("Response - " + result + "\n");
20      }
21
22      // Get an order
23      log:printInfo("---------------Get an existing order-----------------");
24      var getResponse = orderMgtBlockingEp->getOrder("100500");
25      if (getResponse is error) {
26          log:printError("Error from Connector: " + getResponse.reason().
            toString());
28      } else {
29          string result;
30          grpc:Headers resHeaders;
31          [result, resHeaders] = getResponse;
32          log:printInfo("Response - " + result + "\n");
33      }
34  }
```

On line 7, we use a generated client endpoint definition to call the gRPC service. Line 11 defines the sample order request form of the `orderInfo`, which is defined in the `orderMgt_pb.bal` file. Line 12 invokes the `addOder` remote function, and lines 13 to 15 handle errors. If there are no errors, we extract the result from the response and print it to console. To retrieve an order, we invoke `getOrder` in line 24, and then lines 25 to 28 cover the error handling. If there are no errors, we print the result to the console.

Now let's use the following steps to run this sample.

To start the gRPC service, go to the grpc_service_project directory and run the following commands:

```
$ ballerina build order_mgt
Compiling source
    lakmal/order_mgt:0.1.0

Creating balos
    target/balo/order_mgt-2019r3-any-0.1.0.balo

Running tests
    lakmal/order_mgt:0.1.0
[ballerina/grpc] started HTTP/WS listener 0.0.0.0:9090
I'm the before suite function!
I'm the before function!
I'm in test function!
I'm the after function!
I'm the after suite function!
    1 passing
    0 failing
    0 skipped

Generating executables
    target/bin/order_mgt.jar

$ ballerina run target/bin/order_mgt.jar
[ballerina/grpc] started HTTP/WS listener 0.0.0.0:9090
```

We can use the gRPC client application that was implemented earlier to test the addOrder and getOrder functionalities.

```
    $ ballerina build order_client
Compiling source
    lakmal/order_client:0.1.0

Creating balos
    target/balo/order_client-2019r3-any-0.1.0.balo

Running tests
    lakmal/order_client:0.1.0
```

```
I'm the before suite function!
I'm the before function!
I'm in test function!
I'm the after function!
I'm the after suite function!
    1 passing
    0 failing
    0 skipped

Generating executables
    target/bin/order_client.jar
```

```
$ ballerina run target/bin/order_client.jar
```

You will see log statements similar to what is printed here on your terminal as the response:

```
INFO  [grpc_client] - -------------------Add a new order-------------------
INFO  [grpc_client] - Response - Status : Order created; OrderID : 100500

INFO  [grpc_client] - -------------------Get an existing order-------------
INFO  [grpc_client] - Response - id=100500 name=XYZ description=Sample order
```

Summary

In this chapter, we studied the basics of computer networks, distributed programming concepts, and distributed architectures. We also learned how to write network-distributed applications by using Ballerina.

Next, we will be looking at how we can do secure programming by using Ballerina.

CHAPTER 9

Information Security

Information is now more accessible than ever before. Before the advent of electronic media, we stored and shared information mainly on paper media. For example, knowledge was exclusively shared by means of books and newspapers. People bought these or borrowed them from a library. Even further back, communication media consisted of sending letters and telegrams. In those days, if you wanted to secure some information, you would physically lock it up in a secret storage location, such as a locked cupboard or a safe. Secure messaging could be done by using a trusted courier, who would not share the information with anyone else and would share it only with the correct recipient.

The introduction of electronic media and communication has taken information sharing to greater heights. Also, with the advent of public networks and the Internet, we can now share information and communicate instantly in the comfort of our own homes. But this convenience has created new risks. We are now at risk for our information being stolen, modified, or destroyed altogether because of its wider accessibility. To mitigate these risks, we have to build security mechanisms and policies that need to be followed.

Core Concepts

The widely accepted concepts for information security are confidentiality, integrity, and availability, commonly known as the CIA triad. The concepts related to using our secure information are authentication, authorization, and nonrepudiation.

A. Fernando and L. Warusawithana, *Beginning Ballerina Programming*,
https://doi.org/10.1007/978-1-4842-5139-3_9

Confidentiality

If some information is read or copied by someone who is not given explicit access to do so, we see this situation as a loss of confidentiality. This is the most fundamental scenario we try to protect against. The type of information that is susceptible to being stolen includes financial details, medical records, company trade secrets, and so on. To mitigate some of these scenarios, there are rules and regulations to protect the general public. For example, the Health Insurance Portability and Accountability Act (HIPAA) outlines rules to ensure medical records are handled properly, and the General Data Protection Regulation (GDPR) in Europe enforces the data privacy of users.

Integrity

Information can be corrupted, both when it is data at rest and when it is data in transit. This can be due to physical storage media damage or data corruption in unreliable networks. This type of a situation is known as loss of data integrity. Data corruption due to natural causes is usually mitigated using data redundancy techniques in computers, such as error correcting code (ECC) memory and redundant array of independent disks (RAID) technology for hard disks. The checking of data integrity is mainly done with message digests, which check with a high probability whether the data integrity has been violated or not.

Availability

Information that has been deleted or is inaccessible in any way is a loss of availability. This can happen because of natural causes such as hardware faults, or it can be because of malicious users accessing your information and deleting it or creating a large number of requests to a network server and effectively using up all the resources, thus limiting other clients to access the information (known as a denial-of-service attack). This is where we need to use systems such as high availability and load balancing clusters, intrusion detection systems, and data backup systems to handle such scenarios.

Software such as Snort by Cisco Systems can be used in intrusion detection and prevention. It allows us to provide rule sets for identifying specific types of network attacks. Also, availability is one of the main aspects of site reliability engineering (SRE), which has been popularized by Google in its own guidelines for maintaining scalable and highly reliable software systems. A free online book on SRE by Google can be found at `https://landing.google.com/sre/sre-book/toc/index.html`.

Authentication/Authorization

To make information available to certain people who an organization trusts, we need authentication and authorization . Authentication is the act of figuring out who is requesting access to our information. This is usually done by some data only the user knows, such as a username/password combination; something the user has, such as an ID card; or something the user is, i.e., biometrics with fingerprints and iris scans.

Authorization is the act of making sure the identified user has the access and the privileges to see, update, or do a specific action on the information in question. Authentication and authorization are interrelated, where the authorization actions are done after the authentication step takes place. This is simply to say we need to identify who the person is, in other words, authenticate, before we can understand what that person is authorized to do.

Nonrepudiation

In a security system, an action done by an authenticated person cannot challenge the fact that the action in question was done by him. This is called *nonrepudiation*. This basically means being accountable for one's own actions. If a security system doesn't have this quality, it suggests that a person may not take responsibility for their own actions in a consistent manner, even when produced with proof, e.g., a digital signature, thus signaling that the system has a poor security standing.

For example, if you write a check, put your signature on it, and hand it over to someone, the other person can cash this check. At this point, you cannot say that you did not give the person this check or that it is fake. This is because the bank can verify your signature and say that only you could have written the signature, and thus, you cannot refute the act of the other person cashing it. In practice, physical signatures can in fact be forged; however, it is difficult to do this with digital signatures.

Information Security in Action

In this section, we will be looking at the basics of implementing information security using cryptographic technologies in software. We will also look at how Ballerina provides support in implementing the approaches discussed.

Ciphers: Enforcing Confidentiality

Let's look at a scenario where we want to store some data securely, as a secret, so no one will be able to look at it and understand what it is. Only when we want to check the data again should we be able to view it in the original representation.

One of the ways of doing this is to scramble the data. That is, we want to rearrange the data in some way so that others will not be able to make sense of the data that is stored. Later, we can just reverse the scrambling of data to retrieve the original data.

Let's try to calculate an algorithm to do a bit of data scrambling. One approach is to map certain text characters in the input value and convert them to another character, as modeled in Figure 9-1.

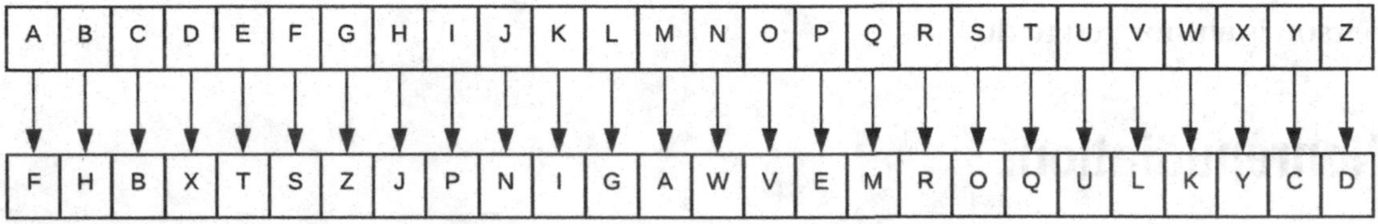

Figure 9-1. *Text scrambling using character substitution*

As shown in Figure 9-1, our text scrambling is done using a character substitution approach. That is, for each alphabetical character, we substitute another alphabetical character. What we end up in the final string is very different from the original.

For example, let's do this character substitution to a few words and see how they look. See Table 9-1.

Table 9-1. *Character Substitution Input/Output*

Input	Output
FACE	SFBT
BED	HTX
THE	QJT

We can see that in Table 9-1 the output column shows the translated text, which does not have any resemblance to the input text. If we want, we can do the reverse operation by following the opposite mapping in Figure 9-1 and get the original text from the output values.

This approach is called a *monoalphabetic* substitution cipher, since it has a constant mapping from the input to the output. A *cipher* is another name for a cryptographic algorithm.

The mapping here does not have to be constant. The letter-to-letter mapping configuration can be given by the user when doing the substitution. In that case, we come up with a custom letter row of 26 characters, similar to the one shown in Figure 9-1. This mapping information is basically a parameter to the encryption algorithm along with the data to be encrypted. We call this a *code* or the *key* of the cipher. Even if someone knows the algorithms used to encrypt some data, they will not know the exact key used to encrypt the data. If the key has a length of 26 characters, each with 26 possible values, the number of possible combinations is 26! ~= 4 * 10^26, which is a pretty big number.

To crack this encryption, one way is to try all the possibilities of the cipher key for the input data, decrypt the data, and see if it gives any meaningful result. But we don't really need to do this; there is an easier way to crack this. This is because, each time, the specific character in the input is always translated to the same character in the ciphertext. This characteristic makes this a weak cipher that is easy to crack by doing a frequency analysis on the cipher text. In any language, there are certain patterns and frequencies for occurrences of individual letters and words. For example, by analyzing a large amount of natural language text, we can identify a frequency distribution in the usage of individual letters of the English language.

The most used letter in the English language is *E*, with a frequency of 12 percent, and this is followed by the letter *T*, with 9.1 percent. So, if we have a sizable cipher text (the resultant text after encryption), we can do a frequency analysis of it and see the frequency distribution of each ciphertext letter. By analyzing the frequency distribution of the ciphertext generated from the key in Figure 9-1, we would identify that the most generated character is *T*, so we can safely assume the source letter of this must be *E*. Also, while cracking such a code, we can use other characteristics of the language, such as the occurrence of two-letter words with the same letters, e.g., EE, SS, and OO, where you wouldn't generally see words with letters like ZZ or KK. These can be used as hints to narrow down and figure out the cipher key.

XOR Cipher

In this section, we will be creating an implementation of a simple cipher, which will take in some binary data, along with a key, to generate the ciphertext. It will also take in ciphertext and the key to decrypt and generate the original data. Let's think of a way to do this.

The cipher key should be responsible for scrambling the input data and creating output that does not look like the input data. Let's make our key size 1 byte, or 8 bits. This will give an instruction to one input byte on how his value should be transformed. So, how can 1 byte of cipher key give some type of scrambling instructions to 1 byte of input data?

Figure 9-2 shows a possible approach to scrambling our input data. This is simply done by telling each bit of the input to either invert its value or not to do so, by the corresponding bit value in the cipher key.

Input	1	0	1	1	0	1	0	1
	XOR	XOR	XOR	XOR	XOR	XOR	XOR	XOR
Cipher Key	1	1	0	1	1	0	1	1
	↓	↓	↓	↓	↓	↓	↓	↓
Cipher Text	0	1	1	0	1	1	1	0

Figure 9-2. *XOR cipher*

For example, we can see that the first bit (rightmost) in the input, which is 1, corresponds to the first value of the cipher key's first bit, which is also 1. This 1 in the cipher key is a directive to the input to tell itself to invert, so the result is 0. We can see the same operation happens in the second bit, where the cipher key tells the input bit 0 to invert, which results in 0. But in the third bit, the cipher key bit value is 0, so it is not telling the input bit of 1 to invert, so the same bit value is put to the resultant cipher text. So, from this, we can see how the cipher key is fully in control and instructs the input to change its value or not. And we can see that the input value itself does not have any say about whether it should change its original value or not; this is fully up to the cipher key. This is an important aspect we need to retain.

Also, you may notice that since the cipher key is simply giving an instruction to invert its value or not, if we do the same operation again to the cipher text, we will get back the original value. This is simply because if the cipher instruction was not to do anything originally, the same original value is there in the cipher text, so again, if we don't do anything, we retain the original value. If the cipher told us to invert the value, we again do what the cipher tells by inverting it again, so we end up with the original value.

The previous operations of the cipher key instructing the input to change its value or not happen to be the same operation we know as the bitwise XOR operation.

Is XOR Cipher Secure?

When using the cipher for a longer sequence of data bigger than its key, it is not a secure cipher. This is because the same frequency analysis can be done on the ciphertext, similar to the scenario we saw with the monoalphabetic substitution cipher. Here, this would actually become easier to crack, because if we figure out a ciphertext section for the input data section, we will be figuring out the cipher key itself that is used with all the data.

If the cipher key is larger or equal to the data that is being encrypted, then this cipher will be fully secure and is unbreakable. This specific scenario is called a *one-time pad* cipher, since it's supposed to be used once, with the same size of the input text, and later the key is to be disposed without using it again. If we reuse the pad, then it opens up the possibility for someone else to do a frequency analysis, and it won't be secure anymore.

Implementation

Let's do an implementation of the XOR cipher using Ballerina, where the input will be an input file path, an output file path, and a cipher key. An encrypted value from this program can be decrypted again using the same program by feeding in the output of the earlier execution as the input of a new execution, with the same cipher key. See Listing 9-1.

Listing 9-1. XOR Cipher

```
import ballerina/io;
import ballerina/lang.'int as ints;

public function main(string... args) returns error? {
    string fileIn = args[0];
    string fileOut = args[1];
    byte key = <byte> check ints:fromString(args[2]);
    io:ReadableByteChannel srcCh = check io:openReadableFile(
                                        <@untainted> fileIn);
    io:WritableByteChannel targetCh = check io:openWritableFile(
                                        <@untainted> fileOut);
    while (true) {
        var result = srcCh.read(100);
        if (result is io:EofError) {
            break;
        } else {
            check writeFully(targetCh, xor(check result, key));
        }
    }
    check srcCh.close();
    check targetCh.close();
}

public function xor(byte[] data, byte key) returns byte[] {
    byte[] result = [];
    int i = 0;
    while i < data.length() {
        result[i] = data[i] ^ key;
        i += 1;
    }
    return result;
}

public function writeFully(io:WritableByteChannel targetCh, byte[] data)
```

```
                               returns error? {
    int written = 0;
    int count = data.length();
    while (written < count) {
        written += check targetCh.write(data, written);
    }
}
```

```
$ ballerina run xor_cipher.bal in out 33
$ ballerina run xor_cipher.bal out out2 33
```

Listing 9-1 shows an implementation of the XOR cipher in Ballerina, and in the previous sample run, the contents of the file `in` are encrypted with the key 33, and the encrypted data will be available in the file `out`. We are then going to run the same operation on `out`, where the file output is `out2`, with the same key. After these operations, you will notice that the contents of `in` and `out2` are the same, because of the behavior of the XOR cipher, and that the decryption of the encrypted data can be done by doing the same operation on the encrypted data with the same key.

Symmetric-Key Ciphers

The basic cryptographic operations we have talked about so far are based on having a single secret key, which is used in both the encryption and decryption of the data. This is known as *private key cryptography* or *symmetric-key cryptography*. The symmetry here is because the same key is used on both sides, for encryption and decryption. These ciphers are categorized into two groups, block ciphers and stream ciphers.

Block Ciphers

A block cipher works by encrypting a fixed block of data at one time. This is mostly 64, 128, or 256 bits. In the case of input messages not aligning to a block size, if required, the data can be aligned to a block boundary by padding the data. For this, there are standard padding mechanisms implemented, such as PKCS5.

Some of the well-known block ciphers are DES, 3DES, Blowfish, and AES. Here, DES employs a 56-bit key length and is considered to be susceptible to brute-force attacks. 3DES is basically an algorithm that runs DES three times, and even though it is much stronger than DES, it is computationally expensive for many practical applications. Blowfish has a variable key length from 32 to 448 bits and has the special property that it is unpatented; thus, it doesn't have any royalty fees associated with using it. Advanced Encryption Standard (AES) is a cipher with 128, 192, and 256 key lengths and is considered the most popular and widely used cipher in the world right now. It is even implemented as CPU instructions in the x86 instruction set, as an extension called AES-NI, in order to make the computations as efficient as possible.

Another aspect of a block cipher is the mode of operation. The cipher provides an approach for encrypting and decrypting a single block of data, but when it comes to a larger dataset that comprises multiple blocks, we need to figure out how the blocks are handled. The simplest approach would be to treat them as fully independent data blocks and do the cipher operations on each block. This mode is defined as Electronic Code Block (ECB), which simply encrypts and decrypts each data block using the cipher key. This operation is illustrated in Figure 9-3.

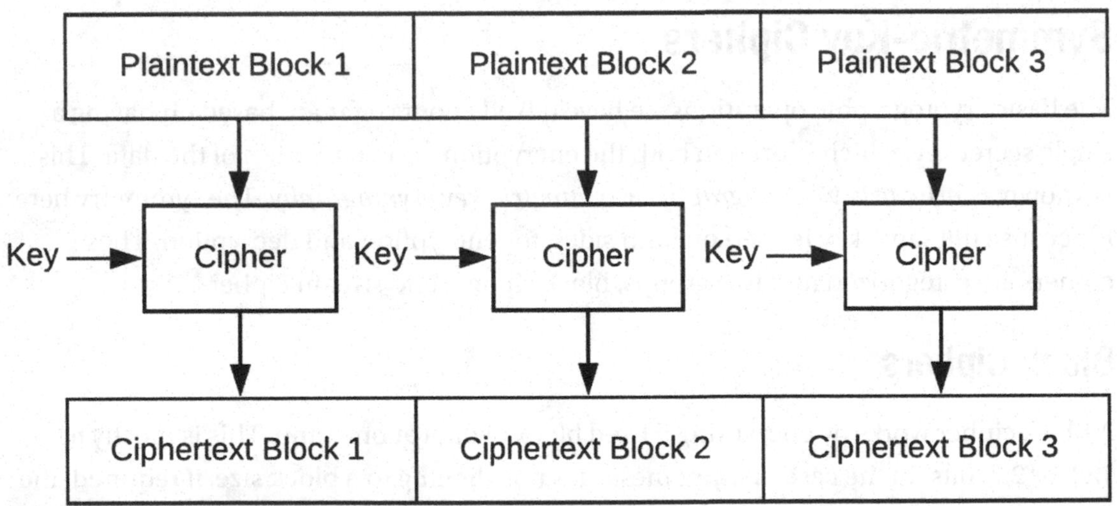

Figure 9-3. *ECB block cipher mode*

Here, you can see that the resultant ciphertext blocks purely depend on one specific source plaintext block and the encryption key. This approach has the issue where, if the same block is repeated, the same ciphertext block will be output. This would result in a situation where by analyzing the resultant ciphertext, someone would be able to find patterns in the source plaintext data, which would ultimately make it easy to crack the encryption.

A more suitable option would be to use a block cipher mode such as Cipher Block Chaining (CBC). In this approach, when encrypting a plaintext block of data, along with the cipher key, it takes the previous ciphertext block contents into account when doing the encryption operation. This operation is shown in Figure 9-4.

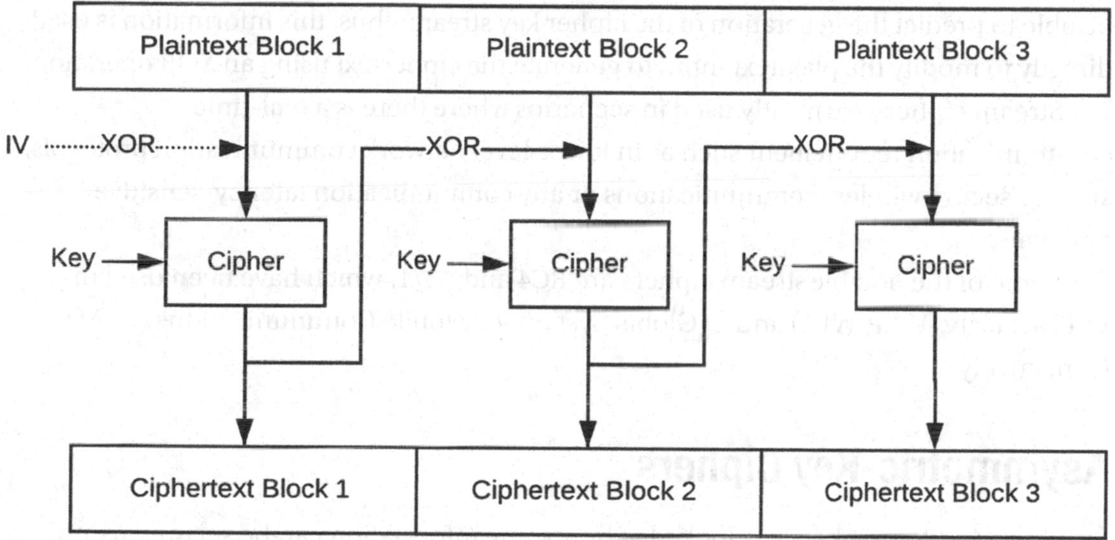

Figure 9-4. *CBC block cipher mode*

Here, the encryption operation is done by XORing the earlier block's ciphertext first with the plaintext block and then applying the encryption operation to the resultant block. In this manner, when a block of plaintext is being encrypted, it takes into account the context of the full previous set of blocks that came before it, and all of them would have had an effect on the block that is currently encrypted. So, at the end, in a given single continuous message, similar plaintext blocks will not have similar ciphertext block values, but rather, the full presentation of the message will end up as a unique ciphertext.

In the case of the same full message itself being repeated, then of course you will get the same resulting ciphertext, with the same blocks as a whole. To mitigate this behavior and to make the full message unique, an initialization vector (IV) can be given as the first value to be used along with the cipher key for encrypting the first plaintext block.

Stream Ciphers

Stream ciphers are used to encrypt data that is flowing continuously as a stream of data. So, for each available byte, we must encrypt it immediately and send it out. This is done by creating a pseudorandom cipher digit stream, which is created by seeding an encryption key. This cipher digit stream is used to XOR with its current cipher digit with the plaintext digit to create the ciphertext stream. The assumption here is that no one will be able to predict the generation of the cipher key stream; thus, this information is used directly to modify the plaintext input to generate the ciphertext using an XOR operation.

Stream ciphers are mostly used in scenarios where there is a real-time communication requirement such as in lower-level network communication protocols, such as secure wireless communications or any communication latency-sensitive applications.

Some of the notable stream ciphers are RC4 and A5/1, which have been used in WiFi security (WEP, WPA) and in Global System for Mobile Communications (GSM), respectively.

Asymmetric-Key Ciphers

In symmetric-key ciphers, we looked at how some information can be secured using encryption and decryption and a single key. This is a good approach when the two parties who are supposed to be involved in the encryption and decryption operations can have access to the private key. For example, if the person who encrypts and decrypts the data is the same person, this approach is ideal. This is the case when you encrypt your hard disk data so no one else can read the data. Here, a single private key is known by a person, and it is used to encrypt and decrypt the data.

Private key cryptography can also be used with multiple parties when the key is shared with the participants beforehand and in a secure way. For example, if two people want to send secure messages to each other at some point, they can meet up beforehand, share a secret key, and later use that key to encrypt and decrypt the messages that are sent between them.

But, what if we didn't have a chance to share a private key to communicate between each other? For example, what if two parties are there in a public network, and there is no way for each other to physically meet or any other way to share the private key to do the communication? This is where an asymmetric-key cipher comes into play. This is also known as *public key cryptography*. In this scenario, we use a pair of keys for the cryptographic operations. The public key is used for encryption, and the private key is used for decryption. These key pairs can be generated by anyone, and they have the special property where, if someone knows one key, the other key cannot be guessed or calculated easily. Also, a value encrypted by one key cannot be decrypted by that key but rather only by the other key of the key pair.

Because of these properties, we can generate a key pair and advertise one key as public so anyone else can use that key to encrypt some values and send that over to the owner of that public key. Now since the owner has the other key, kept as a secret, he can decrypt the messages sent by others. This functionality means we are able to securely communicate with someone without exchanging a private key beforehand.

Figure 9-5 illustrates a scenario where two friends, Sunil and Nimal, are working together, and Sunil wants to be able to send a secure message to Nimal. What if Nimal wants to send a message to Sunil? Sunil could have done the same actions as Nimal in creating a key pair for himself and sending the public key to Nimal. But rather, what we can do is, in the first step of Sunil sending data to Nimal, he can randomly generate a new private key to be used with private key cryptography and share this with Nimal. So now, both have a private key not known by anyone else, and they can use this to communicate with each other by encrypting/decrypting messages with private key cryptography. The private key that is generated and shared through the interactions of public key cryptography is generally referred to as the *session key*.

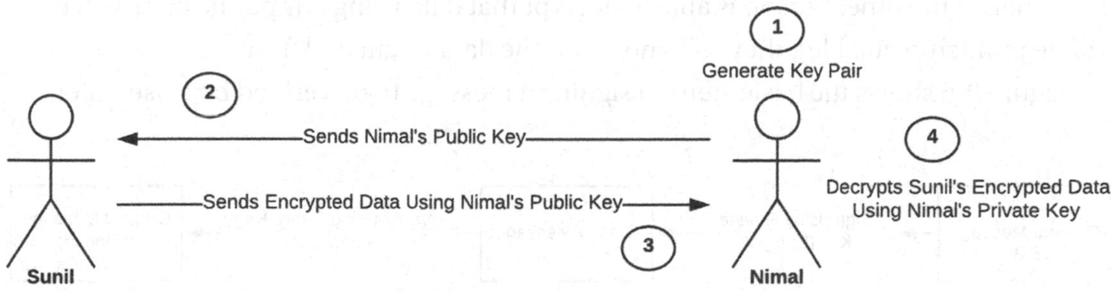

Figure 9-5. *Public key cryptography usage*

We could have used public key cryptography for all the communication, but public key cryptography is considered to be much slower compared to private key cryptography. So, most protocols use the approach of creating a session key first using public key cryptography and then using private key cryptography for further communication with the session key. This is similar to the approach followed by the HTTPS protocol.

The most popular algorithms for public key cryptography are RSA (Rivest, Shamir, Adleman), DSA (Digital Signature Algorithm), and ECC (Elliptic Curve Cryptography). RSA key sizes are usually 128 bits and 256 bits, but ECC is known to be a stronger algorithm and requires smaller key sizes to have similar security compared to RSA.

Digital Signatures: Authenticity, Integrity, and Nonrepudiation

Digital signatures ensure the authenticity of the origin of some data, and at the same time, they can be used to check the integrity of the data. That is, they can make sure the original data is not corrupted or changed along the way. This provides nonrepudiation as a result so the sender cannot dispute the fact that he sent the data.

Digital signatures are implemented using public key cryptography. Earlier we saw how someone's public key can be used to encrypt some data and send that data to the owner of that public key, who also has in his possession the corresponding private key. This private key is used to decrypt the data sent by others. So, this makes sure that only the owner of the public key can decrypt the message. Basically, what we achieve here is to make sure the data will surely go to the owner of the public key. If we do the inverse operation, we can make sure the data came from the owner of the private key. How do we do that? Well, it's simple. Let's say we have a public/private key pair, and rather than encrypt some data using someone else's public key, we encrypt the data using my private key. When some other person is able to decrypt that data using our public key (which will be publicly available), they will know that the data originated from us.

Figure 9-6 shows the basic steps in signing a message to be verified by a user later.

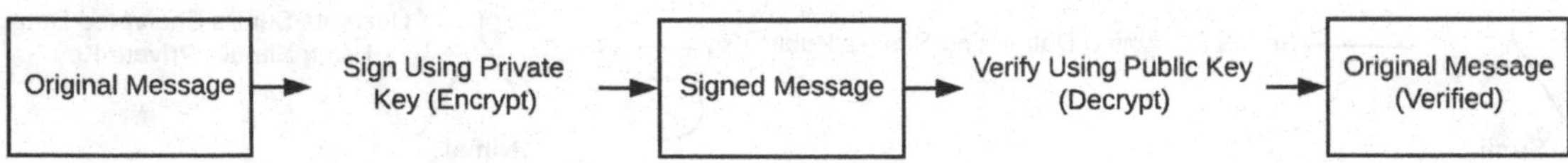

Figure 9-6. *Basic message signing*

But generally, to sign a message, we don't really need to encrypt the full message using our private key. We simply need a representation of our message to be encrypted to be used as the signature of the message. To get a representation of our message, we use a technique known as *hashing*.

A hash value of a message is a one-way value of a variable-sized input payload, which results in a fixed-size numerical value. This size is generally a 128-bit, 256-bit, or 512-bit value. The input can be of any size, and it ensures that every time you generate the hash value of the same payload, you will get the same value. Even if you change one bit of the input value, the output hash value will change a lot, in an unpredictable manner. This makes sure it is nearly impossible to generate a payload that will output a given hash value. So, if you generate a hash value from a payload, then when you are transferring a payload, you will send both the payload and the hash value with the message. Then, on the other size, we can recalculate the hash value from the received payload and compare that value to the received hash value to check whether the hash values are the same. If they are the same, we can say with a very high probability that the payload has not been corrupted, and its integrity is intact. Some of the most popular hashing algorithms are MD5, SHA1, and SHA2.

So, this seems all good. Especially for network communication-based error detection, this works well. But there is still a problem, where we don't know if someone modified the data in the middle of the communication. He could have altered the payload and could have regenerated the hash value for the new payload as well. This is where we can use message signing to solve this problem and also reduce the amount of data we use for the encryption operation required in message signing. The hash value of the message is a good representation of the input payload, and we could simply encrypt this value with our private key to generate the signature.

This signature now encapsulates two bits of information; one is the hash value of the input message, so it represents the input message, and it can be used to check the integrity of the message. It also encapsulates the authenticity of the input message, due to the signing operation, which says it was generated by a specific known entity. Now both of these aspects can be verified by the receiving side of the message. The receiving party gets the plaintext message payload and the signature value. He will generate the hash value from the plaintext message; let's call this the *source hash value*. He will now validate the signature by decrypting the signature value with the public key, and this resultant value has to be equal to the *source hash value*. If this check is successful, our signature is verified, and it certifies that the input message integrity is intact, and the message authenticity is checked as well.

Figure 9-7 shows the high-level steps of how message signing is done and how a signature is verified by the recipient.

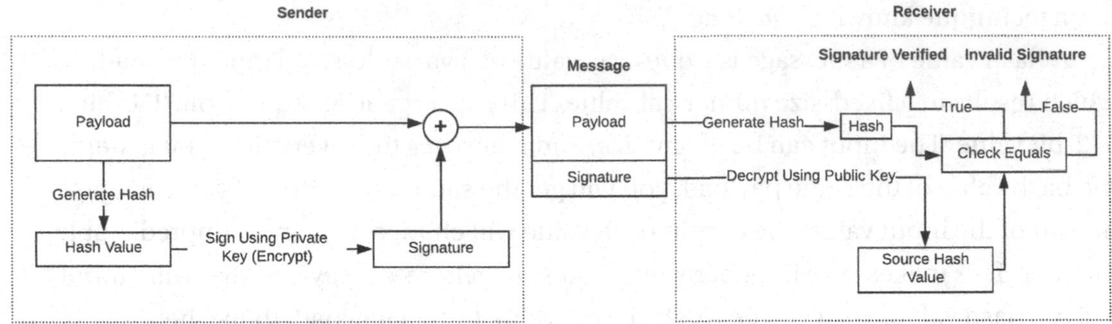

Figure 9-7. *Practical message signing*

Another aspect this process ensures at the end is nonrepudiation. Since the private key is not known by anyone else, after you sign a message, you cannot deny the fact that you sent the message with your signature. This is because you are the only one who can generate that signature.

Public Key Infrastructure

In our usage of the public keys, we assumed that it is owned by a specific entity, user, or device. Unless you personally meet someone and they hand you their public key, you have no way to be sure that a public key is actually owned by someone specific. In other words, we have not seen a clear way to associate an *identity* to a public key. This is what is handled by a public key infrastructure (PKI), which consists of a set of technologies and policies used to solve the problem.

Digital Certificates

An identity is assured for a public key by having a document that states that the public key belongs to a specific entity and by having this document signed by another trusted entity. These documents are called *digital certificates*. They are similar to physical certificates we get to certify something we have. The certificates are issued by an entity known as a *certificate authority* (CA). A certificate authority has its own private key, which is used to sign the certificate attesting to the validity of it, saying a specific identity is surely associated with the public key contained in the certificate. We are now able to validate the certificate signature by using the CA's public key, which will be known by us.

The CA public keys are also stored in their own certificates. The certificates that are signed by a CA contain a reference to the respective CA certificate. A CA certificate also has to be signed by someone; that is, it needs to be guaranteed that the CA certificate is representing the entity it says it is. So, a CA certificate can also be signed by another higher-authority CA certificate, which attests to the identity of the CA certificate in question. So, these certificates can be chained by following the aforementioned pattern to create a chain of trust.

Figure 9-8 shows the basic structure of a certificate. It consists of the following main sections.

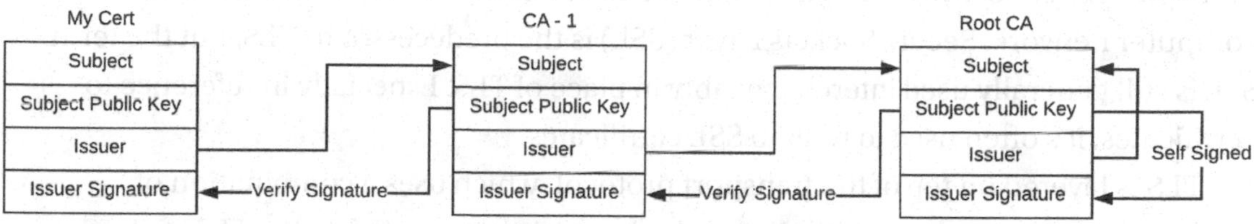

***Figure 9-8.** Certificate chaining*

- **Subject**: The unique identifier of the entity that the CA has issued the certificate to
- **Subject public key**: The public key associated with the certificate
- **Issuer**: The entity name of the CA that has signed this certificate
- **Issuer signature**: The signature of the issuer

As shown in Figure 9-8, each certificate is signed by an issuer. That is, each certificate contains an issuer signature that is generated by the issuer by using his private key. Since in each certificate we have the issuer name and signature, at the point of verifying the signature, we can look up the issuer certificate, extract its public key, verify that our signature is valid, and indeed signed by the said issuer. So, this pattern can be carried on, and chained, as we want. But what about the certificate at the end of the chain? Who is going to sign his certificate and attest to its identity? These are known as *root certificates*, and they are signed by themselves. These are also known as *self-signed certificates*.

They basically use their own private key to sign themselves. So, this does not create any assurances to us regarding the certificate's authenticity. We follow a mechanism where we explicitly note that a few of the root CA certificates are trusted in our system. These are usually stored in web browsers and in the operating system itself. So, if we mark them as trusted in the system, the verification of these certificates is automatically done, and we would trust any other certificates that are signed by these root CA certificates, and so on down the chain to verify other certificates.

SSL/TLS

Transport Layer Security (TLS) is a protocol used for secure communication over a computer network. Secure Sockets Layer (SSL) is the predecessor to TLS, but the term SSL is still generally used interchangeably in place of TLS. Especially in reference to certificates, it's often used to refer to SSL certificates.

TLS is layered on top of the transport protocol, which uses a combination of public key cryptography, certificates, and symmetric key cryptography. TLS is often used to implement secure versions of protocols such as HTTP and FTP, as HTTPS and FTPS, respectively. For example, in HTTPS, it provides data privacy, integrity, and authentication of web servers using certificates. An SSL/TLS certificate uses the X.509 standard in defining its certificates. Using this, a client is able to make sure the data we get from a web site actually originated from the web servers that host the web site.

The basic operation of the TLS protocol is that first the certificate is used for authenticating the web server to make sure we are dealing with the actual domain we were told we are communicating with. Public key cryptography is used to initiate the early communication between the client and the server, which sends a randomly generated key from the client to the server. These initial operations are known as the SSL/TLS *handshake*. This key is now used as a session key for doing symmetric key encryption for the duration of the active connection.

In web browsers, while browsing a web site using HTTPS, we can examine the certificate information by clicking the lock icon that is shown in most of the leading web browsers.

Figure 9-9 shows an example of the TLS/SSL certificate information given when navigating to a web site using HTTPS.

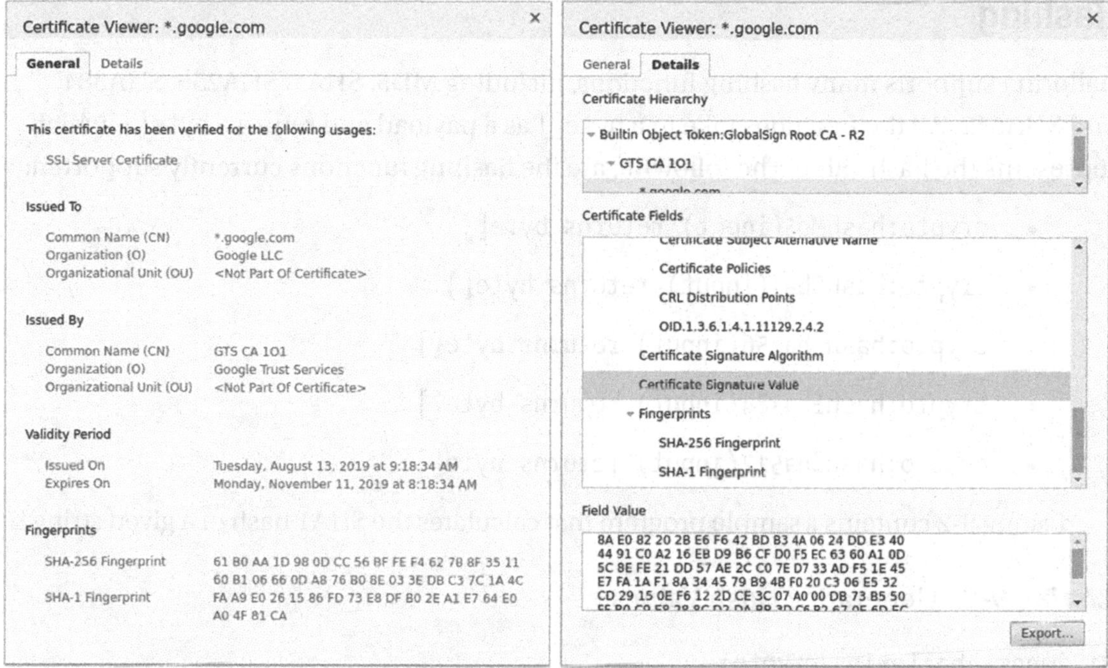

Figure 9-9. *TLS/SSL certificate information*

This certificate mentions that the certificate is issued to any subdomain of `google.com`, and it contains the issuer information, its public key, the signature created by the issuer, and other related information. Basically, from this certificate, we can be sure that the web site data we receive is actually from the `*.google.com` servers, and the browser automatically validates this by comparing it to the domain name of the web page address we are visiting in the browser.

Cryptography API

We have now looked at the basics of cryptography and its derived technologies. Let's look at the features and functionality given by the Ballerina cryptography API, which is available through the module `ballerina/crypto`.

Hashing

Ballerina supports many hashing functions, including MD5, SHA1, SHA256, SHA384, and SHA512. All the functions take in a `byte[]` as a payload and return a `byte[]`, which represents the hash value. The following are the hashing functions currently supported:

- `crypto:hashMd5(input) returns byte[]`
- `crypto:hashSha1(input) returns byte[]`
- `crypto:hashSha256(input) returns byte[]`
- `crypto:hashSha384(input) returns byte[]`
- `crypto:hashSha512(input) returns byte[]`

Listing 9-2 contains a sample program that calculates the SHA1 hash of a given string.

Listing 9-2. Generating Hash Values

```
import ballerina/crypto;
import ballerina/io;

public function main(string... args) returns error? {
    string input = "Hello, World!";
    byte[] hash = crypto:hashSha1(input.toBytes());
    io:println("SHA1: ", hash.toBase16());
}
```

```
$ ballerina run hash.bal
SHA1: 0a0a9f2a6772942557ab5355d76af442f8f65e01
```

Signing

Ballerina's functionality for signing is done using the RSA algorithm, and it combines with one of the hashing functions mentioned earlier to do the signing. To sign the message, we need to get access to an RSA private key. Ballerina supports the archive type PKCS12 (`.p12`), which is used for storing certificates and private keys and is also known as a *keystore* `file`. The signing functions supported in the `crypto` module are as follows:

- `crypto:signRsaMd5(input, privateKey) returns byte[]`
- `crypto:signRsaSha1(input, privateKey) returns byte[]`

- `crypto:signRsaSha128(input, privateKey) returns byte[]`
- `crypto:signRsaSha256(input, privateKey) returns byte[]`
- `crypto:signRsaSha384(input, privateKey) returns byte[]`
- `crypto:signRsaSha512(input, privateKey) returns byte[]`

Listing 9-3 shows how to read a keystore file to extract the private key and do some message signing.

Listing 9-3. Creating Message Signatures

```
import ballerina/crypto;
import ballerina/io;

public function main(string... args) returns error? {
    string input = "Hello, World!";
    crypto:KeyStore keyStore = {
        path: "/usr/lib/ballerina/ballerina-1.0.0/" +
        "distributions/jballerina-1.0.0/examples/crypto/sampleKeystore.p12",
        password: "ballerina" };
    crypto:PrivateKey privateKey = check crypto:decodePrivateKey(keyStore,
                                            "ballerina", "ballerina");
    byte[] output = check crypto:signRsaMd5(input.toBytes(), privateKey);
    io:println("Signature: ", output.toBase16());
}
```

```
$ ballerina run sign.bal
Signature: 605df342f7061064a6b9036cedd75f1b6e546a6e626ca2658a927a0f5df
24e29fd72f527d8cddfd1d720c2986acfed63a9644d11830e7f4d02bf2be783f2fad627
373e3fc75433eab9f118555236eaf252d0b874a776036a7c485f01353d352d2227057
d55bb597de3db109cec2784b92421242e20e40e9e9a8aaedef016103a58424263533388
b9be8735c962ff28a4701f5e9aa647f8fe7acd66f4fb36f590c93aeeb66439db27e7620
1c821b9110d1e1653eba35af53b228808f237f9470fcb27fd66a3504d17f450bb6351
8ebb276af31777c29bdcbafd2d7f63e2a2bf8f199f95283b011295d697d56e6ee8
fbce35ed36cf89d0ef6cc530ad37064a233d
```

HMAC

The Hash-based Message Authentication Code (HMAC) algorithm provides integrity and authentication checks for messages. It uses message hashing and a private key when generating the HMAC. HMAC operations are differentiated with the hashing function that is used in the algorithm. The operations supported are listed here:

- `crypto:hmacMd5(payload, secretKey) returns byte[]`
- `crypto:hmacSha1(payload, secretKey) returns byte[]`
- `crypto:hmacSha128(payload, secretKey) returns byte[]`
- `crypto:hmacSha256(payload, secretKey) returns byte[]`
- `crypto:hmacSha384(payload, secretKey) returns byte[]`
- `crypto:hmacSha512(payload, secretKey) returns byte[]`

A sample usage of HMAC is shown in Listing 9-4.

Listing 9-4. HMAC Generation

```
import ballerina/crypto;
import ballerina/io;

public function main(string... args) returns error? {
    string input = "Hello, World!";
    string key = "mysecret";
    byte[] output = crypto:hmacMd5(input.toBytes(),
                                   key.toBytes());
    io:println("HMAC: ", output.toBase16());
}
```

```
$ ballerina run hmac.bal
HMAC: ecf62c95db159ba7e78064c095fd8602
```

Private Key Crypto

Ballerina provides private key cryptography functionality using the AES algorithm. The Ballerina AES functions are named based on the cipher block modes that are supported. The supported functions are as follows, and all return a byte:

- `crypto:encryptAesCbc(input, key, iv, padding = PKCS5) returns byte[]`
- `crypto:encryptAesEcb(input, key, padding = PKCS5) returns byte[]`
- `crypto:encryptAesGcm(input, key, iv, padding = PKCS5, tagSize = 128) returns byte[]`
- `crypto:decryptAesCbc(input, key, iv, padding = PKCS5) returns byte[]`
- `crypto:decryptAesEcb(input, key, padding = PKCS5) returns byte[]`
- `crypto:decryptAesGcm(input, key, iv, padding = PKCS5, tagSize = 128) returns byte[]`

Listing 9-5 contains a sample code snippet that uses AES encryption/decryption with CBC cipher block mode and with default PKCS5 padding.

Listing 9-5. AES Encryption/Decryption

```
import ballerina/crypto;
import ballerina/io;
import ballerina/lang.'string as strings;

public function main(string... args) returns error? {
    string input = "Hello, World!";

    byte[16] key = [15, 21, 36, 11, 65, 36, 76, 28, 69, 10, 61, 32, 63,
                    14, 55, 6];
    byte[16] iv = [35, 25, 16, 15, 13, 16, 45, 56, 29, 15, 63, 52, 15,
                   44, 51, 15];

```

```
    byte[] encryptedData = check crypto:encryptAesCbc(input.toBytes(),
                                            key, iv);
    io:println("Encrypted Data: ", encryptedData.toBase16());
    byte[] decryptedData = check crypto:decryptAesCbc(encryptedData,
                                            key, iv);
    io:println("Decrypted Data: ", strings:fromBytes(decryptedData));
}
```

```
$ ballerina run aes.bal
Encrypted Data: 3811dd1a1d7e3454eeb1249063df5744
Decrypted Data: Hello, World!
```

Public Key Crypto

Ballerina provides public key cryptography functionality through the RSA algorithm. The RSA encryption/decryption functions that are provided are listed here:

- `crypto:encryptRsaEcb(input, key, padding = PKCS1) returns byte[]`
- `crypto:decryptRsaEcb(input, key, padding = PKCS1) returns byte[]`

A sample Ballerina program using RSA public key cryptography is shown in Listing 9-6.

Listing 9-6. RSA Encryption/Decryption

```
import ballerina/crypto;
import ballerina/io;
import ballerina/lang.'string as strings;

public function main(string... args) returns error? {
    string input = "Hello, World!";
    crypto:KeyStore keyStore = { path: "/usr/lib/ballerina/ballerina-1.0.0" +
                                 "-alpha/examples/crypto/sampleKeystore.
                                 p12",
                                 password: "ballerina" };
    crypto:PrivateKey privateKey = check crypto:decodePrivateKey(keyStore,
                                         "ballerina", "ballerina");
```

```
    crypto:PublicKey publicKey = check crypto:decodePublicKey(keyStore,
                                                 "ballerina");
    byte[] output = check crypto:encryptRsaEcb(input.toBytes(), publicKey);
    io:println("RSA Public Key Encrypted Data: ", output.toBase16());
    output = check crypto:decryptRsaEcb(output, privateKey);
    io:println("RSA Private Key Decrypted Data: ", strings:fromBytes(output));
}
```

```
$ ballerina run rsa.bal
RSA Public Key Encrypted Data: 7d963f26f3dc411a9b91089a72e234375c9f1565
da13fb0131df3c1cf066c5afb91d238003de7e495a91e85385e64f7b8890ef91c5f
3840c1fe218965ae66e27229822c6f35e6685e3ceeadbecc99e4a1e049a4252ff7ca
bda8271f2418fdc56b82fdee0e8a66c7d4ea33464c687cf89e2070072388ea30068af
496567a69d07f12fc35ee2cb919933f351766daffcd28d643729b27f0623b2cc651
98ad2d3d234f5690420ede5175f138006c497385a42bec4c36cac5fcd883b667022061
d07857263ef4643d5f6ac3c61c248ff8ad5b16fc6d86c57bcfc441e1d00e5effb9e1
c73a9bb30aace14d56e850ef74feba02b3f34ab9372380ff723b97c8a257e2d
RSA Private Key Decrypted Data: Hello, World!
```

Listing 9-6 shows how two separate public/private keys are used in encryption and decryption operations.

Identity and Access Control

When we are discussing identity and access control, authentication and authorization play a key role.

Authentication

Single-factor, username/password-based authentication is the most common in the current industry. A user's credentials should check and validate against the stored username and password. These credentials need to send the information across to the backend servers to authenticate. They should not be transferred in an unsecured communication channel. The communication channel should be secured and encrypted from end to end to avoid man-in the-middle attacks. On the backend, password should not be stored as plaintext. To enhance the security and privacy, passwords are saved as a salted hash format. These credentials can be stored in different storage backends such as files, databases, and LDAP.

Let's see how we can use Ballerina to write a simple program to provide file-based basic authentication.

File-Based Basic Authentication

In Ballerina, a service can be secured using basic authentication. The auth provider reads the username and password from a file with the TOML format. For authorization, Ballerina uses the concept of scopes. A resource declared in a service can be bound to one or more scopes. A scope can be declared in the same user-defined TOML file with usernames and passwords.

The following code block shows the contents of the file `sample-users.toml`, which has the required format of usernames, passwords, and scopes, including their mapping:

```
["b7a.users"]

 ["b7a.users.lakmal"]
 password="password1"
 ["b7a.users.anjana"]
 password="password2"
```

In the authorization phase, the scopes of the resource are compared against the scopes mapped to the user. Let's look at the sample shown in Listing 9-7.

Listing 9-7. basic_auth_service.bal

```
import ballerina/http;
import ballerina/log;
import ballerina/auth;

auth:InboundBasicAuthProvider basicAuthProvider = new;
http:BasicAuthHandler basicAuthHandler = new(basicAuthProvider);

listener http:Listener secureBasicAuthEP = new(9443, config = {
    auth: {
        authHandlers: [basicAuthHandler]
```

```
11      },
12      secureSocket: {
13          keyStore: {
14              path: "${ballerina.home}/bre/security/ballerinaKeystore.p12",
15              password: "ballerina"
16          }
17      }
18 });
19
20 @http:ServiceConfig {
21      basePath: "/hello"
22 }
23 service hello on secureBasicAuthEP {
24
25      @http:ResourceConfig {
26          methods: ["GET"]
27      }
28      resource function hi(http:Caller caller, http:Request req) {
29          var result = caller->respond("Hi Greetings!!!\n");
30          if (result is error) {
31              log:printError("Error in responding to caller", err = result);
32          }
33      }
34 }
```

On lines 5 and 6, we create a Basic Auth header handler with the relevant configurations. The endpoint used here is the `http:Listener`, which by default tries to authenticate each request. The Basic Authentication handler is set to this endpoint using the `authHandlers` attribute. It is optional to override the authentication at the service level and/or resource level.

Authentication can be disabled by setting the `enabled: false` annotation attribute.

```
$ ballerina run basic_auth_service.bal --b7a.config.file=sample-users.toml
[ballerina/http] started HTTPS/WSS listener 0.0.0.0:9443

$ curl -k -u lakmal:wrongPassword https://localhost:9443/hello/hi
Authentication failure
```

Authorization

Authorization is the process of establishing which user has the right to access a particular object. To grant authorization, we need to identify the user by using an authentication process.

Role-based access control (RBAC) and attribute-based access control (ABAC) are two major industry-recognized authorization mechanisms.

- **RBAC** is an approach to restricting system access to authorized users. In most RBAC systems, users are assigned particular roles, and through those role assignments they acquire the permissions needed to perform particular system functions. Since users are not directly assigned permissions but assigned through their role, permissions can be managed by simply assigning appropriate roles to a user's account.
- **ABAC** defines an access control paradigm whereby access rights are granted to users through the use of policies that combine attributes. Unlike RBAC, without using predefined roles that carry a specific set of permissions associated with them, ABAC uses policies that express a complex rule set that can evaluate many different attributes.

Let's see how Ballerina can be used to implement simple RBAC with scopes.

Ballerina Basic Auth with Scope

Let's extend the same basic authentication sample we discussed earlier. For authorization, Ballerina uses the concept of scopes. A resource declared in a service can be bound to one or more scopes. A scope can be declared in the same user-defined TOML file with usernames and passwords.

The following code block shows the contents of the file `sample-users.toml`, which has the required format of usernames, passwords, and scopes, including their mapping:

```
["b7a.users"]

 ["b7a.users.lakmal"]
 password="password1"
 scopes="scope2,scope3"
```

```
["b7a.users.anjana"]
password="password2"
scopes="scope1"
```

In the authorization phase, the scopes of the resource are compared against the scopes mapped to the user. Let's look at the sample shown in Listing 9-8.

Listing 9-8. basic_auth_service_scope.bal

```
import ballerina/http;
import ballerina/log;
import ballerina/auth;

auth:InboundBasicAuthProvider basicAuthProvider = new;
http:BasicAuthHandler basicAuthHandler = new(basicAuthProvider);

listener http:Listener secureBasicAuthEP = new(9443, config = {
    auth: {
        authHandlers: [basicAuthHandler]
    },
    secureSocket: {
        keyStore: {
            path: "${ballerina.home}/bre/security/ballerinaKeystore.p12",
            password: "ballerina"
        }
    }
});

@http:ServiceConfig {
    basePath: "/hello",
    auth: {
        scopes: ["scope1"]
    }
}
service hello on secureBasicAuthEP {

```

```
    @http:ResourceConfig {
        methods: ["GET"],
        auth: {
            scopes: ["scope2"]
        }
    }
    resource function hi(http:Caller caller, http:Request req) {
        var result = caller->respond("Hi Greetings!!!\n");
        if (result is error) {
            log:printError("Error in responding to caller", err = result);
        }
    }
    resource function bye(http:Caller caller, http:Request req) {
        var result = caller->respond("Bye Greetings!!!\n");
        if (result is error) {
            log:printError("Error in responding to caller", err = result);
        }
    }
}
```

Authorization is based on scopes. A scope maps to one or more roles. For a user to access a resource, the user should be in the same groups as the scope. To specify one or more scopes of a resource, the `scopes` annotation attribute can be used.

The authentication and authorization settings can be overridden at the resource level. The `hi` and bye resources would inherit the `enabled: true` flag from the service level, which is set automatically. The service-level scope (i.e., `scope1`) will be overridden by the scope defined in the `hi` resource level (i.e., `scope2`). The bye resource inherits the setting in the service level. The user `lakmal` should be able to access the resource `hi` but not the resource bye. The user `anjana` should be able to access the resource bye but not the resource hi.

```
$ ballerina run secured_service_with_basic_auth.bal --b7a.config.
file=sample-users.toml
[ballerina/http] started HTTPS/WSS endpoint 0.0.0.0:9443

$ curl -k -u lakmal:password1 https://localhost:9443/hello/hi
Hi Greetings!!!
```

```
$ curl -k -u lakmal:password1 https://localhost:9443/hello/bye
Authorization failure

$ curl -k -u anjana:password2 https://localhost:9443/hello/hi
Authorization failure
$ curl -k -u anjana:password2 https://localhost:9443/hello/bye
Hi Greetings!!!
```

Access Tokens

An *access token* is a token that contains the security credentials for a login session and identifies the user, the user's groups, and the user's privileges, and in some cases this can be extended to provide additional user information.

JWT

JSON Web Token (JWT) is an open standard (RFC 7519) that defines a compact and self-contained way to securely transmit information between parties as a JSON object. In general, JWTs are used as signed tokens, which are capable of verifying the integrity of the claims contained within them, while encrypted tokens hide those claims from other parties.

Let's implement a secured service with JWT. See Listing 9-9.

Listing 9-9. jwt_service.bal

```
import ballerina/http;
import ballerina/jwt;
import ballerina/log;

jwt:InboundJwtAuthProvider jwtAuthProvider = new({
    issuer: "ballerina",
    audience: "ballerina.io",
    trustStoreConfig: {
        certificateAlias: "ballerina",
        trustStore: {
            path: "${ballerina.home}/bre/security/ballerinaTruststore.p12",
            password: "ballerina"
        }
```

```
    }
});

http:BearerAuthHandler jwtAuthHandler = new(jwtAuthProvider);

listener http:Listener securedEPwithJWT = new(9443, config = {
    auth: {
        authHandlers: [jwtAuthHandler]
    },
    // The secure hello world sample uses HTTPS.
    secureSocket: {
        keyStore: {
            path: "${ballerina.home}/bre/security/ballerinaKeystore.p12",
            password: "ballerina"
        }
    }
});

service hello on securedEPwithJWT {
    @http:ResourceConfig {
        methods: ["GET"],
        path: "/",
        auth: {
            scopes: ["hello"],
            enabled: true
        }
    }
    resource function hello(http:Caller caller, http:Request req) {
        error? result = caller->respond("Hello, World!!!");
        if (result is error) {
            log:printError("Error in responding to caller", err = result);
        }
    }
}
```

On lines 5 to 13, we create an inbound JWT authentication provider with the relevant configurations. On line 17, we create a Bearer Auth handler with the created JWT Auth provider.

In line 19, the endpoint used is `http:Listener`. The JWT authentication handler is set to this endpoint using the `authHandlers` attribute. It is optional to override the authentication and authorization at the service and resource levels.

```
$ ballerina run jwt_service.bal
[ballerina/http] started HTTPS/WSS listener 0.0.0.0:9443
```

Let's access our secured JWT service by using the `curl` command. If we don't provide a valid JWT, it will give an authentication failure.

```
$ curl -k https://localhost:9443/hello/
Authentication failure
```

Let's get a valid JWT token. You can use `https://jwt.io` to get a sample JWT token by providing the following sample data:

HEADER:

```
{
  "alg": "RS256",
  "typ": "JWT"
}
```

PAYLOAD:

```
{
  "sub": "ballerina",
  "iss": "ballerina",
  "exp": 2818415019,
  "iat": 1524575019,
  "jti": "f5aded50585c46f2b8ca233d0c2a3c9d",
  "aud": [
      "ballerina",
      "ballerina.org",
      "ballerina.io"
  ],
  "scope": "hello"
}
```

```
RSASHA256(
  base64UrlEncode(header) + "." +
  base64UrlEncode(payload),
  [public-key or certificate],
  [private-key, only if we want to generate new token. The key never
  leave client/browser]
)
```

Then your sample JWT will look like this:


```
eyJhbGciOiJSUzI1NiIsInR5cCI6IkpXVCJ9.\
eyJzdWIiOiJiYWxsZXJpbmEiLCJpc3MiOiJiYWxsZXJpbmEiLCJleHAiOjI4MTgOMTUwMTksIm\
lhdCI6MTUyNDU3NTAxOSwianRpIjoiZjVhZGVkNTA1ODVjNDZmMmI4Y2EyMzNkMGMyYTNjOWQi\
LCJhdWQiOlsiYmFsbGVyaW5hIiwiYmFsbGVyaW5hLm9yZyIsImJhbGxlcmluYS5pbyJdLCJzY2\
9wZSI6ImhlbGxvIn0.bNoqz9_DzgeKSK6ru3DnKL7NiNbY32ksXPYrh6JpO_O3ST7WfXMs9WVk\
x6Q2TiYukMAGrnMUFrJnrJvZwC3glAmRBrl4BYCbQOc5mCbgM9qhhCjC1tBA5OrjtLAtRW-JTR\
pCKSOB9_EmlVKfvXPKDLIpM5hnfhOin1R3lJCPspJ2ey_Ho6fDhsKE3DZgssvgPgI9PBItnkip\
Q3CqqXWhV-RFBkVBEGPDYXTUVGbXhdNOBSwKw5ZoVJrCUiNG5XDOK4sgN9udVTi3EMKNMnVQaq\
399k6RYPAy3vIhByS6QZtRjOG8X93WJw-9GLiHvcabuid8Olnrs2-mAEcstgiHVw
```


Let's pass JWT to the curl command as a bearer in an authorization header, as shown here:

```
$ curl -k -H "Authorization: Bearer eyJhbGciOiJSUzI1NiIsInR5cCI6IkpXVCJ9.\
eyJzdWIiOiJiYWxsZXJpbmEiLCJpc3MiOiJiYWxsZXJpbmEiLCJleHAiOjI4MTgOMTUwMTksIm\
lhdCI6MTUyNDU3NTAxOSwianRpIjoiZjVhZGVkNTA1ODVjNDZmMmI4Y2EyMzNkMGMyYTNjOWQi\
LCJhdWQiOlsiYmFsbGVyaW5hIiwiYmFsbGVyaW5hLm9yZyIsImJhbGxlcmluYS5pbyJdLCJzY2\
9wZSI6ImhlbGxvIn0.bNoqz9_DzgeKSK6ru3DnKL7NiNbY32ksXPYrh6JpO_O3ST7WfXMs9WVk\
x6Q2TiYukMAGrnMUFrJnrJvZwC3glAmRBrl4BYCbQOc5mCbgM9qhhCjC1tBA5OrjtLAtRW-JTR\
pCKSOB9_EmlVKfvXPKDLIpM5hnfhOin1R3lJCPspJ2ey_Ho6fDhsKE3DZgssvgPgI9PBItnkip\
Q3CqqXWhV-RFBkVBEGPDYXTUVGbXhdNOBSwKw5ZoVJrCUiNG5XDOK4sgN9udVTi3EMKNMnVQaq\
399k6RYPAy3vIhByS6QZtRjOG8X93WJw-9GLiHvcabuid8Olnrs2-mAEcstgiHVw" https://
localhost:9443/hello/
Hello, World!!!
```

As an exercise, you can try to access the secureJWT service by passing an invalid JWT. It will give you an authentication failure.

OAuth 2.0

OAuth 2.0 is an authorization framework for access delegation. In OAuth 2.0, process resource owners can authorize third-party access to their server resources without sharing their credentials. This is done by issuing an access token to third-party clients by an authorization server, with the approval of the resource owner. The third party then uses the access token to access the protected resources hosted by the resource server. OAuth 2.0 is a widely used specification for the authorization aspects of resources in a lightweight manner.

The two token types involved in OAuth 2.0 are access tokens and refresh tokens. The access token is used for authorization to get access to the resources from the resource server, and the refresh token is used to get a new access token when the old one expires. Methods to get access tokens from the authorization server are called *grants*. There are several grant types, namely, Authorization Code, Password (Resource Owner Credentials), and Client Credentials. This book is not going to discuss the details of each grant types, but if you are interested, you can look at the OAuth2 specification for more information. You can find the specification at `https://tools.ietf.org/html/rfc6749`.

Let's see how we can write a Ballerina program with different grant type to access the secured service that is protected by OAuth2.

In Listing 9-10, we will use the Client Credentials grant type to access the online hosted application.

Listing 9-10. oauth_client_credentials_client.bal

```
import ballerina/http;
import ballerina/log;
import ballerina/oauth2;

oauth2:OutboundOAuth2Provider oauth2Provider1 = new({
   tokenUrl: "https://bitbucket.org/site/oauth2/access_token",
   clientId: "mMNWS9PLmM93V5WHjC",
   clientSecret: "jLY6xPY3ER4bNTspaGu6fb7kahhs7kUa"
});
http:BearerAuthHandler oauth2Handler1 = new(oauth2Provider1);

http:Client clientEP1 = new("https://api.bitbucket.org/2.0", {
```

```
13     auth: {
14         authHandler: oauth2Handler1
15     }
16 });
17
18 public function main() {
19     var response1 = clientEP1->get("/repositories/b7ademo");
20     if (response1 is http:Response) {
21         var result = response1.getJsonPayload();
22         if (result is json) {
23             var values = result.values;
24             if (values is json[]) {
25                 var uuid = values[0].uuid;
26                 if (uuid is json) {
27                     log:printInfo(uuid.toString());
28                 }
29             }
30         } else {
31             log:printError("Failed to retrieve payload for clientEP1.");
32         }
33     } else {
34         log:printError("Failed to call the endpoint from clientEP1.",
           err = response1);
35     }
35 }
```

On line 5, we define the OAuth2 client endpoint to call the backend services. The OAuth2 with Client Credentials grant type is set by creating an `oauth2:OutboundOAuth2Provider` object with the relevant configurations passed as a record. The code on line 18, in the `main` function, calls the corresponding endpoint, which will return a successful response.

```
$ ballerina run oauth_client_credentials_client.bal
2019-08-18 12:46:11,877 INFO  [ballerina/log] - {9356828d-6797-496f-975e-3fabaf677214}
```

Let's look at how we can write a client to use the Password grant type. You can define the OAuth2 client endpoint to call the back-end services. The OAuth2 authentication with the Password grant type is set by creating an `oauth2:OutboundOAuth2Provider` object with the relevant configurations passed as a record. If the access token expires or becomes invalid, then it will be automatically refreshed with the provided `refreshConfig`. See the following sample code section:

```
oauth2:OutboundOAuth2Provider oauth2Provider2 = new({
   tokenUrl: "https://bitbucket.org/site/oauth2/access_token",
   username: "b7a.demo@gmail.com",
   password: "ballerina",
   clientId: "mMNWS9PLmM93V5WHjC",
   clientSecret: "jLY6xPY3ER4bNTspaGu6fb7kahhs7kUa",
   refreshConfig: {
       refreshUrl: "https://bitbucket.org/site/oauth2/access_token"
   }
});
http:BearerAuthHandler oauth2Handler2 = new(oauth2Provider2);
```

The following sample code block defines the OAuth2 client endpoint to call the back-end services by using the Authorization code grant type. OAuth2 with direct token mode is set by creating an `oauth2:OutboundOAuth2Provider` object with the relevant configurations passed as a record. If the `accessToken` is invalid or not provided, it will be automatically refreshed with the provided `refreshConfig`.

```
oauth2:OutboundOAuth2Provider oauth2Provider3 = new({
   accessToken: "ya29.GlvQBkqJSOynOzsZm4IIUUzLk3DH1rRiCMKnHiz6deycKm
   TFiDsuoFlFfrmXF8dCbOgyzLyXpnv3VcrIlauj3nMs61CbydaAqMl6RwVIU2r2qg1
   StVVvxRWT9_Or",
   refreshConfig: {
       clientId: "506144513496-dqm5vdqfrfhdjjom1Ormvafb8e3h7rtm.apps.
                 googleusercontent.com",
       clientSecret: "3hw2XN4MfiIRrv6mghX6m5gM",
       refreshToken: "1/UwH3YyYccKTrH9bqj35Y7hMYTK9f3HEC3uzlrleFwPE",
       refreshUrl: "https://www.googleapis.com/oauth2/v4/token"
   }
});
http:BearerAuthHandler oauth2Handler3 = new(oauth2Provider3);
```

Secure Programming

Almost all modern applications interact with a network. Therefore, we need to write more secure programs. The Ballerina compiler is capable of enforcing security precautions. Taint checking plays a major role here.

Taint Checking

Taint checking is designed to increase security by preventing any variable from being modified by an outside user. If we use a variable in another expression without marking it explicitly as untainted (or clean), that second variable will now be marked as suspicious. This kind of analysis is important to prevent SQL injection (such as direct commands to an SQL database or the host computer operating system), path manipulation, file manipulation, unauthorized file access, and unvalidated redirect (open redirect). Since a taint check happens at the compiler stage, the programmer can then redesign the program to erect a safe wall around the dangerous input.

Ballerina has built-in taint analysis in its compiler. As a result of the taint analysis mechanism, the Ballerina compiler identifies untrusted (tainted) data by observing how tainted data propagates through the program. If untrusted data is passed to a security-sensitive parameter, a compiler error is generated.

Let's look at some sample programs. See Listing 9-11.

Listing 9-11. taint-test1.bal

```
import ballerinax/java.jdbc;

public function main(string... args) {

    jdbc:Client customerDBEP = new ({
        //JDBC configs
    });

    var result = customerDBEP->
    select("SELECT firstname FROM student WHERE registration_id = " +
            args[0], ());
    table<record { string firstname; }> dataTable;
    if (result is error) {
```

```
        error e = <error> result;
        panic e;
    } else {
        dataTable = result;
    }
}
```

```
$ ballerina run taint-test1.bal
error: .::taint-test.bal:10:12: tainted value passed to untainted parameter
'sqlQuery'
```

The preceding code block leads to a compiler error. The taint checking mechanism of Ballerina completely prevents SQL injection vulnerabilities by disallowing tainted data in the SQL query. See Listing 9-12.

Listing 9-12. taint-test2.bal

```
01 function userDefinedSecureOperation(@untainted string secureParameter) {
02     // logic
03 }
04 public function main(string... args) {
05     userDefinedSecureOperation(args[0]);
06 }
```

```
$ ballerina run taint-test2.bal
error: .::taint-test.bal:7:32: tainted value passed to untainted parameter
'secureParameter'
```

Line 5 results in a compiler error because a user-provided argument is passed to a sensitive parameter. But after performing the necessary validations and/or escaping, we can use a type cast expression with the `@untainted` annotation to mark the proceeding value as `trusted` and pass it to a sensitive parameter. Then it will pass through the compiler.

```
userDefinedSecureOperation(<@untainted> args[0]);
```

Let's analyze the sample shown in Listing 9-13.

Listing 9-13. taint-test3.bal

```
import ballerinax/java.jdbc;
type Student record {
    string firstname;
};
function userDefinedSecureOperation(@untainted string secureParameter) {
    // logic
}
function sanitizeAndReturnTainted(string input) returns string {
    // transform and sanitize the string here.
    return input;
}
function sanitizeAndReturnUntainted(string input) returns @untainted
string {
    // transform and sanitize the string here.
    return input;
}

public function main(string... args) {
    jdbc:Client customerDBEP = new ({
        //JDBC config
    });
    var result = customerDBEP->
    select("SELECT firstname FROM student WHERE registration_id = " +
              "*", ());
    table<record { string firstname; }> dataTable;
    if (result is error) {
        error e = <error> result;
        panic e;
    } else {
        dataTable = result;
    }
    while (dataTable.hasNext()) {
        var jsonResult = dataTable.getNext();
        if (jsonResult is Student) {
```

```
35             Student jsonData = jsonResult;
36
37             userDefinedSecureOperation(jsonData.firstname);
38
39            string sanitizedData1 = sanitizeAndReturnTainted(jsonData.
              firstname);
40
41             userDefinedSecureOperation(sanitizedData1);
42
43             string sanitizedData2 = sanitizeAndReturnUntainted(jsonData.
               firstname);
44
45             userDefinedSecureOperation(sanitizedData2);
46         }
47     }
48     checkpanic customerDBEP.stop();
49     return;
50 }
```

```
$ ballerina run taint-test3.bal
error: .::taint-test.bal:37:40: tainted value passed to untainted parameter
'secureParameter'
error: .::taint-test.bal:41:40: tainted value passed to untainted parameter
'secureParameter'
```

The return values of certain functions built into Ballerina are decorated with the `@tainted` annotation to denote that the return value should be untrusted (tainted). One such example is the data read from a database. Therefore, line 37 results in a compile error because a value derived from a database read (tainted) is passed to a sensitive parameter.

Line 41 results in a compile error because the `sanitize` function returns a value derived from tainted data. Therefore, the return of the `sanitize` function is also tainted.

Line 45 successfully compiles. Although the `sanitize` function returns a value derived from tainted data, the return value is annotated with the `@untainted` annotation. This means that the return value is safe and can be trusted.

Summary

In this chapter, we learned about the basic concepts of information security: confidentiality, integrity, and availability. We also learned about authentication, authorization, and nonrepudiation come. Then we looked at how Ballerina helps to implement information security and the programming APIs that are related to information security.

CHAPTER 10

Database Programming

Databases are paramount for our day-to-day lives. Every day you will interact with some type of a database. If you go to a supermarket, each time the cashier scans an item, the cashier is looking up the price against a barcode using a database. At the same time, the database is updating its inventory to track its stock of goods. In an airport, if you go through customs, officers will scan your passport; they are looking up all your details in a database and instantly pulling up your information on their screen. All these aspects are possible through the availability of database management systems (DBMSs).

Many database technologies are available. The most mature and widely used technique is the relational database model. There are also other approaches such as document databases, key-value stores, and graph databases. The different types are mainly differentiated by the logical structure that the data is stored in. That is, the different types of databases are optimized to store specific categories of data, and their performance characteristics also change based on this.

In this chapter, we will be looking at the most popular database category, the relational database management system (RDBMS). We will be covering what the relational model is, how to work with databases, and specifically how to work with databases using Ballerina.

Relational Database Model

The main element of a relational database model is a *table*. This is also known as a *relation*. A database table can be visualized as a rectangular data grid, with columns and rows. Each cell in this data grid stores some data value.

Table 10-1 shows an example of a database table.

A. Fernando and L. Warusawithana, *Beginning Ballerina Programming*,
https://doi.org/10.1007/978-1-4842-5139-3_10

***Table 10-1.** Employees*

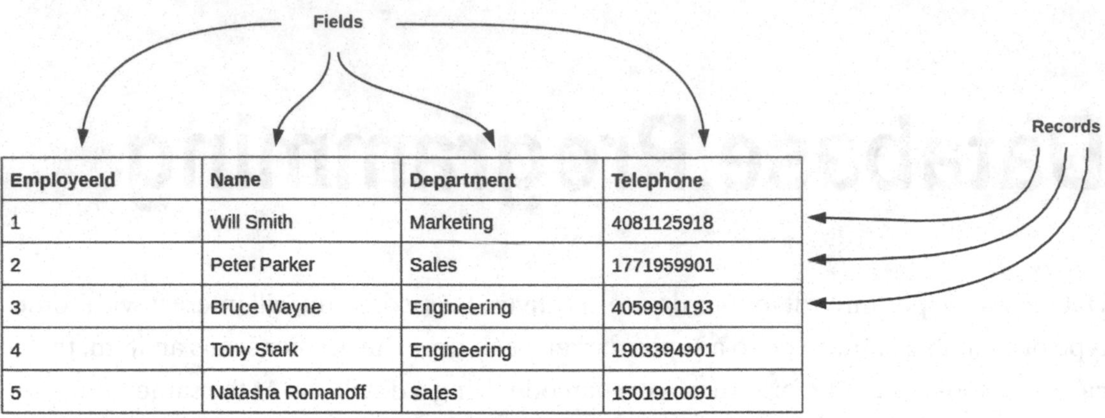

EmployeeId	Name	Department	Telephone
1	Will Smith	Marketing	4081125918
2	Peter Parker	Sales	1771959901
3	Bruce Wayne	Engineering	4059901193
4	Tony Stark	Engineering	1903394901
5	Natasha Romanoff	Sales	1501910091

This table represents data about company employees. So, we call this the Employees table. The table has a fixed set of columns: EmployeeId, Name, Department, and Telephone. Each row in the table represents a set of values for these columns. That is, each row will have a single value for each of the columns defined in the table. We call one of these rows a data *record*. Each cell value of a record is called a record *field*.

Each individual record's field values are related to each other. That is, for example, the first record in the Employee table contains the field's values for the employee Will Smith. That is, it contains Will Smith's name, his department, and his telephone number in field values. The EmployeeId field is present in the table to identify a specific record uniquely. You may be thinking that we could have used the Name field to identify the record uniquely; however, names are not really unique, because two people can have the same name. Therefore, the EmployeeId field just acts as a numerical value to identify a specific row or a record in the table. For example, we can tell the database to give us the record with the EmployeeId equal to 2, and it will return the record value that has Peter Parker's field values.

A unique field that identifies a record in a database table is called a *primary key*. When we mark a database table's column as a primary key, the DBMS creates a unique key index for it and will never store two records with the same primary key value. Also, the DBMS will be able to efficiently look up a record using a primary key value. A primary key can be created by combining two or more fields, which are called a *composite key*. The requirement for a composite key is that the participating fields must always have a combined unique value.

A typical database is created by grouping multiple database tables. Basically, any database table that can be logically grouped together will go to a single database.

If we put all the related data attributes together in a single row, why do we need more tables? Yes, we can actually put all these fields in a single table, but there are a few issues that can come up with that approach. Let's check this with an example.

Our new use case is that in our database we want to extend the department information we are storing. For this, we start by adding an additional field to represent the physical location of the company department, as shown in Table 10-2.

Table 10-2. *Employees (with Updated Department Information)*

EmployeeId	Name	Department	Dept-Location	Telephone
1	Will Smith	Marketing	Building-1	4081125918
2	Peter Parker	Sales	Building-2	1771959901
3	Bruce Wayne	Engineering	Building-1	4059901193
4	Tony Stark	Engineering	Building 1	1903394901
5	Natasha Romanoff	Sales	Building-2	1501910091

In Table 10-2, we can see the new additional field Dept-Location, which says where the employees of the department are housed. We have basically introduced new attributes related to a department. Each time we mention the department information for an employee record, we have to put all the department information properties for every record.

You will notice that each time we repeat the department name for an employee, we also have to repeat the department location value as well as the field values. This approach seems redundant and does not seem efficient when storing values because we have repeated the same values in different records. Also, later, if Engineering is moved to a different building, we will have to update all the records with the Engineering department to reflect the change. While updating these records, if we do not update all the records properly, we can have inconsistent data. For example, check the version of the Employees table in Table 10-3.

***Table 10-3.** Employees (with Inconsistent Department Information)*

EmployeeId	Name	Department	Dept-Location	Telephone
1	Will Smith	Marketing	Building-1	4081125918
2	Peter Parker	Sales	Building-2	1771959901
3	Bruce Wayne	Engineering	Building-3	4059901193
4	Tony Stark	Engineering	Building-1	1903394901
5	Natasha Romanoff	Sales	Building-2	1501910091

Here, we have started to update the department location of Engineering, but due to some program error, we have updated only Bruce Wayne's record, not Tony Stark. This makes the data inconsistent, because in two separate records, the Engineering department has two department locations. The root cause for these complications is the duplication of data in multiple records.

So you may be thinking, from each employee record, what if we have a way to point to a list of field values that represent a unique department, without actually putting all the values in the employee record itself? We can of course do this by creating a separate Departments table. It would have unique records that describe the departments. And the Employees table can simply refer to the Departments table records when an employee needs to be associated with a department. Tables 10-4 and 10-5 demonstrate how to do this.

***Table 10-4.** Employees (Normalized)*

EmployeeId	Name	DeptId	Telephone
1	Will Smith	1	4081125918
2	Peter Parker	2	1771959901
3	Bruce Wayne	3	4059901193
4	Tony Stark	3	1903394901
5	Natasha Romanoff	2	1501910091

Table 10-5. Departments

DeptId	Name	Location
1	Marketing	Building-1
2	Sales	Building-2
3	Engineering	Building-1

We now have a new database table called Departments, as shown in Table 10-5, where each record represents all the information related to a specific department. And each record can be uniquely identified by the field DeptId. So, the primary key of the Department table is DeptId.

Table 10-4 shows the updated Employees table, where its original fields related to department information have been replaced by a single DeptId field. This field basically points to the DeptId field in the Departments table. For example, when we read in the employee information for Tony Stark, we know his DeptId is 3, and in the Departments table, the DeptId with the value 3 says its department name is Engineering, and it is situated at Building-1.

We can see how we simply pointed to a record in an external table from our table's record, thus eliminating the requirement to always repeat the same possible field values. The DeptId field in the Employees table is marked as a *foreign key*. A foreign key is a table field that represents the value of a primary key of a different table. In this case, the DeptId field in the Employees table is a foreign key that points to the primary key of Departments, where its primary key field also happens to have the same field name, DeptId. The reason why a field marked as a foreign key must point to a primary key of a different table is because of the requirement that a unique record must be matched to the current record, rather than having a situation where multiple records are matched to it. The field names do not have to be the same in these tables to create this relationship, but most often, as a convention, they end up having the same name.

This process of finally eliminating redundancy and removing the chance of having inconsistent data is called *normalization*. In the process of normalization, from the Employees table, its records can simply point to a single record that represents the Department data, rather than having multiple copies within themselves. Now in this situation, changing the location of the Engineering department is just a matter of updating a single record in the Departments table.

Entity-Relationship Modeling

We have seen the main components of an RDBMS. When planning to create a database and its tables, the first part is to design the structure of the tables, that is, the fields, data types of the fields, the primary keys, and so on. This is called the *schema* of the database.

A well-known approach for defining the database schema is to use entity relationship (ER) modeling. ER diagrams basically list all the *entities* in the system and the relationships between them. An entity is a person, place, or thing. These entities are represented in RDBMS as tables.

Figure 10-1 represents the ER diagram for the scenario we talked about earlier, related to representing employees and departments in a company.

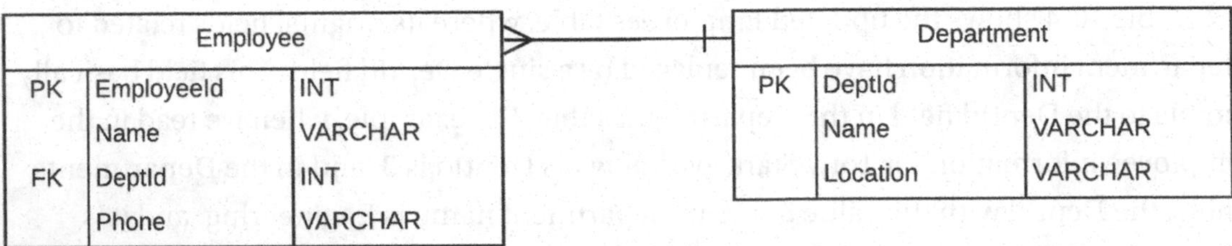

Figure 10-1. *Employee/department ER diagram*

Here we have two entities, Employee and Department, and we basically list all the attributes of each entity. We also attach any additional metadata to the attributes, such as the data type and whether they are primary or foreign keys. The data types of the attributes represent the type of values that can be stored in the respective fields. For example, `INT` means an integer type, meaning only numbers can be stored, and `VARCHAR` is a variable-size string value that can be stored.

Also, using ER diagrams, the relationships between the entities can be clearly visualized by means of lines going between them. These lines have different symbols on either end, symbolizing the type of relationship they have between the entities. This is called the *cardinality* of the relationship. This is basically the number of times an instance (record) of one entity is related to the instances of another entity. For example, in the previous scenario, the cardinality between Department and Employee is said to be *one-to-many*. This means one department will be connected to many employees, and an employee is connected to only one department.

This behavior is accomplished by having a foreign key in Employee, which points to the primary key of Department. That is, multiple employee records can have the same department record linked to them; thus, *many* employee records connect to *one* department record.

The cardinality is shown visually by the endpoints of the line between entities. Figure 10-2 shows the possibilities.

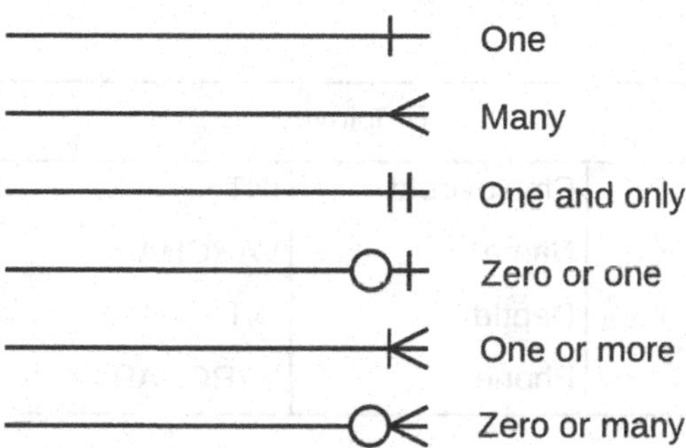

Figure 10-2. *Cardinality*

The list shown in Figure 10-2 illustrates how one side of a relationship is defined with the symbols. In this manner, the previous symbols are used twice (once on each side) in a relation between two entities when defining the cardinality.

Let's bring in another new entity, named Project. This represents a project that an employee will be working on. A project can contain multiple employees, and a single employee can be involved with multiple projects at a given time. Figure 10-3 shows the ER diagram.

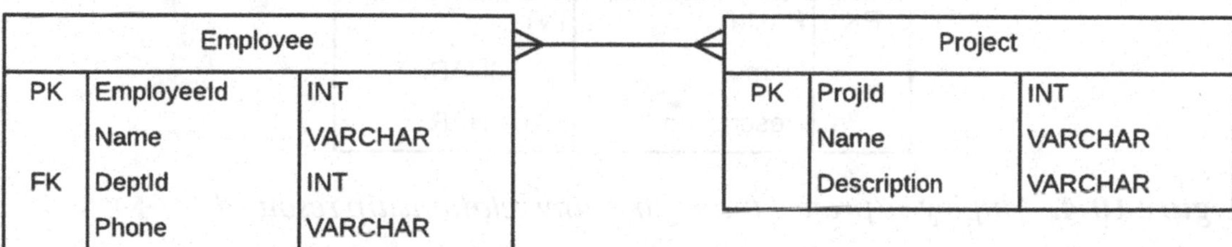

Figure 10-3. *Employee/project ER diagram*

The ER diagram shown here mentions that we need to have a many-to-many relationship between Employee and Project. But it doesn't really list all the attributes and their primary key/foreign key relationships needed to make it work. The reason is that, practically, we can't. Between two entities, when actually implementing the entities as tables in an RDBMS, you can only do at most a one-to-many relationship. So, does that mean we can't do a many-to-many relationship in the RDBMS? We can; we just need another entity, called an *association* entity, to resolve this. Figure 10-4 illustrates the model.

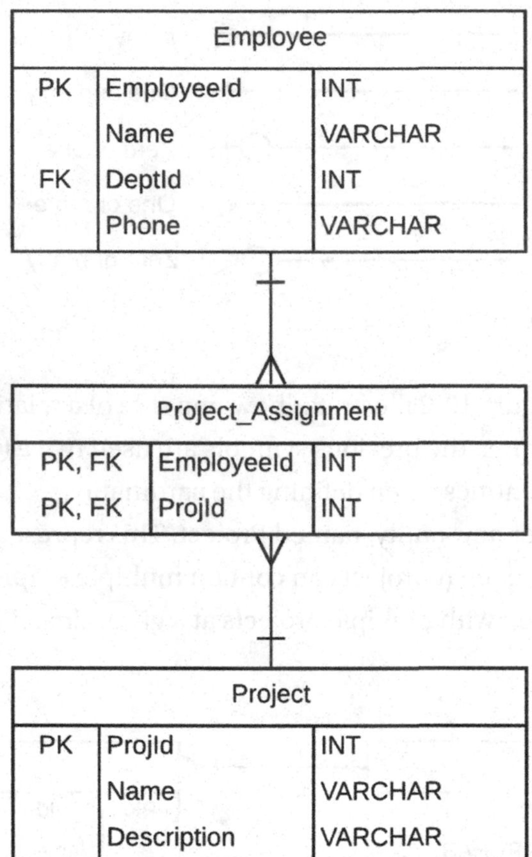

***Figure 10-4.** Employee/project many-to-many relationship resolved*

Here, we have introduced the new entity Project_Assignment, which basically creates the mapping between Employee and Project. It has two fields, EmployeeId and ProjId, which are foreign keys to the tables Employee and Project, respectively. In this way, the records of Project_Assignment can express the association for all the many-to-many connections between Employee and Project. Also, you may notice that both the

EmployeeId and ProjId attributes in Project_Assignment are marked as primary keys. This is because those two attributes together make up a unique value and thus can be used to identify a record unique in Project_Assignment. The two attributes making up a primary key here is the composite key.

Now we have learned the basics of entity-relationship diagrams and how to model a database system. Let's look at how to create the physical representation of these using an RDBMS.

Introduction to SQL

Structured Query Language (SQL) is the de facto standard when working with relational databases. SQL is a declarative language that you can use to define the structure of your data and to access and manipulate the data in a database. A declarative language means that we *say* what we need to be done, rather than *how* to do it. The opposite of declarative is *imperative*, which means we give the step-by-step instructions on how to do something. For example, Ballerina is an imperative programming language, where we tell a computer exactly how to get something done.

SQL is supported by all RDBMS vendors, such as Oracle, MSSQL, MySQL, PostgreSQL, H2, and so on. SQL was adopted as a standard by the American National Standard Institute (ANSI) and also by the International Organization for Standardization (ISO) and is now maintained by the ISO. It is constantly being improved, with new features being added to the standard. But many of the top vendors do not provide full conformance to the SQL standard because of various reasons. This is mainly because of the complexity of the full SQL standard itself and for reasons such as keeping up with backward compatibility of older product versions, which may contain some specific features of the vendor itself. A notable provider for keeping up with the SQL standard is PostgreSQL, where it always aims to be standard compliant.

SQL is a very human-friendly language, because its syntax is created in an intuitive way to work with relational databases. It is divided into two main sections, in relation to the type of operations it can do.

- Data Definition Language (DDL)
- Data Manipulation Language (DML)

DDL is responsible for defining or creating the database tables. DML is used for accessing and manipulating the records of tables. Let's take a closer look at the SQL syntax and usage of each.

Data Definition Language

DDL is all about creating the structure of the database and its objects, such as table indices, stored procedures, and so on. Let's create a database schema based on our earlier Employee/Department/Project scenario. Figure 10-5 shows the final ER diagram for this scenario.

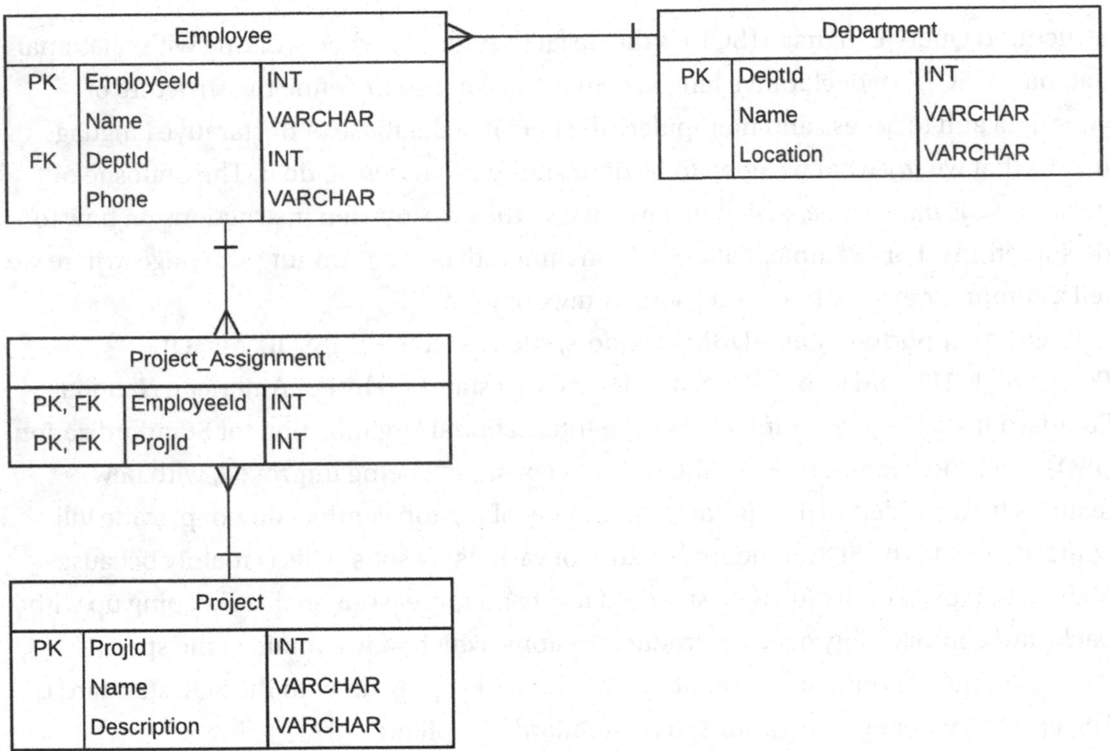

***Figure 10-5.** Employee/Department/Project final ER diagram*

Creating Tables

Tables are created in SQL using the `CREATE TABLE` statement, which has the following structure:

```
CREATE TABLE <table_name> (<column1> <datatype>, <column2> <datatype>,...);
```

The SQL statement for creating the Employees table is as follows:

```
CREATE TABLE Departments (DeptId INT, Name VARCHAR(200), Location
VARCHAR(200), PRIMARY KEY(DeptId));
```

Here, with the previous DDL SQL statement, we have created the Departments table with its attributes and data types. We have also mentioned that our primary key is represented by the field DeptId.

Table 10-6 shows the possible data types that can be used in table columns (fields). This is not meant as an exhaustive list, but it lists some of the main types you will use on a daily basis. Also, some of the names can be different in each DBMS, and they can contain their own specialized data types as well.

Table 10-6. *SQL Data Types*

SQL Type	Description
`INT`	An integer type, usually a 4-byte value, but the size depends on the DBMS.
`BIGINT`	An integer type, which can hold larger values, in relation to the `INT` value. This is usually an 8-byte value, but it depends on the DBMS.
`FLOAT`	A single-precision floating-point value.
`DOUBLE`	A double-precision floating-point value.
`BOOLEAN`	A Boolean type, with either a true or false value.
`CHAR (n)`	A fixed-size string, e.g., `CHAR(100)`.
`VARCHAR (n)`	A variable-size string, e.g., `VARCHAR(100)`.
`DATE`	Represents a type to store a date value; the format depends on the DBMS.
`TIME`	Represent a type to store a time value; the format depends on the DBMS.
`DATETIME`	A combination of a date and a time; the format depends on the DBMS.
`BLOB`	Binary Large Object; this is used to store a large binary value.
`CLOB`	Character Large Object; this is used to store a large string value.

The DDL statement required to create the Employees table is shown here:

```
CREATE TABLE Employees (EmployeeId INT, Name VARCHAR, DeptId INT,
Telephone VARCHAR, PRIMARY KEY(EmployeeId), FOREIGN KEY(DeptId) REFERENCES
Departments(DeptId));
```

Here, we are marking the DeptId field as a foreign key, which points to the field DeptId in the table Departments. This creates the link between the tables, and it also has the added benefit of the DBMS validating the field values when data updates are done. For example, when a new entry is added to the Employees table, the DBMS checks whether the DeptId value given is actually an existing value in a record in the Departments table. We call this maintaining the *referential integrity* among the tables.

In a similar manner, the following contains the SQL statements required to create the Projects and Project_Assignments tables:

```
CREATE TABLE Projects (ProjId INT, Name VARCHAR (200), Description VARCHAR
(200), PRIMARY KEY(ProjId));

CREATE TABLE Project_Assignments (EmployeeId INT, ProjId INT,
PRIMARY KEY(EmployeeId, ProjId), FOREIGN KEY (EmployeeId) REFERENCES
Employees(EmployeeId), FOREIGN KEY (ProjId) REFERENCES Projects(ProjId));
```

Data Definition Language

DDL is where you access and manipulate the data you have in tables. The operations we can do consist of four operations. They are the create, retrieve, update, and delete (CRUD) operations. Let's see the SQL statements that are used to accomplish the previous actions.

SQL INSERT

The SQL INSERT statements are used to populate data in a table by adding new rows/records to a table. The INSERT statements have the following format:

```
INSERT INTO <table_name> (column1, column2,...) VALUES (value1,
value2,...);
```

Let's see a few SQL INSERT statements used to populate data in our earlier defined database tables.

```
INSERT INTO Departments (DeptId, Name, Location) VALUES
(1, 'Marketing', 'Building-1');
INSERT INTO Departments VALUES (2, 'Sales', 'Building-2');

INSERT INTO Employees(EmployeeId, Name, DeptId, Telephone) VALUES
(1, 'Will Smith', 1, 4081125918);
INSERT INTO Employees(EmployeeId, Name, DeptId, Telephone) VALUES
(2, 'Peter Parker', 2, 1771959901);

INSERT INTO Projects (ProjId, Name, Description) VALUES
(1, 'SaveTheWorld1', 'Save the world for the first time');

INSERT INTO Project_Assignments VALUES (1, 1);
INSERT INTO Project_Assignments VALUES (2, 1);
```

Here, we start by populating the Departments table by adding two records to it. You will notice that the list of columns followed by the table name does not exist in the second query. This is valid syntax, because we can omit the list of columns when we are providing values for all the columns/fields of the table, but we must give the values in the same order as when the table columns were defined.

If we do not give the full list of columns in the table, and in turn its values, these values will be set to NULL in the record. A NULL value is saying there is no value there for the specific field. An example of this scenario is shown here:

```
INSERT INTO Employees(EmployeeId, Name, DeptId) VALUES (10, "John Wick", 2);
```

At this point, the data in the table Employees will look similar to Table 10-7.

Table 10-7. *Employees Table*

EmployeeId	Name	DeptId	Telephone
1	Will Smith	1	4081125918
2	Peter Parker	2	1771959901
10	John Wick	2	NULL

A point to note here is that the value NULL is not similar to the string value "NULL", which has four characters defining that value. NULL is a special value, and it will be simply shown in table data renderings with the NULL representation. Providing string values in SQL statements is always done with quotes, which makes it possible to distinguish between the NULL symbol and a possible string value such as "NULL".

Using the same pattern, the previous SQL statements add records to the Projects and Project_Assignments tables. The ordering of the inserts is important here; before adding records that have foreign keys, make sure the tables and the records that are referenced in the foreign keys are added first. Otherwise, you are trying to refer to a record that has not been added yet, and this breaks the referential integrity rule. This is shown where we first added the Projects and Employees records before adding the Project_Assignments records, which has foreign keys to both the Projects and Employees tables.

Identity Columns

In database tables, numerical primary key columns, such as the ones we have used in our tables earlier, are often marked as identity columns. These are also called *auto-incrementing columns*. This signals the DBMS to generate an automatically incrementing number to be added to the column value. The exact mechanism that does this is different between DBMSs. For example, in MySQL/H2, this is done in the following manner:

```
CREATE TABLE Departments (DeptId INT AUTO_INCREMENT, Name VARCHAR(200),
Location VARCHAR(200), PRIMARY KEY(DeptId));
```

If the table is created in the previous manner, when you are inserting records to the table, the DeptId column value can be omitted, and the DBMS will automatically set a unique incremental value for the record. This behavior makes generating a unique value for the primary key much easier for the user and delegates this responsibility to the DBMS.

SQL SELECT

The SELECT statements are used to retrieve data in a database. Here, we can instruct the DBMS which database table or tables to retrieve data from and optionally give some conditions on how to filter the records in a table. The general format of an SQL SELECT statement is as follows:

```
SELECT <column1>, <column2>,... FROM <table> WHERE <conditions>;
```

The WHERE clause is optional, but is required for filtering records in a table.

A simple statement for retrieving all the records from the Departments table is shown here:

```
SELECT DeptId, Name, Location FROM Departments;
```

The result of executing such an SQL statement against a DBMS will result in what is known as a *record set* or a *result set*. It is basically a set of records returned, that is, a table structure representing the result. The result of the previous code is shown in Table 10-8.

Table 10-8. *SQL SELECT of Departments Result Set*

DeptId	Name	Location
1	Marketing	Building-1
2	Sales	Building-2
3	Engineering	Building-1

Table 10-8 represents the result set you would get with the previous SELECT statement. Notice that it is the same as the whole database table. This is true because we asked the DBMS to return all the records in the database table and all the columns/fields.

A shortcut for retrieving all the fields in an SQL SELECT statement is to use the * character in place of listing the table columns. So, the following statement returns the same result as the previous one:

```
SELECT * FROM Departments;
```

As you probably have guessed by now, if we list only a subset of the columns in the table in the SELECT statement, the result set will contain only those columns and their values. The following statement and its result set shown in Table 10-9 shows this behavior:

```
SELECT DeptId, Name FROM Departments;
```

Table 10-9. *SQL SELECT of Departments Result Set with Limited Columns*

DeptId	Name
1	Marketing
2	Sales
3	Engineering

Filtering Records

Record filtering while retrieval can be done with the WHERE clause in SELECT statements. The following SQL statement shows how to select all the departments that reside in Building-1 (see Table 10-10):

```
SELECT Name FROM Departments WHERE Location = "Building-1";
```

Table 10-10. *SQL SELECT of Departments Residing in Building-1*

Name
Marketing
Engineering

More operators such as <, >, >=, <=, IS NULL, IS NOT NULL, and LIKE can be used when defining the predicates. Also, more complex conditions can be created by combining predicates using AND and OR operators. For example, the following query lists all the departments that live in either Building-1 or Building-2 (see Table 10-11):

```
SELECT Name FROM Departments WHERE Location = "Building-1" OR Location =
"Building-2";
```

Table 10-11. *SQL SELECT of Departments Residing in Building-1 or Building-2*

Name
Marketing
Sales
Engineering

Since we have only two buildings, this returns all the departments in our result set.

Joining Tables

Let's say we want a result set in which we retrieve all the employee information, as well as the department name that is associated with each resultant record. If we simply list all the records in the Employees table, we would get the following (see Table 10-12):

```
SELECT * FROM Employees;
```

Table 10-12. *SQL SELECT of Employees*

EmployeeId	Name	DeptId	Telephone
1	Will Smith	1	4081125918
2	Peter Parker	2	1771959901
10	John Wick	2	NULL

The result set of Table 10-12 has only the DeptId, not the actual name of the department. Because of our normalization effort, we have put the actual department information in a separate Departments table. When we retrieve data, we want it back like our older way, where the department name there instead of just a department ID. So, we need to merge the data between the two tables to get what we want. This is done by table *joins*. We basically tell the tables to join the records of one table with the records of another table, and we can give some conditions saying how this joining of records should happen.

In this scenario, we want the tables Employees and Departments to join in a way that records that have the same DeptId from both table's records should join together. Let's see how this SQL statement looks:

```
SELECT E.EmployeeId, E.Name AS EmpName, D.Name AS DeptName, E.Telephone
FROM Employees E, Departments D WHERE E. DeptId = D.DeptId;
```

We can see that, in Table 10-13, all the employee information with its respective department names is available in the result set.

Table 10-13. *Table Join Between Employees and Departments*

EmployeeId	EmpName	DeptName	Telephone
1	Will Smith	Marketing	4081125918
2	Peter Parker	Sales	1771959901
10	John Wick	Sales	NULL

When joining tables, the previous SQL query used table aliases E and D to refer to their respective table fields; otherwise, we would have a problem of ambiguous table column names, because we have the requirement of addressing specific columns. Also, we can provide aliases for the column names that are returned in the result set by using the `AS` keyword in front of the table column. This is also used to make the result set clearer; otherwise, both the Name values in the Employees and Departments tables would be called Name in the final joined result set. So, we give separate aliases to better identify the resultant columns in the result set.

The exact nature of how the join operation happens can be visualized by first considering the records of the first table, Employees; each record individually tries to combine or join with the records in the second table, Departments. Each record in Employees cannot join with all the records in the Departments due to the explicit condition given that it should match each table's DeptId value. This makes it so that only one record from Department matches exactly one record in Employees (with the specific department ID), and it merges all the columns in those records and creates a new record. This is the final record where we will select the columns to be returned in the result set. When a joining condition is not given, each record in the first table will match with all the records in the second table and will create new records for all of these merged columns. We call this the Cartesian product of the two tables, which means if there are n records in the first table and there are m records in the second table, we will get n * m records in the final result set with the table join. And of course, table joins can be done with more than two tables, and the same pattern will hold true for those situations as well.

SQL UPDATE

The UPDATE operation is used for, as it sounds, to update the records in a table. The format for the UPDATE statements is as follows:

```
UPDATE <table_name> SET <column1>=<value1>, <column2>=<value2>,... WHERE
<conditions>
```

This SQL statement provides the target table, the set of columns, and the new values of those columns in each record. The WHERE clause is optional; it is used to filter the records that the update operation will be applied on. If this is not given, all the records in the table will be updated with the new given values for the columns. As an example, the following SQL UPDATE operation is used to update the location of the Engineering department:

```
UPDATE Departments SET Location = "Building-3" WHERE Name = "Engineering";
```

After the previous SQL statement is executed, the data in the Departments table will be similar to Table 10-14.

Table 10-14. *Table Departments After an SQL UPDATE Operation*

DeptId	Name	Location
1	Marketing	Building-1
2	Sales	Building-2
3	Engineering	Building-3

SQL DELETE

The removal of records from a table is done with the SQL DELETE statement. The format of the statement is shown here:

```
DELETE FROM <table_name> WHERE <conditions>
```

The WHERE clause is optional, and if we do not give any conditions with it, the DELETE statement will remove all the records from the given table.

In the following example, a DELETE statement is used to remove all the records in the Employees table, which does not have a Telephone value set, i.e., NULL.

```
DELETE FROM Employees WHERE Telephone IS NULL;
```

After the previous statement is executed, the records in the Employees table will look like Table 10-15.

Table 10-15. *Table Employees After an SQL DELETE Operation*

EmployeeId	Name	DeptId	Telephone
1	Will Smith	1	4081125918
2	Peter Parker	2	1771959901

Ballerina SQL API

We have learned the basics of relational database modeling and how to access databases using SQL. It's time to get our hands dirty with some actual code.

The Ballerina SQL API is based on the Java Database Connectivity (JDBC) API. This is an SQL-based database abstraction API used in the Java runtime. Thus, for the JVM-based Ballerina runtime jBallerina, we use this to get our SQL API functionality. The Ballerina module `ballerinax/java.jdbc` provides the aforementioned functionality.

The JDBC module provides the general SQL API, which will interact with any supported DBMS with its database driver configured. These drivers are JDBC drivers, which are provided as Java archive (`.jar`) files, that needs to be packaged with our Ballerina projects. For our samples for this chapter, we will be using H2 as the database engine. This DBMS is implemented in Java and can work as an embedded database, which stores the database data in the local file system, thus not requiring a separate server to be executing.

Database Client Initialization

Listing 10-1 shows the initialization of the H2 client and provides the connection-related properties in order to initialize it.

Listing 10-1. dbtest.bal (Client Initialization)

```
import ballerinax/java.jdbc;

jdbc:Client db = new ({
    url: "jdbc:h2:file:./mydb",
    username: "user",
    password: "pass"
});
```

The previous code snippet starts by creating a global variable `db`, which represents the JDBC database client. The connection properties are passed into the constructor of the client. In typical server-based DBMSs, such as Oracle, MSSQL, or MySQL, the `url` property will contain a remote network URL that points to the database server. But in this situation, the URL simply points to a local file system location to initialize and use as the database. Also, in this case of using an embedded H2 database, the username and the password values can be given as any value, since this is the first time we are creating the database.

JDBC Drivers

Ballerina depends on JDBC to find the required database driver for connecting to the target database. JDBC drivers are automatically looked up and used by analyzing the JDBC URL, which is the `url` property we used in our JDBC client configuration. The general structure of the JDBC URL is as follows:

```
jdbc:<subprotocol>:<subname>
```

The `subprotocol` is used to identify the DBMS and in turn the driver that is used to communicate with the database. The `subname` part is basically dependent on the subprotocol, which can pass in any additional properties it requires, such as a network address or a location in the local file system. For example, the subprotocol `h2` is used to identify the H2 database driver to be used in this client. This mapping between the subprotocol and the driver implementation happens automatically by the JDBC drivers, which automatically register themselves with the runtime context when they are loaded into the Ballerina/JVM environment. Basically, when we add any JDBC driver as a Ballerina project dependency, it registers itself as the provider for its subprotocol. For example, MySQL connection URLs take the form `jdbc:mysql://localhost:3306/<database>`, and by adding the MySQL JDBC driver as a project dependency, it registers itself as the provider for the `mysql` subprotocol.

The H2 database driver by default ships with the Ballerina runtime; thus, this driver is already registered in the environment, and we do not have to explicitly add it to our Ballerina projects as a dependency.

Database Client Operations

The Ballerina SQL interface is divided into two main API actions.

- Data read actions
    - **select**: Supports executing `SELECT` SQL queries
- Data and schema update actions
    - **update**: Supports executing other non-`SELECT` SQL queries, i.e., operations used to create/insert/update/delete data
    - **batchUpdate**: Update operations done in record value batches for increased performance/throughput
- Stored functions/procedures
    - **call**: Executes stored functions/procedures found in a database

We will be concentrating here on `select`, `update`, and `batchUpdate` actions supported in the Ballerina SQL API. Let's start with the `update` remote method when creating and populating the database tables.

Update

The `update` remote method has the following parameters:

- **sqlQuery**: This is the SQL statement to be executed, given as a string value.
- **parameters**: This is a rest parameter, used to provide parameter values in an SQL statement.

The previous remote method also returns a value of the type `jdbc:UpdateResult|error`. An `error` value will be returned in an error situation, or else the `sql:UpdateResult` value is returned that specifies the number of records updated/created and any automatically generated keys by the DBMS.

Let's continue the example in Listing 10-2 to create the tables in the database. Note that we will be making the primary keys in all of our tables as identity columns with the use of `AUTO_INCREMENT`.

Listing 10-2. dbtest.bal (Creating Tables)

```
public function initTables() {
    var result = db->update("CREATE TABLE Departments (DeptId INT AUTO_INCREMENT,
                             Name VARCHAR(200), Location VARCHAR(200),
                             PRIMARY KEY(DeptId))");
    io:println("Result: ", result);
    result = db->update("CREATE TABLE Employees (EmployeeId INT AUTO_INCREMENT,
                        Name VARCHAR, DeptId INT, Telephone VARCHAR,
                        PRIMARY KEY(EmployeeId),
                        FOREIGN KEY(DeptId) REFERENCES Departments(DeptId))");
    io:println("Result: ", result);
    result = db->update("CREATE TABLE Projects (ProjId INT AUTO_INCREMENT,
                        Name VARCHAR (200), Description VARCHAR (200),
                        PRIMARY KEY(ProjId))");
    io:println("Result: ", result);
    result = db->update("CREATE TABLE Project_Assignments (EmployeeId INT,
```

```
                               ProjId INT, PRIMARY KEY(EmployeeId, ProjId),
                               FOREIGN KEY (EmployeeId) REFERENCES
                               Employees(EmployeeId),
                               FOREIGN KEY (ProjId) REFERENCES Projects(ProjId))");
    io:println("Result: ", result);
}

public function main() {
    initTables();
}
```

```
$ ballerina run dbtest.bal
Result: updatedRowCount=0 generatedKeys=
Result: updatedRowCount=0 generatedKeys=
Result: updatedRowCount=0 generatedKeys=
Result: updatedRowCount=0 generatedKeys=
```

When executing our sample program, it will initialize the H2 SQL client and create the tables in the database with the call to the `initTables` function.

Let's look at how we can insert data into tables. One of the approaches is to execute code similar to the following:

```
var result = db->update("INSERT INTO Departments (Name, Location) VALUES
('Marketing', 'Building-1')");
```

This code has embedded the field values of the record into the SQL statement itself, i.e., Marketing and Building-1. What if these values are not known at compile time and are available only in the runtime as variables? Then, we can do the following:

```
string deptName = "Sales";
string deptLocation = io:readln("Sales Location: ");
result = db->update("INSERT INTO Departments (Name, Location) VALUES (' +"
+ deptName + "', '" + deptLocation + "')");
```

In this approach, we have simply emulated our earlier SQL statement with the values embedded by generating the same SQL statement by concatenating the field values to the same string value.

However, this approach is very dangerous and can cause malicious attacks known as *SQL injection attacks*. This happens when an external value such as `deptLocation`, which is read in from the user, modifies the SQL statement that is going to execute. Since we are appending the user input value directly to the SQL statement string, we can update the SQL string or otherwise extend the SQL statement by adding more statements to be executed. For example, let's say the user entered the following value:

```
"Building-2'); DELETE FROM Departments; INSERT INTO Departments (Name,
Location) VALUES ('A','B"
```

This is a carefully created value for the final SQL statement to not have any syntax errors while injecting the user's own logic into the statement. The final SQL statement that will result from this value is the following:

```
INSERT INTO Departments (Name, Location) VALUES ('Sales', 'Building-2');
DELETE FROM Departments; INSERT INTO Departments (Name, Location) VALUES
('A','B')
```

Here, the malicious user has added extra SQL statements into the same statement by using the ; character to terminate SQL statements so they can keep adding new statements to the same string. In this manner, the user was able to execute a `DELETE` statement that deletes all our records in the table, and they have put another dummy statement at the end to match the ending of our previous SQL string template to avoid a syntax error.

How can we avoid such SQL injection attacks? The answer is to not create a string template as shown previously but rather to pass in the parameters to the SQL statement separately. This approach is demonstrated here:

```
result = db->update("INSERT INTO Departments (Name, Location) VALUES (?,
?)", deptName, deptLocation);
```

The previous code snippet shows how the SQL statement is marked with ? values as placeholders for the parameter values. The actual parameter values are passed into the `update` remote method as values to its rest parameter. In this way, the DBMS explicitly knows the final structure of the SQL statement and that the parameter values passed in are only the values of the parameters for the placeholder field values, not an extension of the SQL statement.

Listing 10-3 shows the full code to populate the data in the tables.

Listing 10-3. dbtest.bal (Populating Data)

```
public function populateData() {
    var result = db->update("INSERT INTO Departments (Name, Location)
                             VALUES ('Marketing', 'Building-1')");
    io:println("Result: ", result);
    string deptName = "Sales";
    string deptLocation = io:readln("Sales Location: ");
    result = db->update("INSERT INTO Departments (Name, Location)
                         VALUES (?, ?)", deptName, deptLocation);
    io:println("Result: ", result);
    result = db->update("INSERT INTO Employees(Name, DeptId, Telephone)
                         VALUES ('Will Smith', 1, 4081125918)");
    io:println("Result: ", result);
    result = db->update("INSERT INTO Employees(Name, DeptId, Telephone)
                         VALUES ('Peter Parker', 2, 1771959901)");
    io:println("Result: ", result);
    result = db->update("INSERT INTO Projects (Name, Description)
                         VALUES ('SaveTheWorld1',
                          'Save the world for the first time')");
    io:println("Result: ", result);
    result = db->update("INSERT INTO Project_Assignments VALUES (1, 1)");
    io:println("Result: ", result);
    result = db->update("INSERT INTO Project_Assignments VALUES (2, 1)");
    io:println("Result: ", result);
}

public function main() {
    // initTables();
    populateData();
}
```

```
$ ballerina run dbtest.bal
Result: updatedRowCount=1 generatedKeys=DEPTID=1
Sales Location: Building-2
Result: updatedRowCount=1 generatedKeys=DEPTID=2
```

```
Result: updatedRowCount=1 generatedKeys=EMPLOYEEID=1
Result: updatedRowCount=1 generatedKeys=EMPLOYEEID=2
Result: updatedRowCount=1 generatedKeys=PROJID=1
Result: updatedRowCount=1 generatedKeys=
Result: updatedRowCount=1 generatedKeys=
```

We can see that when inserting records into tables with identity columns, the execution result of the remote method returns the generated key values, along with the count of the updated rows. Now that we have created and populated the tables, let's see how we can use the SQL API in Ballerina to read in the records.

Select

The `select` remote method in the SQL API is used to execute any `SELECT` SQL statement in order to retrieve records from database tables.

The `select` remote method has the following parameters:

- **sqlQuery**: The SQL statement to be executed, given as a string value.
- **recordType**: Type of the returned table. This is used to do data binding with a record type given by the user. In this way, each record can be returned as a record value when we are iterating the table. This can also be given as a `nil - ()` value; in this situation, you cannot iterate the table but can only do direct conversions to types such as JSON.
- **parameters**: A rest parameter, used to give provide parameter values in an SQL statement.

The return value of this operation is `table|error`.

Let's see an example of how a `select` operation can be executed, as shown here:

```
var result = db->select("SELECT DeptId, Name, Location FROM Departments", ());
if (result is error) {
    io:println("Error: ", result);
} else {
    io:println(jsonutils:fromTable(result));
}
```

The following is the result of this code:

```
[{"DEPTID":1, "NAME":"Marketing", "LOCATION":"Building-1"}, {"DEPTID":2,
"NAME":"Sales", "LOCATION":"Building-2"}]
```

Here, the select operation retrieves all the records from the Departments table, without providing a `recordType` value (given as `nil`), which causes the execution to not do any data binding operations. So, we have opted to directly convert the table structure to a JSON value using the `jsonutils:fromTable(result)` function. The result of converting the table structure into a JSON array is that every element is a JSON object representing every record in the result set, and each attribute in the JSON object represents each field in the record.

Let's update our earlier example code to select employee records by means of data binding to a record, as shown in Listing 10-4.

Listing 10-4. dbtest.bal (Retrieving Data)

```
type Employee record {
    int id;
    string name;
    string department;
    string telephone;
};

public function queryData() {
    table<Employee>|error result = db->select("SELECT E.EmployeeId as id,
                                  E.Name as name, D.Name AS department,
                                  E.Telephone as telephone FROM Employees E,
                                  Departments D WHERE E.DeptId = D.DeptId",
                                  Employee);
    if (result is error) {
        io:println("Error: ", result);
    } else {
        foreach var entry in result {
            io:println("ID: ", entry.id);
            io:println("Name: ", entry.name);
            io:println("Department: ", entry.department);
```

```
            io:println("Telephone: ", entry.telephone);
            io:println("=========================");
        }
    }
}

public function main() {
    //initTables();
    //populateData();
    queryData();
}
```

```
$ ballerina run dbtest.bal
ID: 1
Name: Will Smith
Department: Marketing
Telephone: 4081125918
=========================
ID: 2
Name: Peter Parker
Department: Sales
Telephone: 1771959901
=========================
```

We have now seen the basics of using the SQL API in Ballerina and how we can execute CRUD operations. In the next section, we will dive into some more advanced features of database programming by demonstrating them in the context of creating data services.

Creating Data Services

Data services are a mechanism where your data access and manipulation operations are shared through the network as a service. In this way, you can better manage your data access and share the functionality across multiple projects/customers without duplicating code and data.

As we have seen, Ballerina specializes in making network access operations productive and intuitive to the developer. So, creating a data service in Ballerina is a trivial task compared to most other general-purpose languages.

In the sample scenario we are going to discuss, we will dive deep into more advanced scenarios of our SQL API, such as implementing batch insert scenarios and transactions. To effectively demonstrate these, we will be creating a new use case based on customer accounts management in a bank. This will of course be a simplified view of how a real-world implementation would turn out. Figure 10-6 shows the single entity we will be using to implement our scenario.

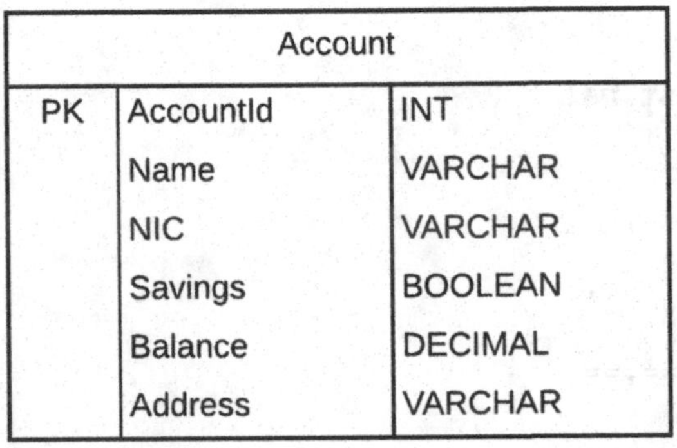

Account		
PK	AccountId	INT
	Name	VARCHAR
	NIC	VARCHAR
	Savings	BOOLEAN
	Balance	DECIMAL
	Address	VARCHAR

Figure 10-6. *Account ER diagram*

Designing the Data Service

The first thing to do is to plan the resources we will be exposing through the data service. This will represent the functionality that is exposed. We will be creating an HTTP service, with each resource path and HTTP method to represent the operation.

- Create Account
  - **Path**: `/account`
  - **HTTP Method**: POST
  - **Request Payload Type**: JSON

    ```
    {
        "name": $name,
        "nic": $nic,
    ```

```
        "savings": $savings,
        "balance": $balance,
        "address": $address
    }
```

- **Response Payload Type**: JSON

```
{
    "AccountId": $accountId
}
```

- Retrieve Account Details
    - **Path**: /account/{accountId}
    - **HTTP Method**: GET
    - **Response Payload Type**: JSON

```
{
    "accountId": $accountId,
    "name": $name,
    "nic": $nic,
    "savings": $savings,
    "balance": $balance,
    "address": $address
}
```

- Retrieve All Account Details
    - **Path**: /accounts
    - **HTTP Method**: GET
    - **Response Payload Type**: JSON

```
[{
    "accountId": $accountId,
    "name": $name,
    "nic": $nic,
    "savings": $savings,
    "balance": $balance,
    "address": $address
},...]
```

- Retrieve Account Details with NIC
    - **Path**: `/search?nic=?`
    - **HTTP Method**: GET
    - **Response Payload Type**: JSON

```
{
    "accountId": $accountId,
    "name": $name,
    "nic": $nic,
    "savings": $savings,
    "balance": $balance,
    "address": $address
}
```

- Update Account Details
    - **Path**: `/account/{accountId}`
    - **HTTP Method**: PUT
    - **Request Payload Type**: JSON

```
{
        "name": $name,
        "nic": $nic,
        "savings": $savings,
        "balance": $balance,
        "address": $address
}
```

- Delete Account
    - **Path**: `/account/{accountId}`
    - **HTTP Method**: DELETE
- Create Accounts Batch
    - **Path**: `/accounts`
    - **HTTP Method**: POST
    - **Request Payload Type**: JSON

```
[{
    "name": $name,
    "nic": $nic,
    "savings": $savings,
    "balance": $balance,
    "address": $address
},...]
```

- **Response Payload Type**: JSON

```
[{
    "AccountId": $accountId
},...]
```

- Transfer Funds
    - **Path**: `/funds_transfer`
    - **HTTP Method**: POST
    - **Request Payload Type**: JSON

```
{
        "fromAccount": $fid,
        "toAccount": $tid,
        "amount": $amount
}
```

Implementing the Data Service

Now that we have designed the structure of the data service, let's get into creating the actual implementation as a Ballerina service. We will start with the initial skeleton of the HTTP service in Ballerina, with the database client and the other structures we will need. See Listing 10-5.

Listing 10-5. accounts_ds.bal (Initial Skeleton)

```
import ballerinax/java.jdbc;
import ballerina/http;

type Account record {
    int accountId = -1;
    string name;
    string nic;
    boolean savings;
    decimal balance;
    string address;
};

type TransferInfo record {
    int fromAccount;
```

```
    int toAccount;
    decimal amount;
};

jdbc:Client db = new ({
    url: "jdbc:h2:file:./accounts_db",
    username: "user",
    password: "pass"
});

type dbfield string|int|boolean|decimal;

@http:ServiceConfig {
    basePath: "accounts_ds"
}
service AccountsDS on new http:Listener(8080) {

    function sendNotFoundError(http:Caller caller, string msg) returns
    error? {
        http:Response resp = new;
        resp.statusCode = 404;
        resp.setPayload(msg);
        check caller->respond(resp);
    }

}
```

Initializing the Database

Now that we have the skeleton code for our accounts data service, let's start implementing the service resources. Here, we will create a special resource for initializing the database schema. In real-world scenarios, we will not have this; we would have initialized the database schema by using external database tools to create its tables, etc. Since we are using an embedded database, we will be initializing the database explicitly using the code in Listing 10-6.

Listing 10-6. accounts_ds.bal (Database Initialization)

```
01 resource function initDB(http:Caller caller, http:Request request)
   returns error? {
02      _ = check db->update("CREATE TABLE ACCOUNTS (ACCOUNT_ID INT AUTO_
           INCREMENT,
03                                             NAME VARCHAR(200),
04                                             NIC VARCHAR(20),
05                                             SAVINGS BOOLEAN,
06                                             BALANCE DECIMAL,
07                                             ADDRESS VARCHAR(200),
08                                             PRIMARY KEY(ACCOUNT_ID))");
09      _ = check db->update("CREATE INDEX ACCOUNTS_NIC on ACCOUNTS(NIC)");
10      check caller->respond("Database Created.");
11 }
```

Listing 10-6 shows how we are executing a few SQL queries to create the database objects we will need. First, in line 2, we create the table ACCOUNTS, which will hold our account data. It contains a single primary key, which is an auto-incremented value. Also, in line 9, we have created an index to the column NIC, which is used to hold a national identification number, which identifies a person uniquely in a country.

When to Create an Index

An index is created to efficiently retrieve records by giving a conditional value to a specific column.

In the previous code, we created an index to the column NIC. In this way, in an SQL statement, we can look up a record by giving a value of the NIC field. For example, we can execute the following SQL statement:

```
SELECT * FROM ACCOUNTS WHERE NIC='481895819v';
```

Here, the DBMS will look up the records where its NIC field equals the given value. If we did not have an index created for this field, the DBMS would need to go through all the records in the table to find all the matching records. That is, we need to do a linear search to scan all the records. When we have a large number of records, this is an expensive operation to do each time we search for a specific record. But when we have an index defined, the system checks the index to find the record locations that match the given field value, and the DBMS can quickly jump to the locations where it matches the given value. So, it will no longer require us to go through all the records but rather uses the index to look up the values. This is similar to an index you find in books, where you look up pages that contain specific terms in the book, rather than reading through the whole book!

The next question would be, when should we create these indices? We should create an index for a column when it is often used to look up values based on it and when this column has a large number of unique values. The number of unique values for a field is its *cardinality*. The higher the cardinality, the more unique values for that column. This is not to be confused with the cardinality concept of ERDs, which is used in a different context. For example, you may be thinking the savings field can be indexed as well, because this field is used to signal if this is a savings account or not. This is a Boolean value and thus contains just two values, `true` and `false`. This has a low cardinality and is therefore not suitable for creating an index. It would be better to do a table scan to find all the matching records rather than going through an index to do this operation. The reason is that traversing the index structure also takes up processing time, and this computation will take longer compared to doing a linear scan of the table. The other implication is that creating unwanted indices increases the processing when inserting records, since it requires additional computations to populate the indices and requires more memory to store the information. Therefore, we need to carefully choose which columns need to be indexed.

Making Requests

We now have our base implementation for our data service. The only resource we can use at the moment is `initDB`, which is used to populate and initialize our database. For this, we will execute our Ballerina service, and we can send HTTP requests to invoke its resources.

HTTP requests can be sent through a tool such as `cURL` or through browser-based tools such as Advanced REST Client or Postman. Here, I will be using Advanced REST Client to show the commands and their results.

The following shows the Ballerina program execution and the request/response we get from our clients (see Figure 10-7):

```
$ ballerina run accounts_ds.bal
Initiating service(s) in 'accounts_ds.bal'
[ballerina/http] started HTTP/WS endpoint 0.0.0.0:8080
```

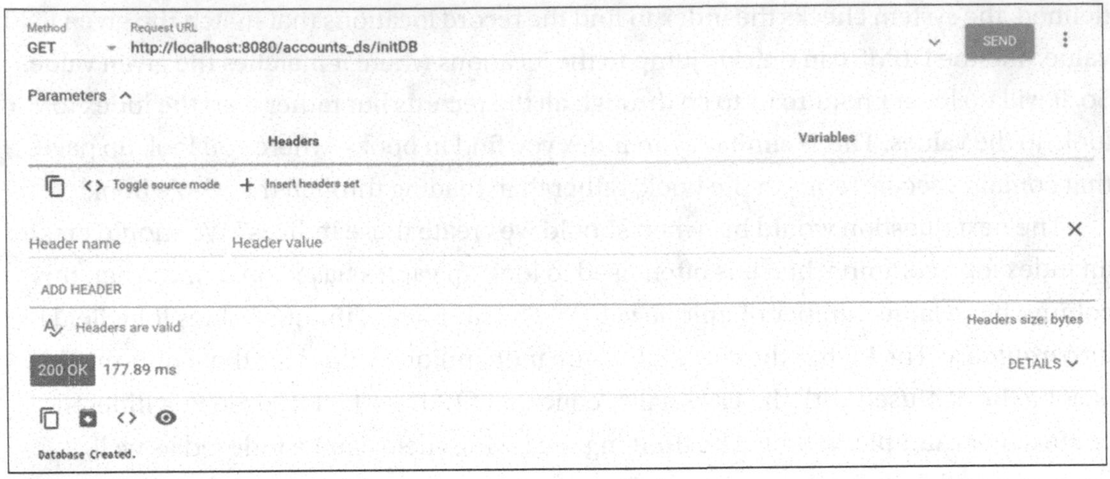

***Figure 10-7.** HTTP request/response for initDB resource*

Creating Accounts

Account creation can be done in two modes, in a single record creation or in batch creation. We have created separate resources for the two scenarios. Let's look at how they are implemented in Listing 10-7.

Listing 10-7. accounts_ds.bal (Account Creation)

```
@http:ResourceConfig {
    path: "/account",
    methods: ["POST"],
    body: "account"
}
resource function addAccount(http:Caller caller, http:Request request,
                             Account account) returns error? {
    var result = check db->update("INSERT INTO ACCOUNTS (NAME, NIC, SAVINGS,
                                  BALANCE, ADDRESS) VALUES (?, ?, ?, ?, ?)",
                                  account.name, account.nic, account.savings,
                                  account.balance, account.address);
    check caller->respond({"AccountId":
                          <int> result.generatedKeys["ACCOUNT_ID"]});
}

```

```
@http:ResourceConfig {
    path: "/accounts",
    methods: ["POST"],
    body: "accounts"
}
resource function addAccounts(http:Caller caller, http:Request request,
                              Account[] accounts) returns error? {
    dbfield?[][] params = [];
    foreach var account in accounts {
        params[params.length()] = [account.name, account.nic, account.
        savings,
                                   account.balance, account.address];
    }
    var result = db->batchUpdate("INSERT INTO ACCOUNTS (NAME, NIC, SAVINGS,
                                 BALANCE, ADDRESS) VALUES (?, ?, ?, ?, ?)",
                                 false, ...params);
    check caller->respond(result.length().toString() + " account(s) added");
}
```

In Listing 10-7, the resources addAccount and addAccounts represent the single account creation and the batch account creation operations, respectively. In the addAccount resource, we do an INSERT SQL query, and in our response to the caller, we return the generated key value. In the same manner, the batch update operation groups all the parameters for the multiple records and does a single call to the batchUpdate operation in the SQL API.

Benefit of Batch Operations

So, why do we need batch operations? We could have simply called the general update operation multiple times to add many account entries. This has to do with the efficiency we experience when we bundle many things together and do them in a single trip. This is compared to doing something one item at a time, making one trip for each item. Making one trip for each single item will create overall more overhead, compared to bundling up more items for a single trip.

Let's take a real-life example. Say we have a mango farm in our backyard, and the time comes to harvest the mangoes and sell them to a neighboring shop. The general process is that we get a payment for a mango and acquire a receipt. We can call this the *protocol* we follow. So, we have hundreds of picked mangoes in the farm, and one way to sell these would be to take one mango at a time, go to the shop, receive the payment, and receive a receipt for the goods. But as you probably have guessed, this is a waste of time, and we would have to make lots of trips. Instead, it would be easier if we take a larger batch of mangoes, like 50 mangoes in a bag, and go through this process. This would be much more efficient, and we would sell many more mangoes per day. We basically increased the efficiency of the operation by reducing the total overhead that will incur. The main overhead comes when we carry just a single mango and do all the paperwork just for a single item, when we could have done that paperwork together for a whole bunch.

This is similar to what happens in our SQL batch scenario. For each record insertion, it will parse the SQL query, optimize it, validate the input data, and do disk operations, all in a single network round-trip for each operation. But in a batch operation, in a single network round-trip, we can parse the SQL query, optimize it one time for multiple records, and also do a more optimized disk operation for the data in a batch of records, compared to multiple disk operations for many requests. The bottom line is that, in a data/record batching scenario, the performance and throughput are much higher because of our efforts in lowering the other overhead incurred in doing the actual work.

Accounts Creation in Action

Figure 10-8 shows the sample runs done to insert account records into the database.

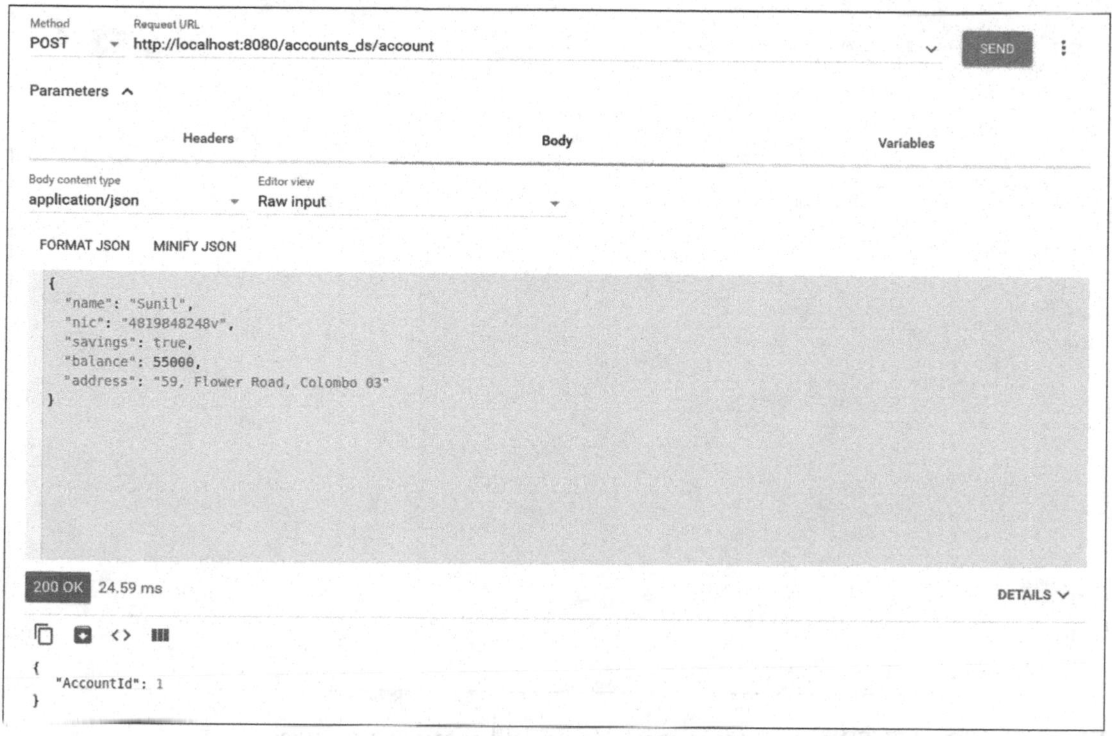

Figure 10-8. *HTTP request/response for addAccount resource*

Here, the information for a single account is added by giving the payload as a JSON object. The result contains a JSON object with the attribute `AccountId`, which contains the autogenerated key value to uniquely identify the account entry.

The request shown in Figure 10-9 takes in an array of JSON objects, where each object is similar to the payload shown in our earlier request in Figure 10-8. The list of account details is executed as a single batch operation from the SQL API.

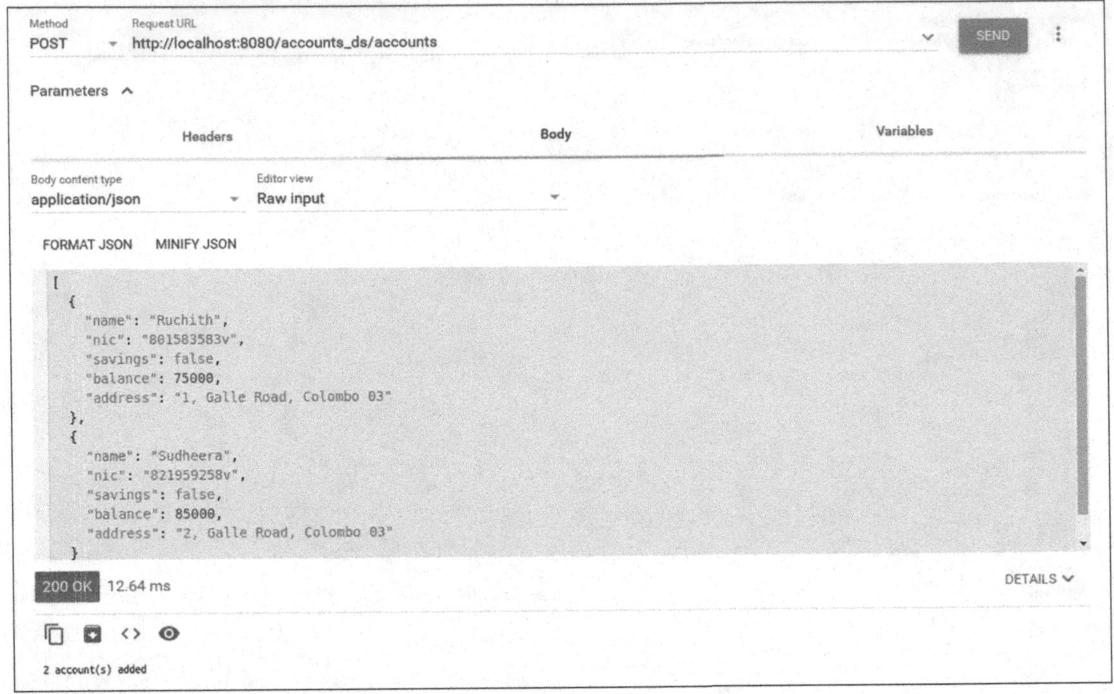

Figure 10-9. *HTTP request/response for addAccounts resource*

Retrieve Account Information

Account information can be queried using the resources `getAccount`, `getAllAccounts`, and `getAccountByNIC`, as shown in Listing 10-8.

Listing 10-8. accounts_ds.bal (Accounts Retrieval)

```
@http:ResourceConfig {
    path: "/account/{accountId}",
    methods: ["GET"]
}
resource function getAccount(http:Caller caller, http:Request request,
                              int accountId) returns error? {
    table<Account> result = check db->select("SELECT ACCOUNT_ID as accountId,
                                              NAME as name, NIC as nic,
                                              SAVINGS as savings,
                                              BALANCE as balance,
```

```
                                                    ADDRESS as address
                                                    FROM Accounts WHERE
                                                    ACCOUNT_ID = ?",
                                                    Account, accountId);
    if (result.hasNext()) {
        check caller->respond(<@untainted> check json.constructFrom(
                                result.getNext()));
    } else {
        check self.sendNotFoundError(caller, "Account not found: " +
                                        accountId.toString());
    }
}

@http:ResourceConfig {
    path: "/accounts",
    methods: ["GET"]
}
resource function getAllAccounts(http:Caller caller,
                                   http:Request request) returns error? {
    table<Account> result = check db->select("SELECT ACCOUNT_ID as
    accountId,
                                                    NAME as name, NIC as nic,
                                                    SAVINGS as savings,
                                                    BALANCE as balance,
                                                    ADDRESS as address
                                                    FROM Accounts", Account);
    check caller->respond(<@untainted> check json.constructFrom(result));
}

@http:ResourceConfig {
    path: "/search",
    methods: ["GET"]
}
resource function getAccountByNIC(http:Caller caller,
                                   http:Request request) returns error? {
```

```
    var nic = request.getQueryParams()["nic"];
    if (nic is string[]) {
        table<Account> result = check db->select("SELECT ACCOUNT_ID as accountId,
                                                  NAME as name, NIC as nic,
                                                  SAVINGS as savings, 01
                                                  BALANCE as balance,
                                                  ADDRESS as address
                                                  FROM Accounts WHERE NIC = ?",
                                                  Account, nic[0]);
        if (result.hasNext()) {
            check caller->respond(<@untainted> check json.constructFrom(
                                        result.getNext()));
        } else {
            check self.sendNotFoundError(caller, "Account not found with NIC: "
                                             + nic[0]);
        }
    }
}
```

Accounts Retrieval in Action

Figure 10-10 shows the HTTP requests/responses for account retrieval operations in the data service.

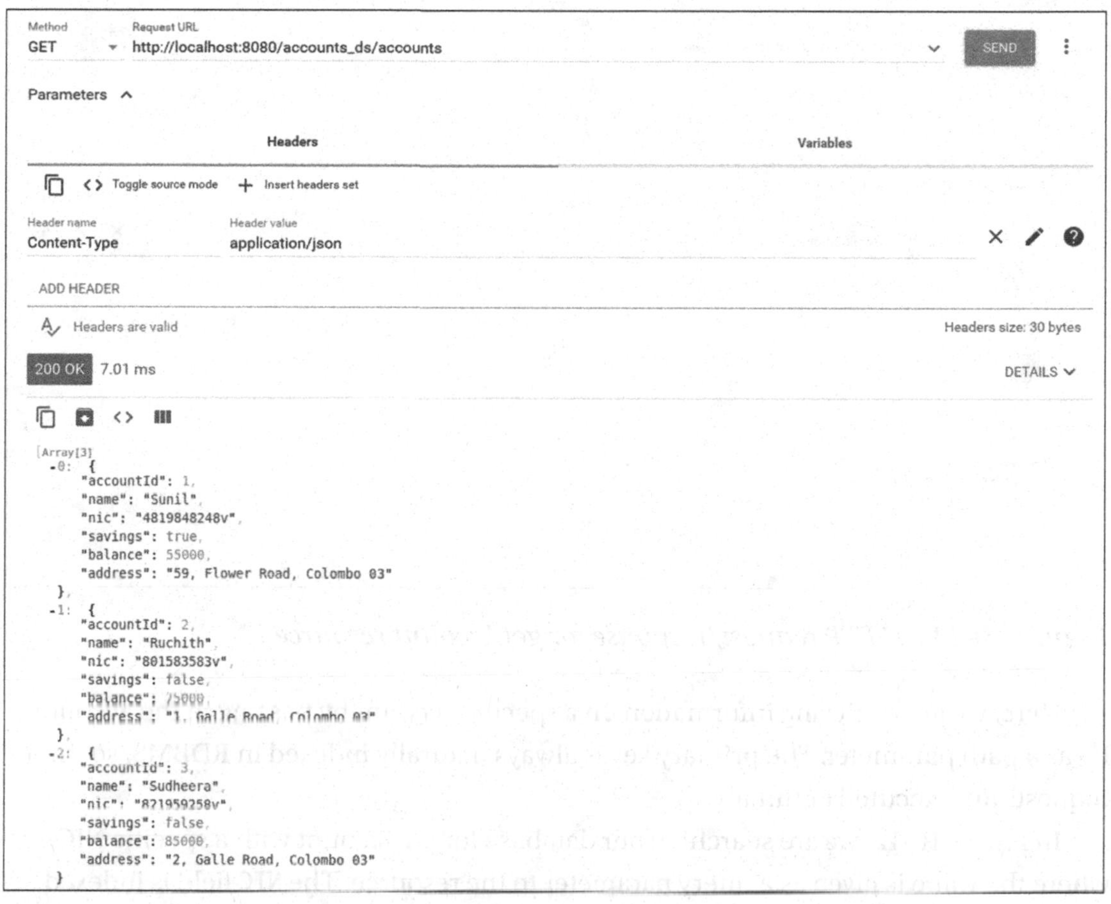

***Figure 10-10.** HTTP request/response for getAllAccounts resource*

The previous request invokes the `getAllAccounts` resource and retrieves information on all the accounts in the database. The response is returned as a JSON array of objects, with each object containing information about a single account. See Figure 10-11.

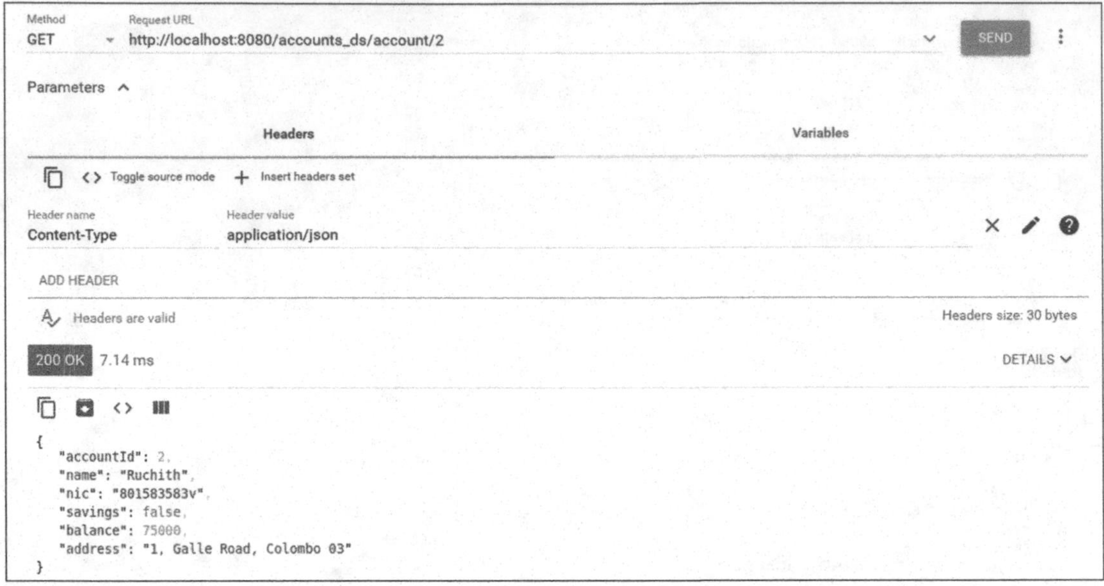

Figure 10-11. *HTTP request/response for getAccount resource*

Here, we are retrieving information on a specific account by passing in the account ID as a path parameter. The primary key is always naturally indexed in RDBMS, so these requests are executed optimally.

In Figure 10-12, we are searching our database for an account with a specific NIC, where the value is given as a query parameter to the resource. The `NIC` field is indexed explicitly in the database table, so this should provide consistent and fast lookup performance, even in a situation where a large number of records are stored in the table.

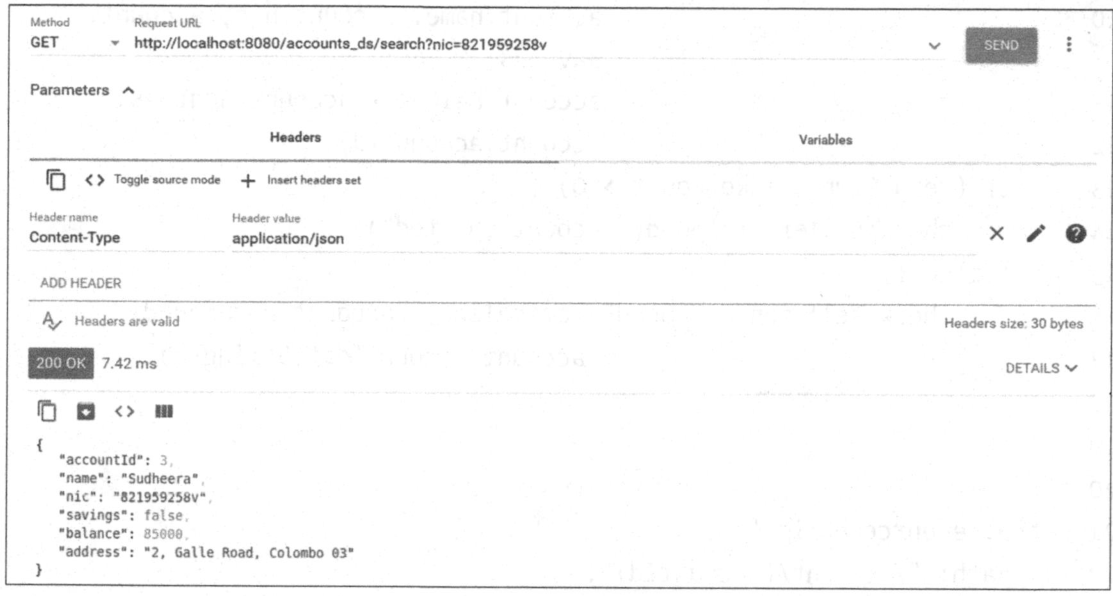

Figure 10-12. *HTTP request/response for getAccountByNIC resource*

Update and Delete Account Information

Listing 10-9 shows the code for the resources `updateAccount` and `deleteAccount`, which represent the functionality for updating and deleting accounts, respectively.

Listing 10-9. accounts_ds.bal (Accounts Update/Delete)

```
@http:ResourceConfig {
    path: "/account",
    methods: ["PUT"],
    body: "account"
}
resource function updateAccount(http:Caller caller, http:Request request,
                                Account account) returns error? {
    var result = check db->update("UPDATE ACCOUNTS SET NAME=?, NIC=?,
    SAVINGS=?,
                                BALANCE=?, ADDRESS=? WHERE ACCOUNT_ID=?",
```

```
                                        account.name, account.nic, account.savings,
                                        account.balance, account.address,
                                        account.accountId);
    if (result.updatedRowCount > 0) {
        check caller->respond("Account updated");
    } else {
        check self.sendNotFoundError(caller, "Account not found: " +
                                        account.accountId.toString());
    }
}

@http:ResourceConfig {
    path: "/account/{accountId}",
    methods: ["DELETE"]
}
resource function deleteAccount(http:Caller caller, http:Request request,
                                        int accountId) returns error? {
    var result = check db->update("DELETE FROM ACCOUNTS WHERE ACCOUNT_ID=?",
                                        accountId);
    if (result.updatedRowCount > 0) {
        check caller->respond("Account deleted");
    } else {
        check self.sendNotFoundError(caller, "Account not found: " +
                                        accountId.toString());
    }
}
```

Accounts Update/Delete in Action

Figure 10-13 illustrates how an account record can be updated, followed by Figure 10-14 which shows the retrieval of the updated record. In similar manner, Figure 10-15 shows how an entry can be deleted from the database, followed by Figure 10-16 which shows the attempt to retrieve the deleted record. Note that, in real life, in a similar situation, these entries will not be physically deleted; rather, information such as account information will be marked as deactivated, for example, in the event of an account closure. These are aspects you need to consider when designing a database and the operations that go with it.

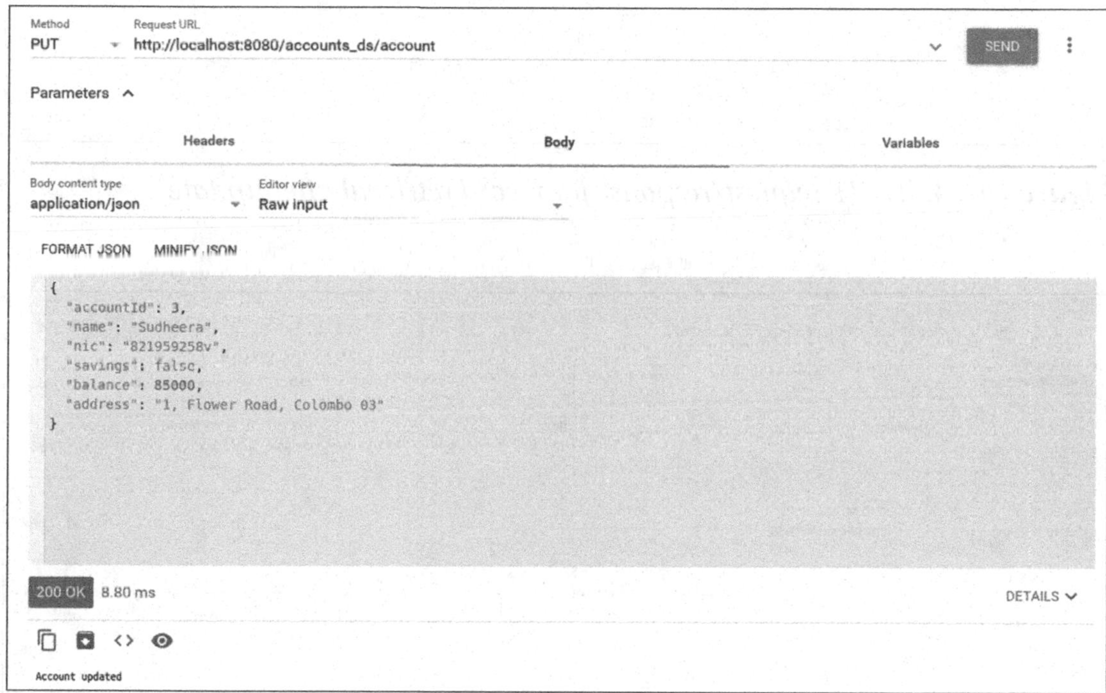

Figure 10-13. *HTTP request/response for updateAccount resource*

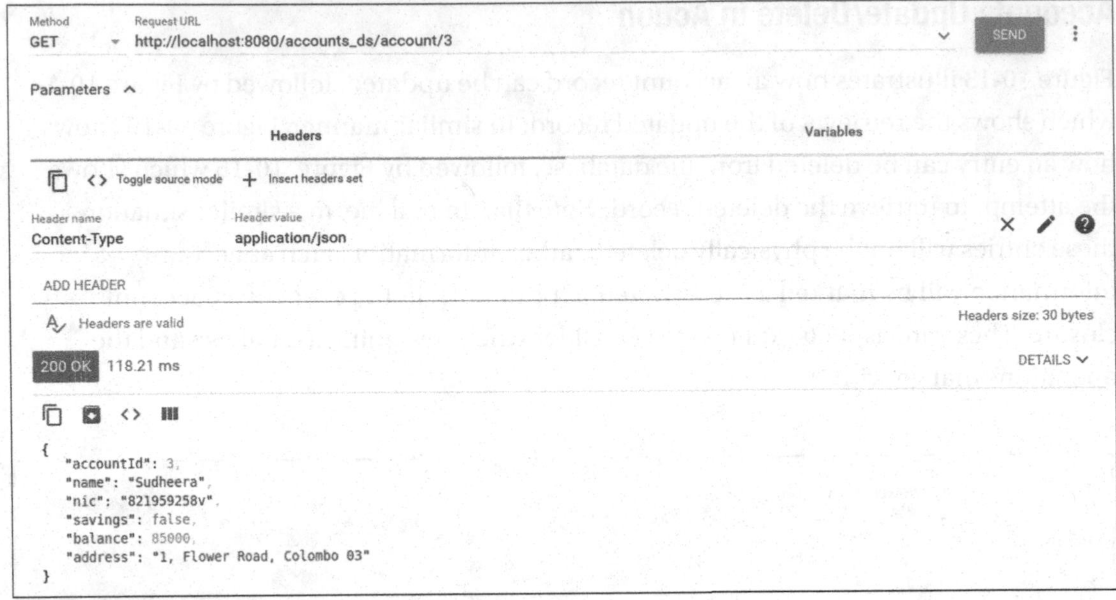

Figure 10-14. *HTTP request/response for record retrieval after update*

Figure 10-15. *HTTP request/response for deleteAccount resource*

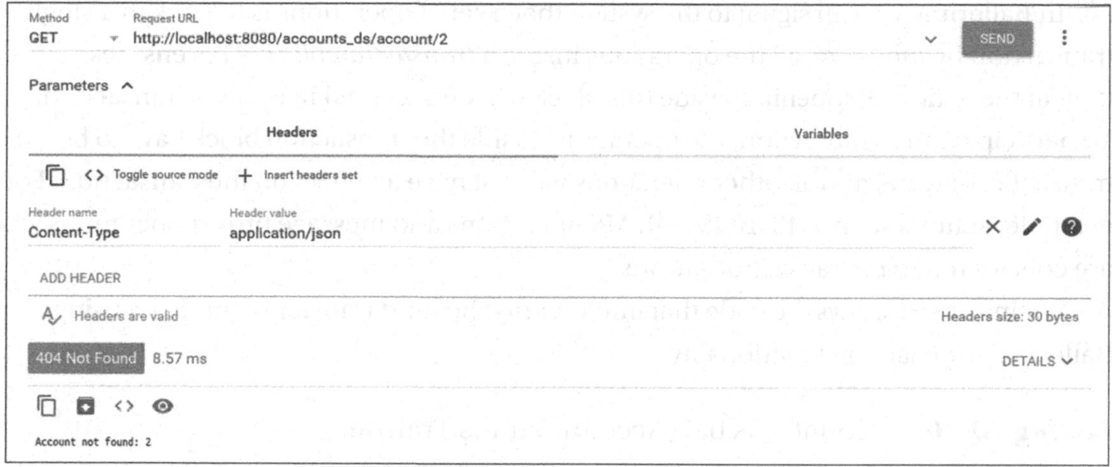

Figure 10-16. *HTTP request/response for record retrieval after delete*

Funds Transfer

The funds transfer scenario is where a certain amount is transferred from one account to another account. So, this operation should credit one account and debit the other account the same amount. This is a critical operation, and it shouldn't fail in the middle. For example, if the operation fails after we subtract the amount from one account and before adding to the balance of the other account, then the money is effectively lost. So, we need to make sure the transfer fully happens or doesn't happen at all. This is where we need transactions in databases.

Transactions

In a DBMS, we can group a set of database operations into a single transaction. This guarantees that either all the operations in the group will succeed or all of them will fail. That is, if we have multiple operations and in the middle one of the operations fails, then all the earlier succeeded operations will be rolled back, and it will be as if no operations took place. So, in our fund transfer scenario, if the first "balance subtract" operation succeeds and the "fund addition" operation fails for some reason, the first operation will also be rolled back so the account balances are at the original amounts. Basically, transactions make sure our data consistency is never compromised.

In Ballerina, we can signal to the system that a set of operations is to work in a single transaction by including all the operations inside a *transaction block*. This ensures that all the actions happening inside this block will be executed in a single transaction. To participate in a transaction, the operations inside the transaction block have to be transaction-aware, and all other operations will not have an effect on the transaction. For example, actions such as RDBMS SQL API operations and message broker operations are considered to be transaction-aware.

Listing 10-10 shows the code that implements the fund transfer scenario by using Ballerina's transaction functionality.

Listing 10-10. accounts_ds.bal (Account Funds Transfer)

```
@http:ResourceConfig {
    path: "/funds_transfer",
    methods: ["POST"],
    body: "transfer"
}
resource function transferFunds(http:Caller caller, http:Request request,
                               TransferInfo transfer) returns error? {
    transaction {
        _ = check db->update("UPDATE ACCOUNTS SET BALANCE=BALANCE-? WHERE
                            ACCOUNT_ID = ?", transfer.amount,
                             transfer.fromAccount);
        _ = check db->update("UPDATE ACCOUNTS SET BALANCE=BALANCE+? WHERE
                            ACCOUNT_ID = ?", transfer.amount,
                             transfer.toAccount);
    }
    check caller->respond("Funds Transfer Successful");
}
```

Funds Transfer in Action

Figure 10-17 shows the requests sent to do a funds transfer between two accounts, and Figure 10-18 shows the account information operation done to check the updated balance in the accounts.

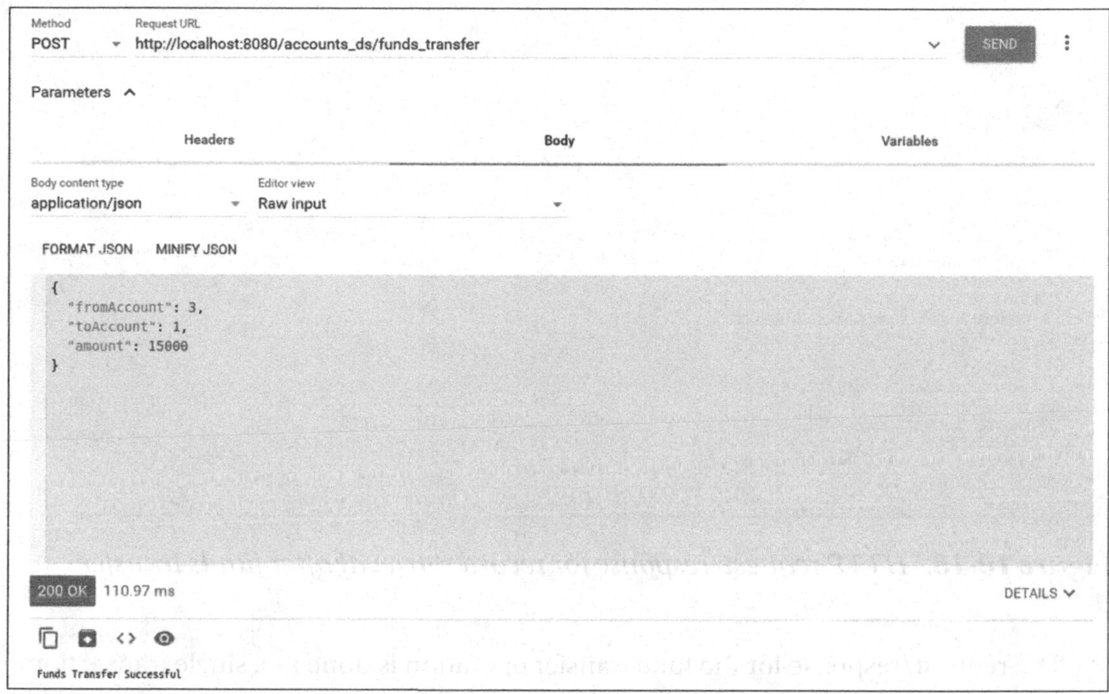

Figure 10-17. *HTTP request/response for transferFunds resource*

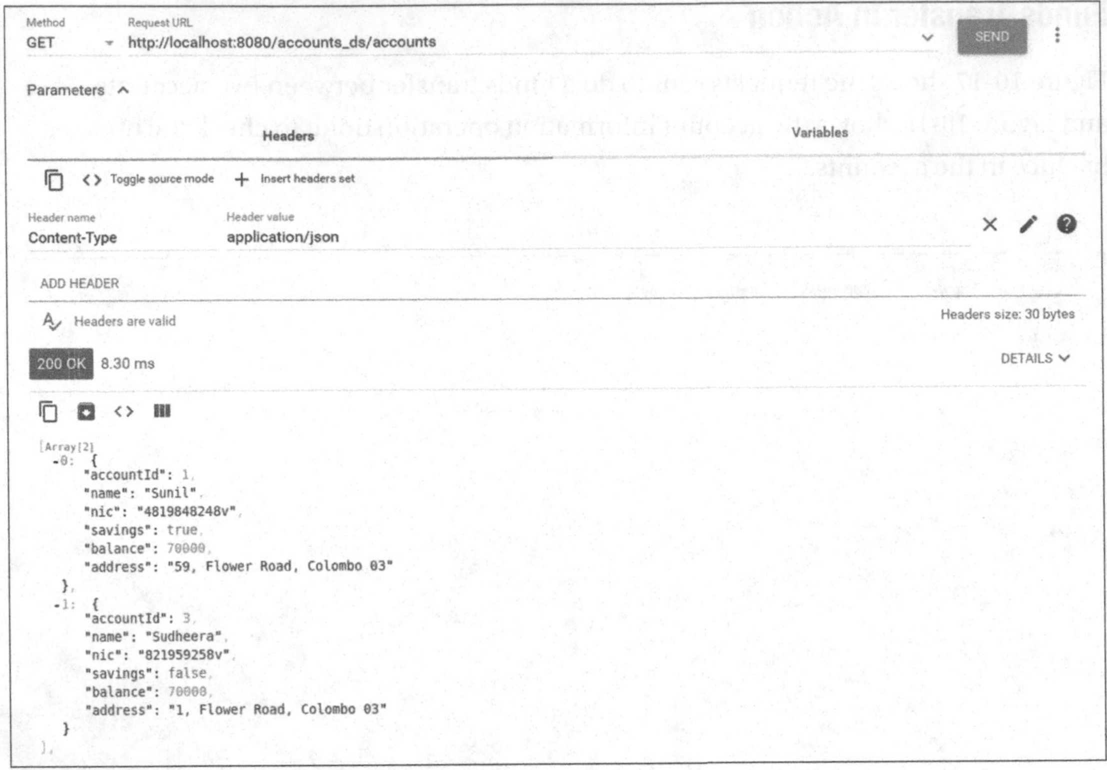

Figure 10-18. *HTTP request/response for record retrieval after funds transfer*

The request/response for the fund transfer operation is done as a single transaction, and the bank account balances have been updated accordingly.

Summary

In this chapter, we looked at what databases are, when to use them, and the basics of database modeling with entity-relationship diagrams. SQL was introduced as the de facto language in relational database querying and data manipulation. Then we looked into the SQL API available in Ballerina to access databases using computer programs.

We also looked at some of the best practices in database index usage and extended features such as batch updates and database transactions. Finally, we looked at how to write data services, in order to expose our data and their operations as network services.

APPENDIX A

Numbers and Representation

In this appendix, we will dig a bit deeper into how different number types are represented in Ballerina, explaining how integers and floating-point numbers are actually stored in memory. This knowledge is not strictly required, but it is always good to know how things work under the hood.

Signed Numbers and Two's Complement Notation

A Ballerina integer is a 64-bit signed number. An unsigned number memory representation is straightforward, where its numeric value is just the value of the binary number, considered a positive value.

Let's look at how we represent a signed value as a binary value. For simplicity in representation, we imagine our values are 8-bit integers. First, the bit positions are considered from the smallest-value digit to the highest-value digit. This is the same as how we write base 10 numbers. So, the rightmost bit has the lowest value of 2^0=1. In general numbering in Ballerina programming, we start indices with 0, not 1. So, something that has eight slots will have indices from 0–7. Going with the same model, the high-order bit is the digit that has the largest value in the number, with 2^7=128 at index position 7 (from the right).

A. Fernando and L. Warusawithana, *Beginning Ballerina Programming*,
https://doi.org/10.1007/978-1-4842-5139-3

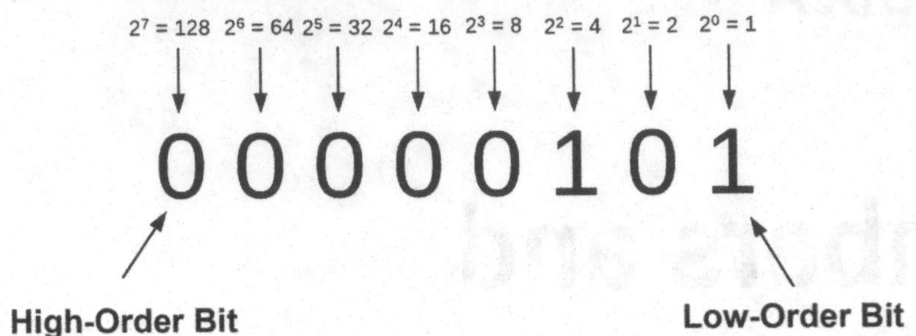

In a signed number, for a positive value, the value is represented by the first 7 bits, and the high-order bit is always 0. That means the high-order bit represents whether the number is positive or negative, and we call this the *sign bit*. For negative values, the sign bit would be 1.

Using this scheme, the numbers $[0\,0\,0\,0\,0\,0\,0\,0]_2$ to $[0\,1\,1\,1\,1\,1\,1\,1]_2$ would be 0 to 127. Here's an example:

$$[0\,0\,0\,1\,0\,1\,1\,1]_2 = 23$$

That looks simple enough, right? So, the obvious way to represent negative numbers would be to simply flip the sign bit and keep the rest of the 7 bits read in the same way. So ideally, we should be able to get -23 by just changing the sign bit of the previous number; then it should be $[1\,0\,0\,1\,0\,1\,1\,1]_2$. But in general computer systems, this is not the case, and for an 8-bit number, this value would be $[1\,1\,1\,0\,1\,0\,0\,1]_2$. This is called the *two's complement* notation negative integer.

You get the two's complement negative number by inverting the digits of the positive version of the binary number and adding 1 to it. You can do the opposite of getting the positive value of a negative number by doing the same thing.

The two's complement notation allows the calculations to be simpler from the electronics side, where it can use the same circuitry to do addition and subtraction of numbers. Basically, in the A - B scenario, the CPU can do A + (-B), where -B would be the two's complement negative value representation of B. So, the actual operation implemented in the CPU is just the addition logic, and a dedicated subtraction logic is not required.

Floating-Point Numbers

In Ballerina, real numbers—that is, numbers that have fractional parts—are represented using the `float` and `decimal` types. Almost all of the programming languages and computer hardware follows the standard defined by IEEE 754 for encoding these numbers. Ballerina also uses the same standard and has two precision levels, which are 64-bit double-precision binary and 128-bit decimal numbers with `float` and `decimal` types, respectively.

Why are they called *floating*? This is because the binary representation is simply a binary number with the decimal point position also given in the value. That is, in the value encoding, we actually give where the decimal point should be, which means it can move around, or it can "float." This format was adopted because, with a reasonable memory size, we can store pretty large numbers and also smaller numbers with a very high accuracy.

The encoding is basically a number written in scientific notation. Let's take the value 99.115 and write it in binary. We convert this to binary by first taking 99 and converting it to binary, which gives 1100011. Then we are left with the value .115. In binary, values after the dot (.) represent ½, ¼, and ⅛ values, and so on, similar to base 10 numbers, where they represent 0.1, 0.01, 001, etc. So when we work out the fractional value of 0.115 in binary, we get 0.000111011.

Therefore, our full binary value for 99.115 is 1100011.000111011. But, if we calculate the base 10 value again from the binary value, we will get 99.115234375. This is because the binary representation cannot represent the fractional values exactly since it works with 2^{-1}, 2^{-2}, and 2^{-3} values, therefore, it won't be able to represent the decimal values perfectly unless it has values such as 0.5, 0.25, 0.125, which are decimal fractional values created from the addition of binary fractional value components (i.e., 2^{-1}, 2^{-2}, 2^{-3}, etc.). Also, we've used only 9 bits to represent the fractional part; if we had used a higher number of bits, it would have been a closer match to 99.115.

Let's get back to our binary value by writing it in scientific notation. This time, we're going to use a larger 23-bit value to represent the fractional component, which would make it $1.10001100011101011100001 * 2^6$.

An IEEE 754 number has three components in it, called the *sign bit*, the *significand*, and the *exponent*. There are multiple formats defined, for example, single-precision and double-precision floating-point formats, which have different significand and exponent sizes for different levels of number size and accuracy. The following illustration shows how the floating-point number components are mapped into the scientific notation.

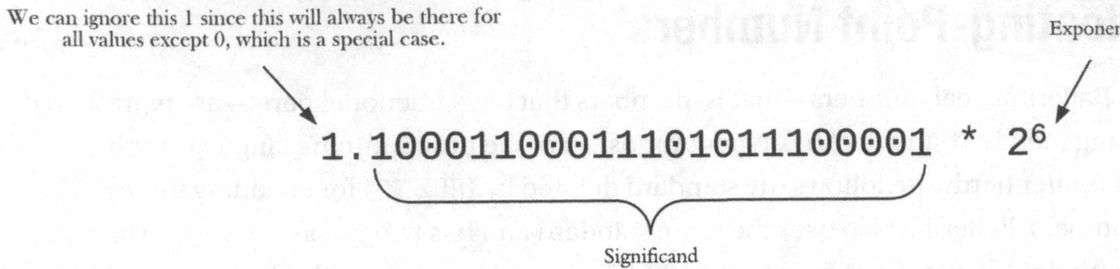
We can ignore this 1 since this will always be there for all values except 0, which is a special case.
Exponent
1.10001100011101011100001 * 2^6
Significand

IEEE 754 Single-Precision (32 bit) Encoding Components for 99.115:

- *Sign (1 bit)*: **0**
- *Exponent (8 bits)*: Bias (127) + **6**
- *Significand (23 bits)*: **[10001100011101011100001]**$_2$

The exponent value has a bias added to it, so it can also represent negative exponent values while still encoding this value as an unsigned (non-negative) integer value. For example, exponent bias value for single-precision numbers is 127. So if our number has an exponent of -1, the actual encoded exponent value in a single-precision IEEE 754 number would be 126. In the previous example, the encoded exponent value would be 127 + 6 = 133, whereas in binary, it would be $[10000101]_2$.

The final 32-bit single-precision floating-point value for 99.115 is encoded as the following binary value: $[01000010110001100011101011100001]_2$.

Index

A. Fernando and L. Warusawithana, *Beginning Ballerina Programming*,
https://doi.org/10.1007/978-1-4842-5139-3

D

E

J, K

L

M

N

O

P, Q

R

S

T

U

V, W, X, Y, Z

Printed in the United States
By Bookmasters